ANNE FRANK

Ronald Wilfred Jansen

Anne Frank

SILENT WITNESSES

Reminders of a Jewish girl's life

RWJ-PUBLISHING

' I WANT TO GO ON LIVING EVEN AFTER MY DEATH ! '
(Anne Frank)

CONTENTS

PROLOGUE
FRANKFURT AM MAIN
AACHEN
AMSTERDAM
THE SECRET ANNEX
CAMP WESTERBORK
AUSCHWITZ-BIRKENAU
BERGEN-BELSEN
EPILOGUE
PHOTOS
ITINERARY
OVERVIEW OF MONUMENTS
OVERVIEW OF PEOPLE
BIBLIOGRAPHY
WEBSITES
SPECIAL THANKS TO...
COLOPHON

PROLOGUE

Annelies Marie 'Anne' Frank (hereafter referred to as Anne) has come to symbolise the Holocaust, and her diary has conquered the world. A plethora of biographies and books containing historical photos have been published on her life. The travelling exhibition *Anne Frank—A History for Today*[1] is the most visited Dutch exhibition outside of the Netherlands. The exhibition *Anne Frank: Her Life in Letters* (2006)[2] depicts her life in hiding with an impressive, panoramic video presentation of excerpts from her diary. Less well known to the public is the physical trail of Silent Witnesses, which serves to remind us of Anne in the (urban) landscape.

My interest in the persecution of Jews in general and of Anne in particular came about gradually. From 1994 to 1996, I participated in international voluntary projects through the Dutch volunteer foundation SIW—projects in the former concentration camps Sachsenhausen and Dachau[3] located in Germany. I wanted to enter into a dialogue with young adults from different countries. I was edging towards the second half of my thirties, whilst most of the others were in their early-twenties. Fortunately, one is never too old to learn.

We discussed Nazism and the dangers of neo-Nazism, with all of us horrified by the stories told by former camp prisoners and members of the resistance. A number of historians led discussions in the presence of local residents. Fortunately, some of them had the courage to face up to this black page in German history. Many (elderly) Germans, however, remain unwilling to face their past. We also participated in excavations and other activities; such activities were intended to foster mutual understanding, but with the secondary aim of facilitating fun together.

What struck me during these activities was the contrast between the current silence in the former concentration camps, combined with the hardships of the prisoners, on the one hand, and the harsh shouts of the camp guards during the war, on the other. I was struck by the cruelty of the Nazi regime. Especially shocking were the lampshades made of human skin. Some of the younger participants were unable to deal with the horrors of the Nazi regime. American army videos displayed shocking images of the corpses of former prisoners in Buchenwald and other camps.

I visited the Achterhuis (the Secret Annex) for the first time in 2001. Visitors tend to be deeply impressed when they visit the Secret Annex, and I was no exception. I could feel the tension of the people in hiding, and I quickly realised Anne had become caught in the Nazi web: she had been snatched away from her usual environment. Anne had a keen interest in culture, religion, science and social matters, and was always concerned with the welfare of others. As a German refugee, she felt at home in Amsterdam and was eager to reach maturity. Her murder just because she was Jewish leaves a very bitter taste in my mouth. Her life was nipped in the bud.

I felt the urge to record Anne's life, not by means of a biography or a book containing old photographs—after all, so many of those have already been published—but in a different manner.

In 2008 and 2009, I went on a memorial tour, visiting Anne's various places of residence (hereafter referred to as main locations): her addresses in Frankfurt am Main and Aachen, the Merwedeplein in Amsterdam, the Secret Annex in Amsterdam where she went into hiding, and the Westerbork, Auschwitz-Birkenau and Bergen-Belsen concentration camps where she was imprisoned.[4] I converted this historical journey into a (photo) book.[5]

The publication of the photo book proceeded with difficulty. The Anne Frank Fonds in Basel only permitted the use of five of Anne's quotes.[6] I wanted to publish the photo book in 2009, the year Anne would have celebrated her 80th birthday. Since I was unable to find a regular publisher for the book, I decided to publish it myself. I quickly made a selection of photographs and edited them with the use of Photoshop; I purchased historical photographs from a stock agency; I did the layout myself and published the book in 2009 through a POD[7] publisher. For the English version of the book, I had to pay Random House[8] a (modest) amount of money because I had used a few quotations from Anne's diaries. Unfortunately, however, my attempts at obtaining subsidies were fruitless.

Nevertheless, I was not put off. I positioned several historical photographs next to current ones taken from the same perspective, which painfully revealed the void left behind by Anne. Many people thought this approach was challenging, and consequently wanted to bring my photo book to the attention of the general public.[9] Hanna 'Hanneli' Elisabeth Goslar (born in 1928, hereafter referred to as Hanneli) was a friend of Anne's and liked my photo book.

The Anne Frank Stichting (The Anne Frank House) noted my original approach[10], and the Anne Frank Fonds in Basel remarked that my photographs bridge the gap between past and present.[11] In spite of this, however, neither organisation was prepared to publish my book[12], which was a great pity. I decided, however, that I would not be deterred by any of this, and would add a final sequel to the photo book and booklet.

This book will be my last work on Anne, and it will be a supplement to the existing historiography of Anne. I wrote this book as a result of getting to know more about the main locations and the surrounding environment of Anne's residences, her hiding place, and various locations she liked to visit.

Another reason for writing this book is that time is running out for people who knew Anne to tell their story. In a similar vein, the book pays specific attention to the reasons behind why the places that remind us of Anne are disappearing.

The major monuments erected after the war, which commemorate Anne, the war and the persecution of the Jews, are mentioned in this book but not elaborated upon since its central theme is Anne's residential environment. These monuments serve to illustrate how Anne, along with other war victims, is being commemorated.

Various sources were consulted during the course of writing this book. Since the book is being financed by private funds, it does not include any photographs of Anne purchased from stock agencies or elsewhere.[13] Ad Tiggeler[14] allowed me to use his collection of old postcards to illustrate this book. It contains excellent images, some less well-known, including photographs of De Wolkenkrabber ('The Skyscraper', a block of flats looking out on Merwedeplein, Amsterdam). My gratitude also goes out to Jos Wiersema, who allowed me to use historical photographs from his collection[15]; images that go beyond the usual pictures.

Some materials from the photo book have been reused in this publication, supplemented by current photos of a number of places Anne visited, which I learnt of in 2010 and 2011 and had overlooked when making the photo book.

Anne maintained a scrapbook with photographs. Some of the places depicted in these photographs have not been identified exactly, even if they show Anne in front of a clearly recognisable background. Following the war, so much attention went to publishing *The Diaries* that not all old pictures were researched adequately with regard to their origin. The bitter fruits of this are now being harvested: the location of some of the buildings can no longer be established with certainty. Fortunately, however, I was able to recognise some of the places in these photographs when I was physically tracing Anne's footsteps.

For other photographs, however, I have not been able to establish location. One black-and-white photograph[16] shows an informal yet slightly uneasy gathering of three teenagers looking into the camera. Both boys are wearing neat suits that are in sharp contrast with their decrepit environment of bare vegetable gardens and unpainted sheds. The youngest boy is wearing clogs. A girl in a light dress gives the photographer a rather surly look whilst pulling one of the cords on her cardigan. This girl is Anne. The two boys standing next to Anne are Herbert Wilp (1928-2002, hereafter referred to as Herbert) and Hermann Wilp (1925-1945, hereafter referred to as Hermann), who came from Neuwied near Koblenz. Following the Kristallnacht[17], Herbert and Hermann fled to Amsterdam. It is unknown where this picture was taken or what relationship existed between Anne and these boys.

Prior to travelling across Anne's locations, I studied the relevant literature in order to garner insight into what has been written about

Anne and where she stayed. Many books have been written about Anne. Melissa Müller's biography is well-structured and contains a wealth of background information on Anne.[18] The level of other writings differs greatly[19], with practically all writers elaborating on others' themes.

The biography by Carol Ann Lee (hereafter referred to as Carol) contains several mistakes.[20] A meticulous description of Amsterdam locations reminiscent of Anne may be found in Bob Polak's book *Naar buiten, lucht en lachen! Een literaire wandeling door het Amsterdam van Anne Frank* [Outside: fresh air and laughter! A literary walk through Anne Frank's Amsterdam] (Amsterdam, 2006). His book was of great use to me. My book also contains information published before, supplemented by new facts about Anne's places of residence and presented from a new perspective.

The Letters[21] and *The Diaries*[22] Anne wrote are the main primary sources for reconstructing Anne's day-to-day environment, and are influenced by the opinions and interpretations of Anne, who, in turn, was influenced by her upbringing, environment and the spirit of her time. There is no information on how the others experienced the hiding: with the exception of Otto Frank (1889-1980, hereafter referred to as Otto), none survived the extermination camps. In spite of the chaotic circumstances in the Secret Annex during the fatal raid on August 4, 1944, excerpts of Anne's diaries remained intact. Many of the letters Anne wrote whilst living at Merwedeplein have undoubtedly been lost.

Margot kept a diary in the Annex[23] that most probably also has been lost, or perhaps Margot's diary is still hidden somewhere under the floorboards of the building at 263 Prinsengracht, in an old forgotten attic or orphaned in an archive that has escaped inventory. Who knows?

New information about Anne still occasionally crops up from hidden places. In 2008, one of Anne's postcards turned up in a gift shop in Naarden, the Netherlands[24], along with a picture of a former admirer.[25] The YIVO Institute for Jewish Research[26] discovered some letters by Otto, revealing that he wanted to flee the Netherlands with his family.

The period from December 6, 1942 up to December 22, 1943[27] is absent from the A version of *The Diaries*. The A version is the first version of *The Diaries*; the B version is the version rewritten by Anne herself, which she planned to publish in the form of a novel after the end of the war. The B version was never completed, probably because Anne was arrested, and ends on March 29, 1944. I prefer to take the A version, written by Anne between June 12, 1942 and August 1, 1944 as a point of reference because it is the uncensored version in which Anne wrote down her thoughts unreservedly and without consideration of her audience. In some places, the B version contains information that is lacking in the A version.

Otto contributed to a C version of *The Diaries*: The 1947 Dutch edition of Het Achterhuis [The Secret Annex], published by Contact, from which certain sensitive passages were removed by Otto[28]. The academic publication of *The Diaries*[29], meant to scientifically refute the accusations by far-right extremists who claim *The Diaries* to be a forgery[30], contains sensitive extracts written by Anne, which Otto had systematically kept out of previous publications.

A booklet containing difficult words that Anne wrote down[31] and the card catalogue of books[32] kept by Anne and Margot have not been found. An accounts book in which Anne noted down texts that appealed to her whilst she was in hiding has been preserved: the *Mooie Zinnenboek*, her Book of Beautiful Sentences (Amsterdam, 2004). (Please refer to the Bibliography section, Translator's Note, for more information on English editions and translations of titles in the). Some separate notes from the *Secret Annex* by Anne were preserved, and she also wrote stories, and in 1944 worked on a novel whilst hiding in the Annex. These were published in Dutch as *Verhaaltjes, en gebeurtenissen uit het Achterhuis. Met de roman in wording Cady's leven* (Amsterdam, 2005), and in English as *Tales from the Secret Annex. Including her Unfinished Novel Cady's Live* (Halban Publishers, 2010). The stories this book contains are partly anecdotes from the Annex, partly made-up fairytales and partly derived from memories of the Jewish grammar school she attended, the Joods Lyceum. Both her stories and her prospective novel contain autobiographical elements: 'It isn't sentimental nonsense for it's modelled on the story of Daddy's life.'[33]

Anne does not elaborately describe her residential environment in her writings, presumably because it was a given to her—just like it is a given for us that we are free to walk down the street. One only notices that something is missing when it is gone. It was the same for Anne. During her period in hiding, she became more aware of the value of nature, fresh air and having some elbow room, and she described the chestnut tree, the birds and the sky above Amsterdam. Comparably, Anne did not write about her residential environments in Aachen and Frankfurt in any detail; she lived there only very briefly, and may not have remembered much about those places of her early childhood. During her hiding period, Anne mainly felt Dutch and probably did not feel any need to be reminded of her native country.

I was unable to obtain permission to consult the Frank family archives. I am unsure as to whether this would have proven useful; the exhibition *Anne Frank—Her Life in Letters* in the Amsterdam Museum in 2006[34] did not lead to new insights into Anne and her places of residence. Moreover, some other authors have already conducted extensive research in the Anne Frank Stichting archives.

I was unable to find specific sources, such as postcards or letters, Anne may have written in one of the concentration camps. She may have been prevented from writing—or perhaps she came to lack the strength. Many of the materials from the camps in which Anne stayed have been lost to posterity, meaning that her life in the camps can only reconstructed through the eyewitness accounts of others.

I sought contact with people who (superficially) knew Anne and who were able to tell me about locations she had visited but did not mention in her writings. Whilst travelling along Anne's locations generally went fine, the contact with her former friends and acquaintances was more difficult. At times, their memory failed them, and they would make contradictory statements. Asking additional question occasionally led to irritations.

Even today, some people continue to argue about who was or was not a friend of Anne's.[35] Some people who knew Anne and Margot are tired of the war and the attention that goes out to Anne.[36] Some do not like to be reminded of the loss of their family.

Some who were born during or shortly after the war are too young to remember anything concrete about that time. For many survivors, a visit to their old neighbourhood, the Rivierenbuurt, is very difficult. Hilde Goldberg-Jacobsthal (born in 1925, hereafter referred to as Hilde) had not been to her neighbourhood since 1943.[37]

Sometimes a person's health prevented me from having any contact; they understandably wanted to be left alone. Unfortunately, I had not been able to contact Hermine 'Miep' Santruschitz (1909-2010) before she passed away. Miep was the last surviving helper of the people in the Annex.

In 2010, I had a telephone conversation with Anne's friend Hanneli. This led to some new information on Anne's places of residence in Amsterdam. I am grateful to her and to the many others who helped me, such as Bernard 'Buddy' Elias (born in 1925, hereafter referred to as Buddy), all of whom are mentioned in the 'Special thanks to...' section of this book.

Various websites offered me the opportunity to publish a general request for information about Anne and her residential environment.[38] Through the 'Zuidelijke Wandelweg'[39] and 'Anne in de buurt'[40] community projects, I was able to reach people who did not belong to Anne's direct circle of friends but who did have important information on her previously unknown places of residence. 'Zuidelijke Wandelweg' and some other websites contain valuable information on the Rivierenbuurt, where Anne spent many years of her life.

Several German papers[41] only wanted to publish my request for sharing information about Anne if I paid them for it, which I declined because Anne is not a commercial product to me. What she left us is public cultural heritage.

Persons who have (in)direct experience of the war in Amsterdam provided me with a large amount of useful information about the war.[42] Karel N. L. Grazell (born in 1928, hereafter referred to as

Karel), who became one of Amsterdam's municipal poets, and Max C. van der Glas (born in 1938, hereafter referred to as Max)[43], who is a writer and Holocaust survivor, did not know Anne in person, but they do know Amsterdam and its history extremely well.[44]

I reached people through the internet whom I would not have been able to reach through any organisation. I would gather information on the architecture of buildings and neighbourhoods in Amsterdam mainly from websites of the *Nederlands Architectuurinstituut* (NAI, the Netherlands Institute of Architecture)[45], *Gemeente Amsterdam Bureau Monumenten & Archeologie* (BMA, the Amsterdam municipal agency for monuments and archaeology)[46] and *Joods Amsterdam* (Jewish Amsterdam).[47] Some elements that have disappeared from our landscape for good can be reconstructed virtually. I was fortunate enough to see Anne's chestnut tree 'live' from the Annex before it was blown down in 2010, but it can also still be admired in The Secret Annex Online.[48] The Secret Annex Online also served as a reminder during my reconstructions, and I would highly recommend it to anyone who has difficulty walking and would otherwise not be able to visit it.

I did not find any local papers that the Franks may have read during the war. Presumably, local papers were not distributed during WWII because paper was scarce and the strict German censorship suppressed their publication. Anne does not mention the *Amstelodamum* magazine that appeared during the war. However, an entrepreneurs' magazine dated January 11, 1940 states that Anne solved their puzzle and could collect her prize.[49]

However, consulting archives, reading, interviewing people or looking up information on the internet did not suffice for the purposes of this book. Travelling deepened my connection with Anne's environment, the distance between her places of residence, the size of her living space, and the elements reminiscent of her in the (urban) landscape. I could only experience the void Anne left behind by perceiving the world from her point of view.

I visited Amsterdam and Aachen again in 2010 and 2011 for the purpose of gathering additional information. The persons and organisations involved provided permission to visit and record the locations inside and out, and I am very grateful to them.

Hopefully, the reader will be inspired to visit Anne's places of residence and share their experiences with others so that more people will take up an interest in Anne's cultural heritage, which extends beyond the Secret Annex, her diaries, and old photographs.

This book will hopefully contribute to the inventory and the preservation of the monuments that remind us of Anne. Private individuals, cultural institutions, research institutes and the government can contribute to this. A great deal of information about Anne is scattered, and there are things we still do not know.

It is important that the study of Anne's cultural heritage stimulates research into the physical traces left behind by other war victims so that they all get the attention they deserve[50]; after all, Anne is just one of millions of Holocaust victims.

[1] http://www.annefrank.org/en/Education/Travelling-exhibition/Introduction-international-exhibition/.
[2] http://www.ymere.nl/ymere/index.asp?id=125 (Dutch only).
[3] I published a small report on my journey in the Dachau Newsletter by the Foundation for Friends of Former Dachau Prisoners: *Nieuwsbrief Dachau* (Stichting Vriendenkring van Oud-Dachauers. Nr. 9 – December 1994) pp. 8-9. (Dutch only).
The local media also covered the *Jugendbegegnungszeltlager* (youth gathering) in which I participated (Süddeutsche Zeitung, 10 August 1994), p. 7 (German only).
[4] Reports of my journey were published on http://joodsactueel.be/2011/01/03/in-de-voetsporen-van-anne-frank-1929-1945/ and in a heritage magazine: Jansen, Ronald Wilfred. Stille Getuigen. Sporen van Anne Frank in het (stedelijke) landschap [Silent Witnesses. Reminders of Anne in the (Urban) Landscape], in: *Monumenten. Hét tijdschrift voor cultureel erfgoed* [Monuments. *The* Cultural Heritage Magazine] (Volume 32, issue 5, May 2011) (both Dutch only).
[5] My English photo book: Jansen, Ronald Wilfred, *Anne Frank. A Memorial Tour in Current Images* (2009) and its Dutch original are listed in the catalogue of the German National Library (http://d-nb.info/998592757). The English version is part of the United States Holocaust Memorial Museum library collection.
(http://catalog.ushmm.org/vwebv/search?searchCode=GKEY%5E&searchType=0&searchArg=memorial+tour+in+current+images).

'In his photo book, Ronald Jansen reveals how our physical landscape contains reminders of Anne's arrival and departure, presence and absence. Jansen tours Anne Frank's home addresses, her hiding place and the concentrations camps where she was imprisoned, i.e. Westerbork, Auschwitz-Birkenau and Bergen-Belsen. In his report of this project, which he himself describes as a memorial tour or historical journey, Jansen takes old photos from the archives and puts them next to the pictures he has recently taken from the same perspective. One of the photographs, taken in the summer of 1932, shows three-year-old Anne playing with water in her garden. The photo taken decades later portrays the stones that were once a part of this scene. The building and the courtyard [Ganghoferstrasse 24, Frankfurt am Main, Frank family residence] are still there, but there are no children playing. In this way, Jansen captures the void Anne left behind.' (Borgman, Erik and Liesbeth Hoeven, *Sporen van afwezigheid. Gedenken in stemmen, stenen en stilte* [Traces of Absence: Commemorating in Voices, Stones and Silence] (Zoetermeer, 2011), p. 55.

The residence stated in the books published by Unibook—which have been withdrawn from the market—is incorrect: Anne did not reside at 5 Liebfrauenstrasse in Eschweiler at this time but at 5 Elsa-Brändström-Strasse in Aachen. I am grateful to the Anne Frank Stichting for pointing this out to me (email dated 14 August 2009).
The paperback edition available through CreateSpace does state the correct address and also contains a current photo of the building. This English edition is available in full colour (ISBN 9781466281936) or in black and white (ISBN 9781463714345).

Since 2011, my photo book has been available in the Netherlands and Belgium through POD publisher www.mijnbestseller.nl (ISBN 9789491080555 (English version) and ISBN 9789491080432 (Dutch version)). In 2011, I also published a black and white paperback booklet on Anne Frank at Mijnbestseller: *In de voetsporen van Anne Frank* (Following the footsteps of Anne Frank, ISBN 9789081423847).
[6] Email from the Anne Frank Fonds, 16 February 2009.

[7] POD stands for 'Print on Demand'. In POD, the author generally provides the text and layout. Most POD publishers in the Netherlands will provide registration at the central distribution centers in the Netherlands and Belgium (Centraal Boekhuis and Libris respectively). More information can be found on https://portal.boekhuis.nl/cbonline/. The POD publisher will often take care of sales and distribution. Seeking publicity is usually the author's task.
Hoogeveen.nu (2 July 2009), Reformatorisch Dagblad (11 November 2009), Weekblad Meppel (25 August 2009), Auschwitz-Bulletin (53, no. 3, September 2009), the Krant van Midden Drenthe (19 August 2009), De Echo ('Zuid' edition, 3 February 2010), The Frankfurter Rundschau (13 June 2011) and the NIW (31) wrote about my publications. The Hoogeveensche Courant (26 June 2009 and 14 August 2009) wrote an elaborate article on my photo project.
The *Krant van Hoogeveen* (25 August 2009), *Dagblad van het Noorden* (01 July 2009), *Meppeler Courant* (2 July 2009) and various other local (internet) media (www.deloodsboot.nl) and websites (http://anne-frank.startpagina.nl/, http://concentratiekampen.loggy.nl/, http://www.goethe.de/ins/nl/ams/nlindex.htm?wt_sc=nederland, http://www.stiwot.nl/) covered my publications on the internet. My gratitude goes out to all of them for their interest—especially the *Hoogeveensche Courant*.

[8] 'Random House is the exclusive licence holder for all Anne Frank texts in English within the US and Canada. They paid us a lot of money in order to acquire those rights, which is the reason they can decide whether or not to grant publishing rights of English Anne Frank texts and whether or not they want to charge money for it. This is normal procedure in international publishing.' (Email from the Anne Frank Fonds, 1 September 2009).

[9] Verenigingsblad Waffel (June 2010, no. 44).

[10] 'This book contains beautiful photographs. It is an excellent idea to take pictures of the places Anne has been to.' (Translation of a Dutch email from the Anne Frank Stichting, 14 August 2009).

[11] 'So far two members of the board are each holding a copy of your book and they are both very impressed with the book and like it very much.' (Email from the Anne Frank Fonds, 17 August 2008).

[12] Email from the Anne Frank Stichting, 17 February 2009. The Anne Frank Stichting was of the opinion that my book did not fit their objectives. I do not really understand their point, but of course I respect their decision. The Anne Frank Stichting employs its own writers who publish books on Anne and sell them in their shop.

[13] http://www.gettyimages.nl/.

[14] http://members.casema.nl/a.tiggeler/.

[15] http://www.amsterdamsetrams.nl/.

[16] http://www.gettyimages.nl/detail/3229104/Premium-Archive.

[17] The Kristallnacht was a pogrom organised by the Nazis against Jewish people in Germany (9-10 November, 1938).

[18] Melissa Müller does a great job of separating main topics from side ones, structures her book well without losing sight of the chronological order of events and manages to place Anne in a broader context. Dutch edition: *Anne Frank. De biografie* (Amsterdam, 1998) English edition: *Anne Frank: The Biography* (Macmillan 2013).

[19] Even now, new books about Anne are being published, some of which provide a new perspective. An example is Francine Prose's work *Anne Frank. Leven en werk van een schrijfster* (Amsterdam, 2009) which emphasises Anne's artistic talents. English editon: *Anne Frank: The Book, The Life, The Afterlife* (Harper Collins Books, 2009). Anne's life is also

available as a graphic novel (Jacobsen S. and E. Colón, *Anne Frank. The Anne Frank House Authorized Graphic Biography* (Anne Frank House, 2010)).
[20] Carol Ann Lee states that Hanneli and her family emigrated to the US in 1940 (Lee, Carol Ann, *Pluk rozen op aarde en vergeet mij niet. Anne Frank 1929-1945* (Amsterdam, 1998) p. 82). English editon: *Roses from the Earth: The Biography of Anne Frank* (Penguin Books, 2000). In fact, Hanneli was deported to Bergen-Belsen. On page 83, Carol writes that Otto's office was located at Singelgracht, but his office was at Singel (no. 400, Amsterdam). (Lee, Carol Ann, *Pluk rozen op aarde en vergeet mij niet. Anne Frank 1929-1945* (Amsterdam, 1998) p. 68).
[21] Anne Frank Stichting, *Anne Frank. Haar leven in brieven* [Her Life in Letters] (Amsterdam, 2006).
[22] Official English title of *The Diaries*: *The Diary of Anne Frank: The Revised Critical Edition*. The Netherlands Institute for War Documentation (New York, 2003). Original Dutch title: *De Dagboeken van Anne Frank*. Rijksinstituut voor Oorlogsdocumentatie (Amsterdam, 1990/2001).
[23] The Diaries, 28 September 1942.
[24] http://www.geheugenvanplanzuid.nl/tijdtijn/kaartAnneFrank.htm.
[25] De Telegraaf, 26 February 2008.
[26] http://www.yivoinstitute.org/
[27] In *The Diaries* (20 May 1944) Anne describes how a toppled vase ruins some of her work. This may have included entries from her diary.
[28] Otto had recently lost his family, so it is quite understandable that he left out Anne's curses directed at her mother.
[29] *De Dagboeken van Anne Frank*, Rijksinstituut voor Oorlogsdocumentatie (Amsterdam, 2001).
[30] http://www.stormfront.org/forum/t215308/.
[31] 'I learnt same more new words today, 'bordeel' [brothel] and 'cocotte' [floozie], I bought a separate booklet for those.' (*The Diaries*, 28 October 1942).
[32] 'Father made Margot and me a filing box with cards that are blanc on one side. This will become our card catalogue of books; we will both write down what books we have read, by whom they were written and the date.' (*The Diaries*, 27 February 1943).
[33] *The Diaries*, 11 May 1944.
[34] http://www.ymere.nl/ymere/index.asp?id=125.
[35] Eva Schloss' book (*Herinneringen van een joods meisje* [Memories of a Jewish Girl] (Breda, 2005)) states that she became Anne's friend. Eva lived at Merwedeplein during the same period as Anne. Anne does not mention her in her diary.
[36] 'I NEVER read Anne's diary, in spite of the fact that my daughter left it in our house for over a year. And probably I never will. My opinion on all those publications is the subject is being milked out (...) I think history has become too much focused on Anne, while so many other things were going on in the neighourhood [Francien lived near the Franks].' (translation of a Dutch email from Francien Bachra, 21 December 2010).
[37] http://www.geschiedenis24.nl/andere-tijden/afleveringen/2002-2003/Hilde-Goldberg.html
[38] http://www.bijbelaantekeningen.nl/blog/2011/01/19/oproep-informatie-over-anne-frank-gezocht/, De Weekrant Amsterdam 11 January 2011 p. 4, http://www.dichtbij.nl/amsterdam-zuid/regionaal-nieuws/artikel/1882689/gezocht-getuigen-anne-frank.aspx, www.echo.nl 28 December 2010, http://hetverhalenarchief.nl/user-stories, Nieuw Israelietisch Weekblad (NIW) 17 14 January 2011 p.37, http://rivierenbuurt.weblog.nl/2008/05/08/profielschets-stadsdeelvoorzitter/, http://www.seniorennet.nl/forum/viewtopic.php?t=71829&sid=432713e3d58f49e9b534626b863b51a5., http://www.deweekkrant.nl/pages.php?page=1528934, Weekblad De Echo Editie

Amsterdam Oud-Zuid 2 February 2011, http://www.joodswelzijn.nl/de-Benjamin-Joodse-agenda/Oproepjes-activiteiten-ingezonden-door-lezers.aspx.
The *Centraal Joods Overleg* (CJO, the Netherlands Central Jewish Consulting Body) does not have a magazine and only places content on their website that is directly related to the CJO. Some organisations, such as Gedenkstätte Bergen-Belsen and the Stadtbibliothek Aachen, do not have a newsletter. The Westerbork Camp Memorial Centre (Herinneringscentrum Kamp Westerbork) and the Anne Frank Stichting in Amsterdam did not reply when I asked for permission to publish a request for information about Anne.

[39] http://www.zuidelijkewandelweg.nl/.

[40] http://www.anne-in-de-buurt.nl/.

[41] *Frankfurter Allgemeine Zeitung* (www.faz.de), http://www.zeitungsverlag-aachen.de/, http://www.az-web.de.

[42] Max C. van der Glas.

[43] http://www.geheugenvanplanzuid.nl/ingezonden/113.htm.

[44] This also applies to some of Anne's other former neighbours who may have seen Anne without knowing. 'I am afraid I cannot help you because I never met Anne. Still, our paths must have crossed regularly since we lived in Niersstraat across the school that Anne attended for a few years. By coincidence, I worked at Sporthuis Centrum in 1961, and there I became acquainted with a girl from Rotterdam who would travel up and down between Amsterdam and Rotterdam. She later found a room with the Vergnes family at 15 Merwedeplein. This means we know the roof terrace very well, although it was quite a feat to climb up there because it had no regular exit. Incidentally, I married that girl, and that will be 48 years ago this January [2011].' (Translation of email from John Hendriks, 22 December 2010).

[45] http://www.nai.nl/bezoek/info.

[46] http://www.bma.amsterdam.nl/.

[47] http://www.joodsamsterdam.nl/.

[48] http://www.annefrank.org/en/Subsites/Home/.

[49] The periodical's title is *The Consumer* [De consument. Officieel orgaan op verkoopgebied verspreid door winkeliers aangesloten bij de Vakvereniging E.M.M] dated 11 January 1940. Page 7 lists the winners of puzzle 77 and 78. Anne Frank, 37 Merwedeplein won a photo album in group B (to be collected from shopkeeper J. v. Zalingen). In addition to a childrens' page, the periodical contains recipes, a serial and advertisements. Mrs. S. L. L. Fransen presented the periodical as a gift to the Anne Frank Stichting in 1996. (Email from the Anne Frank Stichting, 15 December 2011).

[50] 'Some are able to appreciate that [i.e. memories of Anne]. But we are her contemporaries and we lived in the same neighbourhood. We have seen so many houses being raided and none of those received the same attention. If I had had a say in it, the Merwedeplein residence would just have been rented out or sold.' (Translation of a Dutch email from Francien Bachra, 8 January 2011) Her lively memories of the Rivierenbuurt can be read on: http://www.zuidelijkewandelweg.nl/ingezonden/francienvanderveenbachra.htm.

FRANKFURT AM MAIN

Anne's Jewish ancestors in Germany were confronted with anti-Semitism and economic hardship as far back as the 17th century. Anti-Semitism—hostility against Jews—is as old as the hills.

In 1806, emperor Napoleon I (1804-1815) established equal rights for Jews in Germany. Germany consisted of independent principalities at the time, with Prussia and Austria as its leading states. During the German Empire (1871-1918), Jews could participate in public, economic and social life like all other citizens.

During the course of the 19th century, the German Empire industrialised rapidly; however, not everybody profited equally from these developments, and anti-Semitism rose amongst national-socialists, communists and conservatives. Many anti-Semitists were less successful in (banking) business and science than the Jews, and the government protected the Jewish community because they contributed considerable funds to the treasury.

Industrialisation, capitalism, fierce competition and theories centred on the survival of the fittest became prominent in economic practices. Many European countries sought to expand their territory and were engaged in a fierce battle for colonies and natural resources, which accelerated the rise of nationalism and racial classification theories.

During the German Empire, anti-Semitism was generally not expressed openly. Around 1900, however, the Bahnhofhotel Kölner Hof manager came to hate Jews to the extent that he prohibited them from entering his premises. The beer barrels were inscribed with degrading slogans about Jews, such as: *Der Jude ist nicht ein Teutscher sondern ein Täuscher* (Jews are not Germanic; they are cheaters), *Nicht ein Bürger, sondern ein Würger* (Not citizens but stranglers), *Das Judentum [...] verdient [...] Ausrottung* (Judaism deserves to be exterminated) and *Kauft nicht bei Juden* (Do not purchase from Jews)[1]. In spite of the open hostility against the Jewish, however, many Jews remained loyal to their native country.

Anne's (great) grandparents adopted German customs and habits, working their way up into the well-to-do, educated upper class of Jewish entrepreneurs in Frankfurt am Main.

Because of its strategic location at the river Main, Frankfurt am Main grew into a major trade centre over the course of the centuries.

Otto Frank did not attend a Jewish school. Instead, he attended advanced secondary education at the public Lessing Gymnasium. Following his graduation in 1908, Otto enrolled in a postgraduate course on economics at the Heidelberg University. However, he quit his studies after a few months, choosing to take up a position with a bank; subsequently, through a fellow student, he was offered the chance to gain work experience at Macy's department store in New York. Otto left for the United States in September 1909. Unfortunately, he had to return shortly afterwards because his father passed away on 17 September 1909. Following a brief return, Otto went back to the US. This time, he stayed for two years. He spent his first year working at Macy's department store before taking up a position at a bank. He returned to Germany in the autumn of 1911. Otto started out working for a company in Düsseldorf, which produced window frames. After a while, he joined a company producing horseshoes.[2]

The suppressed frustrations and internal tensions came to a head in WWI: 'Like the majority of Germans, the Jews responded to the August 1914 declarations of war with enthusiastic nationalism'.[3] The *Centralverein deutscher Staatsbürger jüdischen Glaubens* (Central Committee of German Citizens of the Jewish Faith) sent out an appeal:

'To the German Jews! In this fateful hour, our native country is calling its sons to arms. It speaks for itself that every German Jew who is called for duty is prepared to sacrifice his life. Fellow believers! We appeal to you to dedicate your strength to your native country and exceed your duty! Take up arms voluntarily! All of you, men and women alike, should serve your country by personal service of any kind and by providing funds and resources! Berlin, 1 August 1914.'[4]

Incidentally, conscription made enlistment in the armed forces compulsory at this time.

Propaganda by the German empire, as well as the prevailing public opinion in Germany that Russia had started WWI, caused the patriotism of German Jews to increase. Because of the pogroms in Russia and the Russian expulsion of Jews, German Jews felt especially militant.

WWI was the first military conflict on an immense scale in which new technologies and poison gas were deployed. Many young soldiers died in the trenches. Over 17 million soldiers and civilians died during this Great War. Eventually, Germany was defeated.

Otto Frank had been an officer in the German army and took Germany's defeat as a personal failure.

Following WWI, Germany was in an afflicted state. It was suffering from a severe economic crisis and pervasive unemployment. The country had been devastated. The Germans regarded the Treaty of Versailles (1919) as a major defeat. Germany was heavily impacted by its loss of territory, the forced dismantling of its army and the compensatory payments resulting from the Treaty.

During the Weimar Republic (1918-1933), the Jews were formally equal to other citizens; in practice, however, the crisis led to increased nationalism and anti-Semitism. Many blamed the Jews for the military defeat and the resulting hardships.

During this period, the Frank family bank experienced great difficulties as a result of the various restrictions imposed upon the currency trade. Privately, the Franks also experienced major financial losses; their savings had evaporated due to inflation, and their war shares, in which they had invested considerably with a view to German victory, had become void.[5]

The pre-WWII patriotic enthusiasm of German Jews can be compared to the current patriotism of Jews in the Netherlands. Most Dutch Jews support the royal family and happily join in singing the national anthem *Het Wilhelmus* at official gatherings, both domestically and abroad. Notably, however, it was the same in Germany before the onset of WWII.[6]

Following the German defeat, many German Jews devoted themselves to supporting democracy and socialism,[7] with a great number of them actively involved in interest groups, such as the *Reichsbund jüdischer Frontsoldaten* (national league of Jewish front soldiers), established in 1919, which looked after the interests of Jewish WWI veterans. Many Jews in Germany also provided support for the Ostjuden, who were subjected to heavy persecutions in Russia.

As far as I am aware, the Franks were not (very) active in politics. After WWI, Otto reluctantly took over the bank from his mother and his brother Herbert Frank (1891-1987, hereafter referred to as Herbert).[8] Herbert was not a very talented banker, and his eldest brother, Robert Frank (1886-1953, hereafter referred to as Robert),[9] was not interested in taking over.[10]

Otto was not a born banker, either. He had aborted his undergraduate course in economics and, according to Anne, was not particularly good at maths. 'I flatly refuse to do these <u>foul</u> math problems every day. Daddy Agrees that they're horrible. I'm almost better at them than he is, though neither of us is much good and we have to fetch Margot all the time,' Anne wrote whilst in hiding.[11]

The family bank in Germany was performing poorly. In 1923, Otto opened M. Frank & Zonen—a Dutch branch of the German family bank—in a stately building on a canal in Amsterdam (604 Keizersgracht). This was risky business: there was a dire scarcity of currencies in Germany and various restrictions were in force pertaining to banks that wanted to trade currencies.

This coincided with the failed coup by Adolf Hitler (1889-1945, hereafter referred to as Hitler) on 9 November 1923, and his consecutive brief detainment during which he wrote *Mein Kampf*, which was to become the National Socialist bible. It was still relatively quiet in the Netherlands.

On 31 December 1923, Otto registered the bank's Dutch affiliate with the Amsterdam Chamber of Commerce. Otto appointed Johannes 'Jo' Kleiman (1896-1959, hereafter referred to as Johannes) as his main accountant. M. Frank and Zonen did not do well; the bank went into liquidation in 1924.

The premises on 604 Keizersgracht[12] currently host various companies. The old architecture is still visible in many of its details, such as its letterbox and door knobs. There are many beautiful buildings with a rich history on Keizersgracht.

Otto married 25 year old Edith Holländer (1900-1945, hereafter referred to as Edith) on 12 May 1925, his birthday, in the synagogue in Aachen. Photographs show a radiant couple on their honeymoon in Italy. It was a marriage of convenience, and Edith's capital was of great use to Otto. Edith received a monthly allowance from her mother Rosalie 'Rosa' Holländer-Stern (1866-1942, hereafter referred to as Rosa) from Aachen.[13] Otto had been engaged before.[14]

'(...) I think Father married Mother because he thought she was the best replacement for his fiancée (...) it cannot be easy for a loving wife to know that she will never occupy the first place in her husband's heart,' Anne wrote in her diary.[15]

After the wedding, the couple took up residence in the home of Otto's parents at 4 Mertonstrasse in Frankfurt am Main. Otto's father, Michael Frank (1851-1909, hereafter referred to as Michael),[16] had purchased this semi-detached house in 1901. When his father died, his widow, Alice Betty Frank-Stern (1865-1953, hereafter referred to as Alice), was left in charge. The large, stately urban villa was suitable for the well-to-do upper middle class. It was located in an elegant residential area, and had a separate entrance for servants,[17] three balconies at the front, a dome, a central tower, and a large garden.

Otto and Edith had two daughters. Their first child, Margot Betti Frank (1926-1945, hereafter referred to as Margot), was born on 16 February 1926. Halfway through 1927, when Margot had just started walking, the family rented an apartment in a villa at 307 Marbachweg in the Betramshöhe area on the outskirts of Frankfurt am Main in the Dornbusch district—approximately three miles north-east of Mertonstrasse.[18] The rent was affordable for the Franks.[19]

The family lived at 307 Marbachweg, which was a semi-detached home like 4 Mertonstrasse, until late March, 1931. This large residence remains to this day, situated on a crossroads in a Frankfurt am Main suburb. It was built by its former landlord with the support of the Frankfurt am Main Teachers' Association.

The Franks inhabited the left side of the complex. The house actually comprised two separate living spaces, one on the first floor and one on the second, which were connected by a staircase. The family's living room, dining room and library were downstairs. Otto and Edith were not intellectuals, but they did read widely. I suspect Otto was not very interested in Jewish history. In 1922, the *Museum Jüdischer Altertümer*[20] opened in Frankfurt am Main (the Museum of Jewish Antiquities at 14/15 Untermainkai). I do not know whether the Franks visited this museum (with any interest).

In addition, the Franks' residence contained a kitchen, bathroom, and a room for Edith. The small room was furnished with Edith's elegant writing desk, which she had brought from Aachen, and a bookcase in which she kept her Hebrew prayer books. Otto was not interested in Jewish customs or the Torah. Edith's family celebrated Jewish holidays, ate kosher foods[21] and were prominent members of the Jewish community in Aachen. I cannot tell whether Otto's and Edith's parent would have gotten along well.

Otto and Edith's bedroom, Margot's bedroom, Edith's study and the maid's room were upstairs. The guest room at the back of the house had a balcony with potted flowers. Edith loved flowers. At the back of the Marbachweg residence there was an entrance leading to the basement and a play area.

Edith's parents and her brothers, Julius Holländer (1894-1967, hereafter referred to as Julius) and Walter Holländer (1897-1968, hereafter referred to as Walter), often came to visit from Aachen. Anne and Margot's uncles would regularly take them by car to their grandmother in Aachen.

The landlord resided on the ground floor of number 305; the first floor was inhabited by the Stab family. Their neighbours at number 303 were the Naumanns.

On 12 June 1929, when Margot had just turned three, Anne was born in the *Klinik des Vaterländischen Frauenvereins in der*

Eschenheimer Anlage[22] in Frankfurt am Main—a joyful family occasion.

In summer, the family liked to sit on the balcony at the back of the house, which overlooked a small garden and the street. The children would swing or play in the Stabs' sandpit. The Marbachweg area was a green area with plenty of space for children to play.

In October 1929, the year of Anne's birth, share prices at Wall Street crashed, which initiated a worldwide economic crisis that would last for many years. Tens of millions of people suffered because of unemployment and poverty—not only in America but also in Europe. Germany was afflicted the most by the crisis because of the burdensome WWI compensatory payments. The global crisis also severely affected the family bank.

The bank had to move to less costly premises on the edge of the city centre, at 20 Bockenheimer Anlage. In her diary, Anne refers to her parents' financial situation as follows:

'Daddy was born in Frankfurt am Main, his parents were immensely rich, Michael Frank owned a bank and became a millionaire and Alice Stern had very rich and distinguished parents. Michael Frank had not been at rich when he was young, but he duly worked his way up. In his youth Daddy had a real little rich boy's upbringing: parties every week, balls, festivities, beautiful girls, waltzing, dinners, a large home, etc., etc. After Grandpa's death [in 1909] all the money was lost and after the World War [WWI] and the inflation nothing was left at all.'[23]

The crisis and the inability of governments to turn the tide provided fertile ground for fascism in Europe. Hitler's national-socialists were rapidly gaining ground in Frankfurt am Main and throughout Germany and, as usual, blamed the Jews for the crisis and ensuing unemployment. Since Frankfurt am Main was an important financial centre and the Jews had always been very influential there, the national-socialists regarded Frankfurt am Main as the place from which the Jews wanted to establish their worldwide rule.

Jews were increasingly confronted with harassment. Otto's parents were members of the *B'nai B'rith* association.[24] This support group, run for and by Jews, had been established in Amsterdam in 1924. Although Otto was not very interested in Jewish traditions, he was very concerned for the fate of the Jewish people.

According to author Melissa Müller, one-fifth of the population of Westend—a district in Frankfurt am Main—was Jewish, but not many Jews lived in the Marbachweg area.[25] Jewish buildings, however, indicate that a Jewish community *was* active around Marbachweg. On 8 September 1929, the Jewish cemetery at Eschersheimer Landstraße was founded—not even half a mile from 307 Marbachweg. The synagogues taught Hebrew and organised readings. *Der Freisinnige Verein für jüdisches Gemeindeleben*[26] (the Liberal Society for Jewish Community Life) provided education at the Westend Synagogue.

According to Melissa Müller, there was no synagogue close to Marbachweg.[27] The main synagogue was located two and a half miles from Marbachweg, in the inner city. Melissa Müller indicates that the Franks did not attend the main (liberal) synagogue, but rather the Westend one.[28]

The Westend synagogue had been in use since 1910, and was designed by the architect Franz Roeckle (1879-1953). It was located at 30 Freiherr-vom-Stein-Strasse, and was the first synagogue in Frankfurt am Main outside the ancient city walls. There was another synagogue at 21-23 Unterlindau, the Synagoge der Israelitischen Gemeinde (synagogue of the Israelite community)—approximately two miles from Marbachweg.

Both men and women could attend the Westend Synagogue. The inner space and balcony comprised a total of 1,600 seats. Amongst the attendants of this synagogue were descendants of the Jews who had lived in Judengasse—a ghetto. Aside from the orthodox synagogue at Friedberger Anlage, this was the largest synagogue in Frankfurt.

Hitler's popularity grew as a result of the crisis; he continued hammering away at how the Jews were the main cause of the crisis, and in his book, *Mein Kampf*, the dictator revealed his plan to exterminate all Jews. Unemployed working class people, side-tracked military men and industrialists thought they could capitalise on the war industry.

The environment grew increasingly hostile of Jews. Otto decided to move to 24 Ganghoferstrasse when he discovered that his landlord felt sympathetic towards the Nazis. This must have been very painful for Otto: he had fought for his country in WWI and afterwards was discarded by the Germans as a Jew. Otto must have felt betrayed.

From 1930 onwards, Hitler's propaganda blaming the German government for not having eradicated the Jews before WWI became increasingly prominent.

People sometimes say that children were not aware of the danger at hand.[29] Margot and Anne were still very young; nevertheless, they must have sensed Otto and Edith's tensions. Parents did their utmost to keep their children aloof from the Nazi danger.

Another reason why Otto moved to 24 Ganghoferstrasse was the decline of his banking business, which forced him to look for a cheaper apartment. His sister Helene Frank (1893-1986, hereafter referred to as Helene)[30] had moved to Switzerland in 1930 because it provided new job opportunities for her husband Erich Elias (1890-1984, hereafter referred to as Erich). His brother Herbert left the family bank and moved to Paris in 1932. During the move, Anne temporarily stayed with her neighbours and their daughter, Gertrud Naumann (1917-2002),[31] at 303 Marbachweg.

From late March 1931 to late March 1933, the Franks rented a five-room apartment on the ground floor of 24 Ganghoferstrasse. Unlike the one at Marbachweg, the urban villa at 24 Ganghoferstrasse did not have a balcony. It did, however, have a backyard and an inner court where Margot and Anne could play. The house was smaller than 307 Marbachweg. The family had taken their old furniture and furnished their home with pretty steel-blue couches and oval side-tables.[32]

The white building had a protruding façade with window shutters, and was situated in a suburb of Frankfurt am Main that was known as the poets' district: many physicians, lawyers and architects resided here. It was one of the many urban villas in the street.

Ganghoferstrasse was within walking distance from Marbachweg in a north-western direction, on the other side of Eschersheimer Landstraße. Although they lived a mile away from Marbachweg, Anne and Margot kept in touch with some of their old friends from the area. They also quickly made friends in their new neighbourhood. Margot attended the Ludwig Richter Schule (10 Hinter den Ulmen, Frankfurt am Main).[33] At this progressive school, Anne received Jewish religious education.[34]

There used to be a green meadow across the street where the children would play on the sandy hills; now, however, these have been built over. Margot loved to pull Anne on a little sledge. In the (back)yard, the children would play with water in an old metal bucket. The Franks were a tolerant family, and Anne and Margot would play with children from various backgrounds: Catholic, Protestant and Jewish. Margot attended a friend's Communion celebration. When the Franks celebrate Hanukkah, an eight-day Jewish winter festival, neighbouring children would join in. Whenever Anne's cousins, Stephan Elias (1921-1980, hereafter referred to as Stephan) and Bernhard 'Buddy' Elias (born in 1925, hereafter referred to as Buddy), visited, the children would be spoiled and the house would be full of toys.

Some defended the Jews that had fought in the German army during WWI. In 1932, the *Reichsbund jüdischer Frontsoldaten* (National League of Jewish Front Soldiers) handed the German president Paul Ludwig Hans von Beneckendorf und von Hindenburg (1847-1934, hereafter referred to as Hindenburg) the book *Die jüdischen Gefallenen des Deutschen Heeres, der deutschen Marine und der deutschen Schutstruppen 1914-1918. Ein Gedenkbuch.* (Jewish soldiers killed in action serving the German army, the German navy and the German defence troops 1914-1918. A memorial book.).[35] This, however, did not decrease anti-Semitism: 'I [Otto] remember that even in 1932, SA troops would march by singing: 'When Jewish blood splashes off the knife'.[36]

Otto and Edith were burdened by financial problems and the antagonistic atmosphere; however, yet they wanted their children to live a care-free life as much as possible. Their mother would regularly take Anne and Margot shopping in the Frankfurt am Main city centre. Edith would buy clothes for her children, who always looked impeccable. Edith once bought a beautiful, white fur coat for Anne and a pair of patent-leather shoes for Margot. After shopping, they often went to a café on Hauptwache in the centre of Frankfurt am Main. Edith would treat Anne and Margot to *Kaffee und Kuchen* (coffee and cake). Edith and Otto must have noticed the anti-Semitic slogans chalked on the shop windows, indicating the doom at hand.

On 31 July 1932, fourteen million German citizens voted for Hitler, which made his national-socialist party, the Nationalsozialistische Deutsche Arbeiterpartei (NSDAP), the largest party in the new Reichstag parliament.[37] On 30 January 1933, Hindenburg appointed Hitler as the Reichskanzler (national chancellor), heralding the end of the Weimar Republic (1918-1933).

Otto about Hitler: 'We [Otto and Edith] were sitting around the table listening to the radio. Then came the news that Hitler had become Chancellor. This was followed by a report of the SA torch lit procession in Berlin and we could hear the screaming and cheering. Hitler ended his speech with the words, "Just give me four years." Our host then said enthusiastically: "Let's see what that man can do!" I was speechless, my wife stunned.'[38]

On 13 March 1933, the Nazis celebrated their victory in the city hall (Römer) at Römerberg. Swastika flags waved on the porch. Following the takeover by the Nazis, the Jewish mayor, Ludwig Landmann (1868-1945), fled to Berlin and the Nazis instated their own front man. In Anne's times, Römerberg was the city's central square, with medieval buildings and a city hall. Hitler eliminated his opponents and outlawed the Jews.

Soon after the takeover, the SA (*Sturmabteilung*, the paramilitary wing of the Nazi party) barricaded the entrances of Jewish businesses. Otto's (Jewish) family bank was greatly affected by the national-socialist rule and, before long, Otto was unable to afford the rent of 24 Ganghoferstrasse.[39] He and his family temporarily moved in with his mother, Alice, on Mertonstrasse.[40] The urban villa was in the Westend area, close to the synagogue. This was the house in which Otto grew up, and he lived there with his family from late March 1933 to July 1933.

Friedrich Krebs (1894-1961), Frankfurt's new mayor,[41] coordinated the dismantling of Jewish shops and the removal of all Jewish doctors, lawyers, and any other Jewish entrepreneurs, from their posts. The leading Jewish-owned department store Tietz,[42] founded by Hermann Tietz (1837-1907), had branches in all major European cities but, by Nazi order, the Dresdner Bank appointed Georg Karg (1888-1972) as the new director of the enterprise, replacing the Jewish-owned Tietz by Hertie-Warenhausunternehmen. Jews were banned from these 'Aryanised' businesses.

On 1 April 1933, Nazi students and the SA occupied the University of Frankfurt. With the help of these students, Jewish professors and students were expelled from university.

The University of Frankfurt (Goethe-Universität, Senckenberganlage 31)[43] had been founded in 1914. Its campus was located near to Alice's home on Mertonstrasse. 'Shortly after Hitler seized power, the national-socialists expelled from the universities all Jewish and any opposing scientists and students. The University of Frankfurt was particularly adversely affected by these enforcements: teaching permissions of 100 Jewish scientists were withdrawn in the spring of 1933; one-third of all professors were forced to step down; another 16 teachers voluntarily left their posts out of political conviction; many students were expelled from the university and forced to give up their studies. Frankfurt's internationally renowned, liberal university was turned into a 'well-aligned' educational institution.'[44]

The Nazis were very influential in the construction industry; project managers and contractors were eager to accept Nazi projects. In 1930, IG Farben (Interessen Gemeinschaft Farbenindustrie Aktiengesellschaft) moved into a monumental building at 1 Grüneburgplatz, built in the style of the New Objectivity.

IG Farben was a large chemical concern that produced Zyklon B, which would be used by the Nazis to kill millions of Jews in Eastern European extermination camps ten years later.

The Nazis implemented restrictions that isolated Jews from society. The school board refuse to enrol Anne in pre-school because she was Jewish. Margot attended the Varrentrapp school, where she had to sit apart from her non-Jewish classmates; she was seven at the time. Many Jews left Frankfurt am Main after the Nazis had assumed power. The sculptor Benno Elkan (1877-1960), for example, emigrated from Frankfurt am Main to London.[45] After the war, Otto refers to this period in a letter: 'When many of my fellow Germans changed into multitudes of nationalist, cruel, anti-Semitic criminals, I had to draw the obvious conclusion and, although I was very much aggrieved by it, I realised that Germany was not the only place in the world and left my country for good.'[46]

The family banking business continued to decline, and Otto wanted to prevent his property from falling into the hands of the Nazis. He also wanted to protect his wife and children from Hitler's violence.

Otto aimed for Amsterdam because he had some important contacts there. In 1933, Otto's brother-in-law Erich offered him the opportunity to set up a business in the Netherlands, which is why he did not want to leave for Switzerland, London or the United States. Apparently, Otto did not want to send his children to Palestine either. The *Hilfsverein der Deutschen Juden*[47] was a society that supported Jews who wanted to emigrate and Jewish children who wanted to move to Palestine. Alice left 4 Mertonstrasse and moved to Basel. She had a difficult time bidding farewell to 4 Mertonstrasse, having lived there for thirty years.

In Frankfurt am Main, Anne's place of birth, I stayed in Hotel National near the Hauptbahnhof central station, and strolled along many of these places that are reminiscent of Anne.

When Anne was born, approximately 540,000 people lived in Frankfurt am Main, including 30,000 Jews. Frankfurt am Main had the second largest population of Jews in Germany, after Berlin. Three out of four Jews were murdered during WWII, including Anne. There were other communities that also suffered greatly under the Nazi regime, such as the gypsies. Survivors had not just lost their family, but also their homes and possessions. Otto, the only survivor amongst the people hiding in the Annex, lost his wife and children.

The assassination of the German diplomat Ernst vom Rath (1909-1938) on 7 November 1938 in Paris, allegedly committed by the 17 year old Polish Jew Herschel Grynszpan (1921-1942), was a 'good' excuse for the Nazis to destroy Jewish property in Frankfurt am Main during the Reichskristallnacht (8-9 November 1938). The Westend Synagogue was damaged by a fire, and all other Frankfurt synagogues were completely destroyed by the Nazis.

Anne was nine at the time, leading a care-free life at Merwedeplein, oblivious of the horrors going on in her home town. The Nazis did not just damage Jewish properties in Frankfurt am Main, but throughout Germany. They ransacked over 1,600 German synagogues. Even the *Museum Jüdischer Altertümer* was destroyed and looted by gangs. The Gestapo deported the liberal rabbi of the Westend Synagogue, Georg Salzberger (1882-1975),[48] to the Dachau concentration camp. Apparently, he was released: he emigrated to the UK in 1939. The Nazis also confiscated Jewish property. The so-called *Judenvertrag* that took effect on 3 April 1939 compelled Jews to sell their property for next to nothing, and they were held liable for the damage the Nazis had done. The Nazis enjoyed humiliating the Jewish community. Otto's possessions were relatively safe because he had moved to Amsterdam and was running a business at 400 Singel.

Throughout WWII, the Westend Synagogue served as a furniture storage for the citizens of Frankfurt. Anne was already hiding in the Annex when British bombs destroyed Frankfurt am Main's medieval city centre on 22 March 1944. The Westend Synagogue was severely damaged during this air raid, and the Hauptwache[49] and the *Klinik des Vaterländischen Frauenvereins in der Eschenheimer Anlage*[50] did not remain unharmed either. The Untermainbrücke 'arose from its ashes' following the war.

Nothing is left of the old medieval town that Anne would stroll through as a very young child. Many Jewish monuments have also disappeared for good. Some of the old buildings, such as the baroque café on Hauptwache, were reconstructed after WWII. Because of its strategic location at the river Main, Frankfurt managed to recuperate quickly. It is now a modern city and an important financial centre. The horizon is dominated by tall skyscrapers with lots of glass and steel; because of these buildings, Frankfurt am Main is sometimes referred to as Europe's Manhattan. Old and new buildings are scattered randomly across the map in an architectural chaos. The clear medieval street plan no longer exists.

After the war, the *Jüdische Betreuungsstelle der Stadt Frankfurt am Main* (Frankfurt Municipal Care for the Jews)[51] took care of the survivors. In 1945, four hundred of them returned to Frankfurt. On 9 November 1946, the Jews remembered their dead on the Jewish cemetery at 10 Rat-Beil-Strasse.[52]

Only a handful of monuments to the rich, pre-war Jewish life have survived up to the present. For example, the Jewish cemetery at 238 Eckenheimer Landstrasse,[53] founded in 1928, commemorates the 12,000 Jewish citizens of Frankfurt who, like Ann, died during the war, as does the cemetery on Rat-Beil-Straße.

The municipality did not attempt to restore the Westend Synagogue directly after WWII: there was a lack of finances as a result of the war and a lack of faith in the re-emergence of a flourishing Jewish community after the Holocaust. The first post-war religious function in the synagogue was held on 12 September 1945. The sermon was given by Rabbi Leopold Neuhaus (1879-1954), a Theresienstadt survivor. However, many Jews no longer felt at home in Frankfurt am Main, and ended up leaving for the United States and Israel. By 1949, over 5,000 Eastern European Jews had arrived in Frankfurt because they were no longer able to thrive in their own country.

On 6 September 1950, the Westend Synagogue was re-consecrated and, during the 1989-1994 restorations, many original building elements were revealed. The current appearance of the synagogue is very similar to what the Franks would have seen.

Frankfurt University also was heavily damaged during WWII.[54] It was rebuilt after the war and re-emerged as a major, international academic centre. The university has not allowed the Holocaust to pass into oblivion. In 2011, the historian Wolfgang Benz (born in 1941) delivered a lecture at the university's Westend campus—the former premises of IG Farben at 1 Grüneburgplatz—which centred on national-socialist propaganda.

In spite of the heavy bombings on Frankfurt am Main by the allied forces, the IG Farben building survived the war. Since 2000, the Fritz Bauer Institute has been established in this former mass-murder plant. 'The Fritz Bauer Institute is an interdisciplinary, independent research, documentation and educational organisation that studies the history of national-socialist mass crimes in general and the Holocaust in particular, as well as its impact up to the present. The institute is located in the IG Farben building on the Westend Campus of the Goethe University Frankfurt am Main.'[55]

A memorial plate at the entrance of the former plant states: 'This building was designed by the architect Hans Poelzig [(1869-1936)] and erected between 1928 to 1931 as the headquarters of IG Farben Industries. Between 1933 and 1945, as one of the largest chemical concerns in the world, the company increasingly put its scientific knowledge and production technologies into the service of war preparations and the National Socialist regime of terror. From 1942 to 1945, IG Farben, together with the SS, maintained the concentration camp at Buna-Monowitz adjacent to the IG Farben factory at Auschwitz. Of the ten thousand prisoners made to work for the company there, most were murdered. In the Nazi extermination camps many hundreds of thousands of people, mostly Jews, were killed by Zyklon B gas, which was sold by an IG Farben company. From 1945 the building was the seat of the American military government and the High Commissioner for Germany. On 19 September 1945, the State of Hesse was proclaimed here. From 1952 to 1995 the building was the headquarters of the 5th Corps of US Army. Aware of the history of the building, the State of Hesse acquired it in 1996 for the Johann Wolfgang Goethe University. In the future it will be used for teaching and research. Nobody can withdraw from the history of one's people. One should know that the past must not be based on forgetting else it returns and becomes the present.' Visitors can take an architectural tour of this bleak building.[56]

Anne's home at 307 Marbachweg also survived WWII. The Franks lived there until late March 1931. When I arrived there, I noticed that, since the old photographs were taken, the urban villa has hardly changed: it is easy to recognise the windows with their green shutters and the gabled roof. The birch tree in front of the 307 Marbachweg residence has grown tremendously since Anne's times, and now occupies a prominent place in the garden. Anne would look out on a much smaller tree.

One of the current residents allowed me to take photographs outside the building. For security reasons, however, he preferred not to have any pictures taken in the courtyard or inside the house. Of course, I thanked him and respected his wishes. The 307 Marbachweg residence does not have a plate commemorating Anne. She used to have a beautiful view from the balcony, which is now obstructed by cars, fences and the foliage of a tree.

In Frankfurt am Main, the Holocaust is still being studied, and some of the younger citizens are interested in Anne and her legacy. The *Jugendbegegnungsstätte Anne Frank e.V* youth group[57] is located in the Dornbusch district, half a mile from Marbachweg and a mile from Ganghoferstrasse.[58]

Fortunately, the urban villa at 24 Ganghoferstrasse also survived the war: the suburb was never bombed. The Dornbusch district is situated in the north of Frankfurt am Main. Anne lived there from late March 1931 to late March 1933. Most of the buildings in this street still breathe a thirties atmosphere. The upper floor of 24 Ganghoferstrasse allows a nice view of the street and its urban villas. I like such houses; their individual architecture, the history of their residents and the fact that they are not all the same like terraced houses. I simply ignore the cars, asphalt road, street lighting and road marks that remind me of the present.

I was received on a friendly note by the current residents of 24 Ganghoferstrasse. I rang the doorbell and was lucky to find them home because the letter I had sent them through TNT (currently PostNL) came back to me: the villa has multiple inhabitants and I had not directed my letter to a particular person. The current residents informed me that 24 Ganghoferstrasse is visited regularly by students and journalists who are interested in Anne's story.

I asked the inhabitants whether they recognised the place in the old photo that shows Anne and her sister playing with one of their friends. They did, and enthusiastically pointed me to their backyard. When I took a current photograph of the backyard from the same perspective, I could feel the emptiness Anne left behind.

I appreciate the interest the inhabitants of 24 Ganghoferstrasse take in the history of their home and its previous residents; it makes me feel supported in my project. There is more overgrowth at the back of the house now, and most of the paving stones have made way for a lawn. The sandpit Anne used to play in has disappeared from the backyard. The outline of neighbours' house is still partly the same, although the open veranda is now a closed veranda.

Three and a half miles south of 24 Ganghoferstrasse was 4 Jordanstrasse where the Franks stayed with Otto's mother Alice from late March 1933 to July 1933. It is not easy to find 4 Jordanstrasse because the street names changed after WWII. From 1917 through to 1933, Jordanstrasse was known as Mertonstrasse, a name which was then changed to Dantestrasse. Strangely enough, the current Jordanstrasse starts with a number 6. The friendly owner of a café in the current Jordanstrasse handed me an old black-and-white photograph showing the beautiful stately mansions of the 1930 Jordanstrasse. Alice's home was also in this street: it had a large dome and was surrounded by lush overgrowth. Unfortunately, her former house in Jordanstrasse was demolished following WWII. The neighbourhood's old atmosphere is completely gone.

After WWII, some of Frankfurts' inhabitants blamed the Jews for the terrors of the war. Gradually, however, when people were able to look back on the war more objectively, they became a little more understanding towards the Jews.

In 1957, 2,000 teenagers travelled from Hamburg to Bergen-Belsen to commemorate Anne's death. The memorial plate on the façade of 24 Ganghoferstrasse was placed on their initiative. Its inscription reads: 'This used to be Anne Frank's house (born on 12/06/1929 in Frankfurt A. Main). She became a victim of the national-socialist persecution and died in the Bergen-Belsen KZ-Lager in 1945. Her life and death—our obligation. The youth of Frankfurt.'[59] There was a memorial service in the Paulskirche in Frankfurt in the same year.[60]

The plate at 24 Ganghoferstrasse is the only sign I have seen on the former residences of Anne in Frankfurt am Main that commemorates her as a war victim. Although Frankfurt am Main does show some interest in her, there is a noticeable lack of a prominent statue of Anne in the centre of her place of birth.

There are, however, some general references to the war in the city centre. The commemorative plaque on Römerberg reads: 'In this place, on 10 May 1933, national-socialist students burnt the books of literary authors, scientists, essayists and philosophers.' The edge of the plaque reads: 'This was merely a prelude, for where people burn books, people will eventually burn people.'[61] This is a quote from Heinrich Heine (1797-1856). The books burnt by the Nazis had been written by Jewish authors and social critics, such as Sigmund Freud (1856-1939), Stefan Zweig (1881-1942) and Bertold Brecht (1898-1956).

There are a few references to Anne outside of the city centre, such as the Anne Frank School[62] and the Anne Frank Strasse. The Jewish Monument at Battonnstrasse commemorates the Jewish inhabitants of Frankfurt am Main who were murdered, including Anne.[63] It is located next to the former synagogue that was destroyed during Kristallnacht in 1938. The Historic Museum in Frankfurt am Main organised exhibitions about Anne. The exhibition *Anne Frank in the World, 1929-1945* took place in the Paulskirche[64] in 1985.[65]

In 1992, the Jewish Museum in Frankfurt am Main (14/15 Untermainkai)[66] opened the *Museum Judengasse*, which exhibits the history of Judaism in Frankfurt am Main and commemorates the Jewish inhabitants of Frankfurt who were killed by the Nazis. In 2008, I visited a special photographic exhibition *Special Express to Death: Deportation on the German National Railway* about the role the *Deutsche Bundesbahn* (DB) played in transporting Jews and gypsies to the concentration camps. Anne is listed in the *Gedenkbuch Opfer der Verfolgung der Juden unter der nationalsozialistischen Gewaltherrschaft in Deutschland 1933-1945* (Memorial Book: Victims of the Persecution of Jews under the National-Socialist Tyranny in Germany 1933-1945) by the German Federal Archives[67] that accompanied the exhibition.

Anne's photograph was probably not on display in this exhibition since she was not deported directly from Germany to the extermination camps in the east. When she was deported from the Westerbork camp to Auschwitz, however, she will have been transferred onto the German National Railway once she had crossed the German border.

The exhibition also displayed many children of Anne's age group who had lived in Germany or had fled to France and who were killed by the Nazis. Steffi Bernheim, for example, was born on 11 January 1930 in Berlin. The Bernheims fled Germany and went to live in Paris, France, on 60 Rue de Provence. Steffi was arrested during a large-scale razzia and sent to Auschwitz on transport 23 on 24 August 1942, where she joined her mother, who had been imprisoned earlier. Her father, Walter, and brother, Norbert, followed on transport 57 on 18 July 1943.[68] This family's fate is no less tragic than that of the Franks.

I experience my environment best when I walk. I ended up walking many miles to visit Anne's locations. In spite of my hiking shoes, I had blisters on my feet. The current residents of 24 Ganghoferstrasse were considerate enough to offer me a ride back to my hotel near Frankfurt central station, where I could enjoy a good night's sleep.

[1] Source: (various) labels from the Kölner Hof hotel dated around 1900 and containing anti-Semitic texts. Archives of the Jewish Historical Museum, inventory no. 00004698.
[2] http://www.annefrank.org/en/Anne-Frank/All-people/Otto-Frank/.
[3] 'Wie die Mehrheit der Deutschen, reagierten die Juden auf die Kriegserklärungen im August 1914 mit vaterländischer Begeisterung zu machen.' From: Rachel Heuberger and Helgo Krohn. *Hinaus aus dem ghetto…Juden in Frankfurt am Main 1800-1950* [Out of the Ghetto: Jews in Frankfurt am Main 1800-1950] (Frankfurt am Main, 1988), p. 129.
[4] 'An die deutschen Juden! In schicksalsernster Stunde ruft das Vaterland seine Söhne unter die Fahnen. Dass jeder deutsche Jude zu den Opfern an Gut und Blut bereit ist, die die Pflicht erheischt, ist selbstverständlich. Glaubensgenossen! Wir rufen Euch auf, über dass Mass der Pflicht hinaus Eure Kräfte dem Vaterlande nu widmen! Eilet freiwillig zu den Fahnen! Ihr alle –Männer und Frauen- stellet Euch durch persönliche Hilfeleistung jeder Art und durch Hergabe von Geld und Gut in den Dienst der Vaterlandes! Berlin, den 1. August 1914.' From: Rachel Heuberger en Helgo Krohn. *Hinaus aus dem ghetto…Juden in Frankfurt am Main 1800-1950* (Frankfurt am Main, 1988), p. 130.
[5] Melissa Müller, *Anne Frank. De biografie* (Amsterdam, 1998), p. 27. Original German edition: *Das Mädchen Anne Frank. Die Biographie*. English edition: *Anne Frank. The Biography* (Macmillan, 2013).
[6] Max C. van der Glas, email dated 22 December 2010.
[7] Rachel Heuberger and Helgo Krohn. *Hinaus aus dem ghetto…Juden in Frankfurt am Main 1800-1950* (Frankfurt am Main, 1988), p. 147.
[8] http://www.freebase.com/view/en/herbert_frank.
[9] http://www.freebase.com/view/m/073jm1t.
[10] Some authors describe Otto as a born banker. 'Otto was de enige van zijn broers die zich interesseerde voor de bankzaken.' [Otto was the only one amongst his brothers who was interested in banking.] From: Hans Ulrich, *Wie was Anne Frank? Haar leven, het Achterhuis en haar dood* (Laren, 2010), p. 27. English edition: *Who was Anne Frank: Her Life, the Secret Annex and her Death.* (Verbum, 2011).
[11] *The Diaries*, 14 October 1942.
[12] 604 Keizersgracht, see http://monumentenregister.cultureelerfgoed.nl/.
[13] 'Otto did not marry Edith because of her dowry.' Buddy Elias, email dated 30 December 2010.
[14] Cor Suijk (born in 1924, hereafter referred to as Cor) is the former director of the Anne Frank Stichting. In the beginning of the 1980s, he received four original pages from *The Diaries* from Otto's inheritance in which Anne states that Otto never loved Edith much, because he could not forget his first love whose parents would not let her marry him. Otto wanted Cor to receive these papers after his death. Insiders already knew about these pages from the A version of Anne's diary. These four pages, however, were part of the rewritten (B-)version by Anne, which she planned to publish after the war.

Otto Frank, who passed away in 1980, wanted to make these extracts public after his demise. The NIOD added a note to the 8 February 1944 entry of Anne's diary: 'In the 47 lines omitted here [the four retrieved pages] Anne Frank gave an extremely unkind [which is incorrect, Anne shows empathy for her mother] and partly unfair picture [also incorrect, Anne describes her parents' marriage as not characterised by real passion but by correctitude] of her parents' marriage. At the request of the Frank family this passage has been deleted.' From: *De Dagboeken van Anne Frank* [The Diary of Anne Frank: The Critical Edition.] Rijksinstituut voor Oorlogsdocumentatie (Amsterdam, 1990), p. 499.

A nasty quarrel ensued. According to Cor (email dated 13 January 2011), various sources, e.g. the NRC national paper 13 March 2001 issue, incorrectly stated that he had sold the retrieved pages written by Anne Frank to the NIOD.

'When, after a long, antagonistic row between the NIOD, the Anne Frank House and the Anne Frank Fonds about my possession of the pages, the government prosecutor concluded after thorough investigation that I was the legal owner, I donated the pages to the NIOD. Three months later, the Dutch government, as a token of appreciation, decided to support my educational institute in the United States [www.c-hef.org] with a considerable amount of money.'

The Anne Frank Fonds is of the opinion that it holds the rights to the diaries. The missing pages were published in *The Diary of Anne Frank: the Critical Edition* by the Netherlands Institute for War Documentation (1st Dutch ed. Amsterdam 1986, 1st English ed. New York 1989).

[15] *The Diaries*, 8 February 1944.

[16] http://www.freebase.com/view/m/073j4gd.

[17] Melissa Müller, *Anne Frank. De biografie* (Amsterdam, 1998), p. 23.

[18] Melissa Müller, *Anne Frank. De biografie* (Amsterdam, 1998), p. 23. After WWI, Frankfurt am Main expanded and new districts were built, such as Bergen-Enkheim and Frankfurter Berg.

[19] Melissa Müller, *Anne Frank. De biografie* (Amsterdam, 1998), p. 23.

[20] http://juedischesmuseum.de/museumsgeschichte.html?&L=1.

[21] Foods prepared according to Jewish dietary law.

[22] The exact location of this hospital 'of the fatherland's women's association' could not be traced: it was destroyed during WWII. Buddy Elias (email 30 December 2010): 'Yes as much as I know Anne was born in that Klinik. Address unknown to me.'

[23] *The Diaries*, 8 May 1944.

[24] http://www.bnaibrith-amsterdam.org/.

[25] Melissa Müller, *Anne Frank. De biografie* (Amsterdam, 1998), p. 24.

[26] https://www.uzh.ch/khist/static/Online_Docs/100_Jahre_Westend_Synagoge_100_a ni.pdf.

[27] Melissa Müller, *Anne Frank. De biografie* (Amsterdam, 1998), p. 24.

[28] Melissa Müller, *Anne Frank. De biografie* (Amsterdam, 1998), p. 24. Some others doubt whether the Franks attended the Westend Synagogue. 'Ob Familie Frank die Westendsynagoge besuchte weiss ich nicht. Auf jeden Fall war die

Westendsynagoge jedoch seit Ihrer Gründung bis zur Progromnacht eine Liberale Synagoge. Erst nach dem 2. Weltkrieg wird sie als orthodoxe Synagoge benutzt (...)'. [I do not know whether the Franks attended the Westend Synagogue. In any case, the Westend Synagogue was a liberal synagogue from its establishment up to the night of the Pogrom. Only after the Second World War did it become an orthodox synagogue (...)'] Email from Rachel Heuberger, Manager Hebraica and Judaica Collection, Frankfurt university library, dated 27 June 2010.

[29] Melissa Müller, *Anne Frank. De biografie* (Amsterdam, 1998), p. 25.

[30] http://www.freebase.com/view/en/herbert_frank.

[31] http://www.freebase.com/view/en/gertrud_naumann.

[32] Melissa Müller, *Anne Frank. De biografie* (Amsterdam, 1998), p. 33.

[33] http://ludwigrichterschule.de/2009/ (German only). According to Mr. Erhard Claudy (email dated 24 June 2011) the Ludwig-Richter Schule in Frankfurt am Main still owns a poor quality photograph with Margot Frank on it.

[34] http://www.annefrank.org/en/Anne-Frank/Life-in-Germany/Happy-years/.

[35] The 'Bund jüdischer Soldaten' (RjF) was banned by the Nazis in 1938: http://www.bundjuedischersoldaten-online.com/39994.html (German only)

[36] http://www.annefrank.org/en/Anne-Frank/Life-in-Germany/Crisis-and-anti-Semitism/

[37] http://en.wikipedia.org/wiki/German_federal_election,_July_1932

[38] http://www.annefrank.org/en/Anne-Frank/Life-in-Germany/Crisis-and-anti-Semitism/

[39] http://www.frankfurt1933-1945.de (German only)

[40] Melissa Müller refers to this street as the Mertoustrasse (incorrect spelling) Melissa Müller, *Anne Frank. De biografie* (Amsterdam, 1998) p. 36.

[41] http://de.wikipedia.org/wiki/Friedrich_Krebs_(Politiker) (German only).

[42] http://www.fundinguniverse.com/company-histories/HERTIE-WARENUND-KAUFHAUS-GMBH-company-History.html.

[43] Translated from German content on: http://www2.uni-frankfurt.de/38072330/geschichte (German only, an English summary can be found at http://www2.uni-frankfurt.de/43281596/history).

[44] http://www2.uni-frankfurt.de/38072330/geschichte (German only, an English summary can be found at http://www2.uni-frankfurt.de/43281596/history).

[45] http://en.wikipedia.org/wiki/Ludwig_Landmann.

[46] http://www.annefrank.org/en/Anne-Frank/Life-in-Germany/Emigration-plans/.

[47] http://www1.yadvashem.org/odot_pdf/Microsoft%20Word%20-%206371.pdf.

[48] Additional information on Georg Salzberger can be found on http://www.judengasse.de/ehtml/P147.htm (German only).

[49] http://www.annefrank.org/en/Subsites/Tijdlijn/#!/en/Subsites/Timeline/World-War-Two-1939-1945/The-Arrest/1945/The-ruins-of-the-Hauptwache-the-main-police-station-in-Frankfurt-am-Main-AprilMay-1945-/.

[50] http://www.ffmhist.de/ffm33-45/portal01/portal01.php?ziel=t_hm_frank1 (German only).

[51] http://www.ffmhist.de/ffm33-45/portal01/portal01.php?ziel=t_jm_hist_ab1945 (German only).

[52] Rachel Heuberger and Helgo Krohn, *Hinaus aus dem ghetto... Juden in Frankfurt am Main 1800-1950* [Out of the Ghetto: Jews in Frankfurt am Main 1800-1950] (Frankfurt am Main, 1988), p. 202.
[53] http://www.jg-ffm.de/index.php/juedische-friedhoefe (German only).
[54] http://www2.uni-frankfurt.de/38072330/geschichte (German only, an English summary can be found at http://www2.uni-frankfurt.de/43281596/history).
[55] http://www.fritz-bauer-institut.de (German only, a partial English version can be found at http://www.fritz-bauer-institut.de/institut.html?&L=1).
[56] http://www.frankfurt-fuehrungen.de/frankfurt_tour3_e.htm.
[57] http://www.jbs-anne-frank.de/ (German only).
[58] http://www.jbs-anne-frank.de/ (German only).
[59] Translated from German content on: http://jd-f.de/web/index.php?option=com_content&task=view&id=17&Itemid=10 (German only).
[60] http://www.annefrank.org/en/Subsites/Timeline/#!/en/Subsites/Timeline/Postwar-period-1945--present-day/Saved-from-Demolition/1957/Commemoration-of-Anne-Frank-in-Frankfurt-am-Main/.
[61] Translated from German: http://www.stadtgeschichte-ffm.de/service/gedenktafeln/buecherverbrennung.html (German only).
[62] http://www.anne-frank-schule-frankfurt.de/ (German only).
[63] http://www.jg-ffm.de/index.php/juedische-friedhoefe (German only).
[64] http://en.wikipedia.org/wiki/St._Paul%27s_Church,_Frankfurt_am_Main.
[65] http://www.historisches-museum.frankfurt.de/index.php?article_id=73&clang=0 (German only).
[66] http://juedischesmuseum.de/startseite.html?&L=1.
[67] http://www.bundesarchiv.de/gedenkbuch/index.html.en.
[68] Information leaflet *Special Express to Death. Deportation on the German National Railway*.

AACHEN

Whilst Otto was setting up his business in Amsterdam in July of 1933, Anne, Margot and their mother departed for Aachen by train from the *Centralbahnhof* in Frankfurt am Main. Anne would never again see Frankfurt am Main, the city where she was born. Her short story *Paula's Flight* mentions the 'Frankfurt a/M central station'.[1]

In an interview she gave shortly before she died, Gertrud, the girl who lived next door to Anne in Frankfurt am Main, said wistfully: 'I would have loved to hold Anne in my arms once more after she arrived in the Netherlands. I used to change her diapers when she was little, feed her and play with her. I was attached to her and Margot, to the entire family and their friends and acquaintances. Actually, the Franks did not really want to go to the Netherlands. But what else could they do? I knew the Franks and loved them dearly and could never forget them.'[2]

Aachen was a ready choice; Edith's family was from Aachen. Abraham Holländer (1860-1928) (hereafter referred to as Abraham)[3], Rosa's husband and Anne's grandfather, relocated to Aachen in 1890 and began a scrapyard on Grünen Weg. Currently, this is a large industrial area. Anne's other grandmother, Alice, was from Aachen as well. Anne's grandmothers may have met each other at an early stage.

Abraham passed away in 1928, approximately a year before Anne was born. During Anne's residence in Frankfurt, she stayed with Rosa, who lived in a stately detached home they had purchased at 5 Liebfrauenstrasse (currently 5 Elsa-Brändström-Strasse)[4], the same house where Edith was born. Although the Jewish community in Aachen supported each other, Rosa was going through a difficult period. The Holländers were forced to sell the house on 5 Liebfrauenstrasse due to financial reasons in 1932—four years after Abraham's demise—with Otto and Edith's consent since they were partial owners. Since then, Rosa and her three children had been living in rented apartments.[5][6]

The Franks travelled by train to Aachen to celebrate Hanukkah[7] with Rosa. The very young Anne strolled along the streets of the ancient, medieval city centre with her mother and grandmother, where splendid monuments remind passers-by of its imperial past.

The *Aachener Dom* or Aachen Cathedral at Münsterplatz[8] has been an episcopal seat since 1930. Originally, the Dom was constructed as the royal church of Charlemagne (742/748-814). The central octagonal section of the Dom was built between 796 and 804 after Byzantine example. The Dom contains the relics Charlemagne brought from Jerusalem in 799: the Child Jesus' swaddling cloth, Jesus Christ's loincloth, the Virgin Mary's dress and the cloth in which the severed head of John the Baptist is said to have been wrapped. The Dom also contains the vault of Charlemagne, King of the Franks (768-814), who was crowned emperor in 800. The Aachen cathedral became a pilgrimage site in the Dark Ages and is currently on the UNESCO world heritage list.

The Gothic city hall (*Katschhof*)[9] was built in the 14th century and was renovated into a baroque urban palace in the 17th and 18th centuries. The city hall was damaged heavily during the great fires of 1656 and 1883. The northern façade is embellished with sculptures of 50 German rulers; 31 of these kings were coronated in Aachen.

Since 1825, a neo-classicist building on Theaterplatz houses the theatre. In 1920, the city of Aachen became responsible for the building's maintenance. Many renowned artists worked in Aachen and began their career here, such as conductor Leo Blech (1871-1958).

In the evening of 9 November 1938 (*Kristallnacht*), the Nazis watched Giuseppe Fortunino Francesco Verdi's (1813-1901) opera *Il Trovatore* (The Troubadour) at the Aachen Municipal Theatre on Theaterplatz—a restricted area for Jews at the time—on the occasion of Hitler's unsuccessful coup of 9 November 1923.

The Jewish community would meet in the synagogue (on the then Promenadenstraße; currently 23 Synagogenplatz), founded in 1862 and situated only a mile from Pastorplatz. There were pinnacles on both front corners. The sunlight entered the spacious hall through a large circular window high up in the building. The walls were decorated with mosaics and ornaments. Above the entrance, there was an organ loft with space for the choir. The prayer area was divided in two by a wide aisle. On Jewish festival days, the men would wear hats whilst the women would be dressed elegantly.[10] This is the synagogue in which Otto and Edith were married.

After the prayers, visitors would leave the synagogue through its main entrance, accessible through a wrought iron gate decorated with Stars of David. Children used the narrow path around the synagogue to release their excess energy.[11] Next to the synagogue were the other Jewish community buildings: the administrative office, a meeting facility, a youth centre, space reserved for the *Ostjuden* and the caretaker's residence.

After Hitler's takeover on 30 January 1933, the hatred of Jews rose in Aachen and throughout Germany. Margot had already moved to the Amsterdam Merwedeplein in December 1933. A memorial plate in Aachen states that Anne stayed with her grandmother Rosa on Monheimsallee from July 1933 through to January 1934,[12] only a short walk from the Town Hall and market. Anne stayed with Rosa until February of 1934.[13] The following year, Anne went to stay with her grandmother at 1 Pastorplatz, where Rosa rented a terraced house with several rooms along with her sons Walter and Julius, Anne's uncles. About nine households lived at 1 Pastorplatz at that time.[14]

On Saturday 1 April 1933, the general boycott of Jewish businesses in Germany took effect in Aachen as well. The windows of Jewish shops were plastered with Stars of David by the SA. They also wrote slogans on Jewish lawyers and doctors' practices, such as 'Jews, go to hell!', 'Do not purchase from Jews!' and 'Death to the Jews!'.[15] The Nazis prohibited Jews from holding posts at the university. The SA molested Jews on Adalbertstrasse—less than half a mile from Monheimsallee and Pastorplatz. Rosa will have done everything to protect her grandchild from these terrors.

A month before they instated the general boycott on Jewish businesses, the Nazis had established their first concentration camp in Dachau. In spite of this extreme hostility against their people, many

Jews in Aachen and throughout Germany kept their faith in their native country.

On 16 December 1934, the magazine of the Jewish community in Aachen (*Jüdischen Gemeinde Aachen*) stated: 'We strive for a second emancipation and have faith in this, because we believe in a positive development and are convinced that such development will take place by historical-psychological necessity (…).'[16] So many Jews were killed by the Nazis during WWII, however, that after the war many surviving Jews decided to abandon Germany for good and emigrate, such as to Israel (starting from 1948) or the United States, for example.

Nazi leaders formally affirmed the hostile attitude towards Jews by introducing the Nuremberg racial laws on 15 September 1935, which were intended to establish whether someone was Jewish or a pure-blooded Aryan. Jews were deprived of all civil rights, and they were not allowed to interact (or have sexual intercourse) with non-Jewish persons. To the Jews, these were extremely distressful measures since they had actively supported German society and had fought for Germany during WWI. Many Jews even lost their lives fighting for Germany in WWI.

This anti-Jew policy was intended to make the Jews leave Germany by their own 'free' will. Between 1 January 1933 and 30 September 1935, 158 of the 1,345 Jews residing in Aachen left the city, 58 leaving to live in the Netherlands.[17] A silent march in protest of Nazi violence, carried out in 1937, did not lead to any improvement.

During *Kristallnacht* in 1938, mobs destroyed the synagogue on the then Promenadenstraße (currently 23 Synagogenplatz). In 1941, the Nazis began deporting Jews to the extermination camps in the East. Significantly, 700 Jews from Aachen were murdered there, including the head of the local Jewish community, Dr Adolf Rosenthal (1873-1944)[18], who was killed in Auschwitz.[19]

Aachen is situated on the border of Germany, in its western-most area, and was heavily affected by the war. In July of 1941, the first of a series of five air raids on Aachen destroyed most of its city centre.

The city was liberated by the Americans on 21 October 1944, after six weeks of heavy fighting. In 1946, the American occupation was replaced by a Belgian one. Aachen had almost 11,000 inhabitants at that time. A large number of war criminals—who had been responsible for murdering Jewish inhabitants of Aachen—escaped punishment. Not the victims but the perpetrators were being protected. The chief offenders of the Aachen pogrom faced trial on 12 June, 1947, with many of them acquitted of their charges. The national-socialist wartime mayor also got off scot-free.[20] Following the war, many of those who were Nazi leaders during the war obtained lucrative posts in the German government or elsewhere in the world.

A new Aachen city centre was thrown up after the war, which reconstructed most of the old buildings. Many of the original buildings in the centre that were reminiscent of the rich, Jewish life have been lost forever. The city hall's *Krönungssaal* still contains 19th century frescoes by Alfred Rethel (1816-1859) and copies of regalia and of the Gothic and Baroque interior. The new Aachen theatre stages operas, plays, dance performances and concerts. The Roman hot springs have been reinstated, and are now used as healing baths.

Some of the buildings where Anne used to live survived the war. The urban villa at 5 Liebfrauenstrasse (renamed 5 Elsa-Brändström-Strasse in 1937) was damaged heavily during an air raid but was restored after WWII. Rosa's place at 42-44 Monheimsallee did not make it through the war and was replaced by a lawn in a park.

A monument next to the new synagogue commemorates the destruction of the old one (currently 23 Synagogenplatz). The Jewish community has shrunk considerably, and now comprises only 500 members. Many people refuse to learn from history: Jews are still being harassed in many places, with Aachen no exception. There will always be frustrated people who take out their frustrations on minorities. The Aachen synagogue was plastered with swastikas in the night of 4 July 2011.

At 1 Pastorplatz, *Stolpersteine* (cobble stones) have been installed in the pavement in memory of Anne, Margot and Edith who died (i.e. were murdered) in Nazi concentration camps.[21] The brass plates were made on the initiative of the Anne-Frank Grammar School in Aachen by the artist Günter Demnig (born in 1947) on the occasion of Anne's 80th birthday in 2009. Such monuments are slightly raised in comparison to other stones, and may cause one to trip, raising awareness of the surrounding buildings whose former residents were murdered by the Nazis. *Stolpersteine* were made for the Nazi victims: their name, as well as the date and place they were killed (mostly in concentration camps), are engraved on the *Stolpersteine*.[22]

The area surrounding 1 Pastorplatz has become quite decrepit over the course of time. On a Sunday afternoon, I saw homeless people, worn-out benches and an old phone booth. There is a heavy iron gate in front of the building. An iron roll-down shutter serves to discourage burglars. The name plates indicate that a number of entrepreneurs are located at 1 Pastorplatz.

One may find various references to Anne in Aachen, such as public buildings named after her. Students of the Anne Frank Grammar School read her diary and have visited the Secret Annex in Amsterdam.[23] On what would have been Anne Frank's 80th birthday in 2009, the Anne Frank Grammar School, the Aachen police force and the *Volkshochschule* Aachen, its general secondary school, participated in a day of projects on the theme of National Socialism.[24] Plays based on *The Diaries* are being staged: in 2007, the *Grenzlandtheater Aachen*[25] staged such a play for the Anne-Frank Grammar School. Although Anne's memory is alive amongst the younger generation, there is no prominent statue of Anne anywhere in Aachen—as in Frankfurt am Main.

[1] Anne Frank *Verhaaltjes, en gebeurtenissen uit het Achterhuis. Met de roman in wording Cady's leven* (Amsterdam, 2005), p. 70. English edition: *Tales from the Secret Annex. Including her Unfinished Novel Cady's Live* (Halban Publishers, 2010).
[2] Carol Ann Lee. *Anne Frank. Het leven van een jong meisje* [The life of a Young Girl. The Definitive Biography] (Amsterdam, 2009), p. 71.
[3] http://www.freebase.com/view/en/abraham_hollander.
[4] Not to be confused with the current 5 Liebfrauenstrasse, Eschweiler, Germany.
[5] Melissa Müller, *Anne Frank. De biografie* (Amsterdam, 1998), p. 88. Original German edition: *Das Mädchen Anne Frank. Die Biographie*. English edition: *Anne Frank. The Biography* (Macmillan, 2013).
[6] Other sources state that Rosa lived on Monheimsallee since the death of her husband in 1928 (http://www.wgdv.de/wege/monheimsallee.htm, (German only).
[7] http://www.jhm.nl/cultuur-en-geschiedenis/woordenlijst/c/chanoeka (Dutch only), English summary on http://www.jhm.nl/culture-and-history/glossary/h/hanukkah
[8] http://werelderfgoedfotos.nl/fotos/119-dom-van-aken.html.
[9] http://www.aachen.de/EN/ts/140_museums/140_70.html.
[10] Manfred Bierganz and Annelie Kreutz, *Juden in Aachen* [Jews in Aachen] (Aachen, 1988), p. 125 (German only).
[11] Manfred Bierganz and Annelie Kreutz, *Juden in Aachen* (Aachen, 1988), p. 122 (German only).
[12] http://www.aachen.de/de/kultur_freizeit/pdf_kultur_freizeit/gedenktafeln.pdf.
[13] An address book states that Rosa lived on Monheimsallee in 1934 (Email from the Stadtarchiv Aachen [Municipal Archives], 24 November 2010).
[14] Emails from the Stadtarchiv Aachen [Municipal Archives], 23 November 2010 and 24 November 2010.
[15] Original German slogans: 'Juda verrecke!', 'Kauft nicht bei Juden!' and 'Juden den Tod!' Manfred Bierganz and Annelie Kreutz, *Juden in Aachen* (Aachen, 1988), p. 34 (German only).
[16] Manfred Bierganz and Annelie Kreutz, *Juden in Aachen* (Aachen, 1988), p. 51 (German only).
[17] Manfred Bierganz and Annelie Kreutz, *Juden in Aachen* (Aachen, 1988), p. 51 (German only).
[18] Manfred Bierganz and Annelie Kreutz, *Juden in Aachen* (Aachen, 1988), p. 85 (German only).
[19] http://www.holocaust.cz/en/victims/PERSON.ITI.596766.
[20] Manfred Bierganz and Annelie Kreutz, *Juden in Aachen* (Aachen, 1988), p. 72 (German only).
[21] Murder would imply an active act. In the case of the Jews, however, I still refer to this as murder.
[22] http://www.stolpersteine.com/start.html.
[23] http://www.anne-frank-gymnasium.de/?page_id=6 (German only).
[24] http://www.vhs-aachen.de/ (German only).

[25] http://www.grenzlandtheater.de/ (German only).

AMSTERDAM

Following Hitler's appointment as *Reichskanzler* (National Chancellor) on 30 January 1933, the first German Jews migrated to Amsterdam. Many of these refugees joined *Het Nederlands Verbond voor Progressief Jodendom* (The Dutch Association for Progressive Judaism).[1,2] Generally speaking, the Dutch were afraid German immigrants would make it more difficult for them to survive during the crisis, and so the German Jews were not always received with open arms. Some were jealous of the fact that these first German Jews rented houses in the Amsterdam Zuid area, immediately south of the city centre, which could not be afforded by some Dutch Jews. Many of the prejudices against German Jews pertained to their being wealthy and German, rather than Jewish. In the meantime, however, the Dutch government permitted German immigrants to take up residence in Amsterdam if they could afford the residence permit, as they were viewed as being economically self-sufficient and also would bring in money.

The Franks chose to come to Amsterdam. Since the 17th century, the Netherlands had enjoyed a reputation of being a (relatively) tolerant country open to dissenters. There was, however, still a fair degree of discrimination against Jews and other social groups in the Netherlands during the 1930s—even though structural persecution of the Jews, such as in Germany, was unheard of as yet.

Otto had some important business relations in Amsterdam and was familiar with the Dutch language. Edith's family had Dutch roots: their surname 'Holländer' bears witness to this.[3] Still, Edith would never really feel at home in the Netherlands.

Another reason for choosing Amsterdam was the long-standing presence of a Jewish community: approximately 10% of the Amsterdam population was Jewish at around 1930, amongst which liberal Jews were a minority.

Since Hitler's takeover in 1933, an increasing number of liberal Jewish started living in the Rivierenbuurt area. The population of

German Jews was concentrated on Merwedeplein, which is located in the Rivierenbuurt area. Otto and Edith were undoubtedly aware of this newly constructed neighbourhood in Amsterdam Zuid.

Otto also wanted to come to Amsterdam because he could maintain his family there. Unlike in Germany, Jews were still allowed to own businesses in the Netherlands (as yet). In their native country, the Franks could certainly no longer build a private or professional life. Moreover, the Netherlands, like Switzerland, had managed to remain neutral during WWI. Many Jewish immigrants did not think the Netherlands would become involved in a potential war.

The triangular Merwedeplein is the centre of the Rivierenbuurt area in the south of Amsterdam. Its name 'Rivierenbuurt' refers to the wide, orderly lanes bearing the names of rivers in the Netherlands. The Rivierenbuurt is bordered by the Amstel at a walking distance towards the east and the north.

I followed the signs that read 'Rivierenbuurt' and took the S109 exit. There was an event at the RAI conference venue on Europaplein and I became stuck in a traffic jam. Since I was a stranger to the neighbourhood, I decided to ask a traffic policewoman for directions. Even though she lived in Amsterdam, she did not know where Merwedeplein was. I located Jekerstraat, which leads to Merwedeplein, on Google Maps. It was a Sunday, and I parked my car in the last vacant parking space on Merwedeplein, free of charge.

Starting from Merwedeplein, I asked the well-known football player, Wim Kieft (born in 1962), for directions, and a bit further on I asked another gentleman—who is of Anne's generation—who turns out to have lived around the corner from where Anne lived.

Then I noticed a block of flats in the background and recognised the Wolkenkrabber apartment building from the old photographs, which, due to the wide-angle effect of old cameras, seems smaller in relation to its surroundings than in reality. The sun is shining and there is a bright blue sky. It is a quiet area with a few children playing outside.

It would eventually take me eight days to visit all of Anne's locations in Amsterdam.

On my second day in Amsterdam, I forgot to put on my hiking shoes and, after a day's walk, reached the Amsterdam Central Station limping heavily.

On my next outings, I took breaks more often, drank more and made sure I wore my hiking shoes, ensuring my ankles were supported and I could focus on taking photographs and looking around.

There was a lot of construction work going on during the period Edith and Otto came to Amsterdam—particularly the works related to *Plan Zuid,* the 1917 urban development plan by H. P. Berlage (1856-1934, hereafter referred to as Berlage).

The Amsterdam working-class neighbourhoods dating from the 19th century, such as De Pijp in Oud Zuid, contain long rows of small houses on narrow streets. In contrast, the Rivierenbuurt was mainly inhabited by middle-class families in more spacious houses around generous squares, public gardens and playground areas.

The Wolkenkrabber, a block of flats in the Rivierenbuurt, was designed by the versatile Jan Frederik Staal (1879-1940, hereafter referred to as Staal). This twelve-storeyed building—as remarkable a building today as it was back then—still dominates Merwedeplein. The building was constructed using a mixture of concrete, yellow bricks, steel and glass. Construction on the Wolkenkrabber and its 284 apartments began on 12 March 1929—even before Anne was born— and was completed in 1932. When the Franks had just moved to Merwedeplein in 1933, the finishings were still being worked on.

The Wolkenkrabber's main entrance is located on Daniël Willinkplein—renamed Victorieplein in 1946. Its main entrance, staircase and lifts are located in the circular central area, made up of glass and steel. This area actually rises higher than the roof itself and is bordered on both sides by small balconies and large, horizontal windows with steel panes. The brick walls on both ends contain small, vertical windows. The uninterrupted gallery of first-floor balconies highlights the central entrance.

The walls of the buildings on Merwedeplein are typical of the Amsterdam School of Architecture, with protruding façades that have been designed to form a unity. The buildings surrounding the Wolkenkrabber are noticeably lower than the apartment complex itself. The contrast emphasises the tower block's height. In 2009, there was a sign on Victorieplein (formerly known as Daniël Willinkplein) commemorating the large-scale *razzia* on 30 June, 1940, and the deportation of Jews, for example, to extermination camp Auschwitz. On this square, right in front of the Wolkenkrabber, the Germans would round up Jews.

The 'big' kids would meet at the bicycle stand, currently Fysioplus on 2 Deltastraat, situated on the corner of the Wolkenkrabber.

'Something amusing happened yesterday, I was passing the bicycle sheds when someone called out to me. I looked around and there was the nice-looking boy I met on the previous evening at Wilma's home [Wilma de Jong, born 1926. She lived on 41-III Churchilllaan and Eva in Anne's diaries is based on her character.] He came shyly towards me and introduced himself as Hello Silberberg [Helmuth 'Hello' Silberberg, 1926-2011].[4] I was rather surprised and wondered what he wanted, but I didn't have to wait long. He asked if I would allow him to accompany me to school. (…) Hello is sixteen [Anne was 13] and can tell all kinds of amusing stories.'[5] Hello lived with his grandparents at 191-II Rooseveltlaan and was Anne's third boyfriend, the previous ones being Sol 'Sally' Kim(m)el (born in 1928) and Lutz Peter Schiff (1926-1945).

Hello and Sally survived the war. Wilma de Jonge (1926-1943)[6] was gassed in Auschwitz on 10 September 1943, along with her mother and younger sister. Her older brother had already died in August 1942. Her father was murdered in Sobibor in April 1943.[7]

Walking around Amsterdam-Zuid, in the vicinity of Lekstraat, for example, I noticed many Amsterdam School architectural elements, such as the protruding façades, the red bricks, curved walls, and façades adorned with sculptured natural stone.

The buildings on Deltastraat and the higher residential blocks on Merwedeplein were designed by Staal,[8] who is often said to belong to the Amsterdam School. Staal was a bit of an outsider, however: he incorporated New Objectivity into his works—an architectural style that arose around 1920 at the Bauhaus institute in Germany. In essence, New Objectivity was functionally minded, and focused on the idea that an object's form should be in accordance with its intended use. The architectural design of the Wolkenkrabber and the residential buildings on Merwedeplein are expressions of this attitude of New Objectivity.

Although the apartments on Merwedeplein display various features that belong to the Amsterdam School, all houses, including those in which the Franks lived, have a uniform appearance. The straightforward sandstone façades, large windows, white window frames and small balconies are all influenced by New Objectivity.

There is a noticeable symmetry in the layout of the streets around Merwedeplein, between Churchilllaan (known as Noorder Amstellaan up to 1946), Rooseveltlaan (known as Zuider Amstellaan up to 1946)[9] and Scheldestraat, which is lacking in the rest of the Rivierenbuurt area. Deltastraat starts at the Wolkenkrabber, and branches out into two onto Merwedeplein: on the left there is a row of houses with uneven numbers starting from 1; on the right there are even numbers starting from 2.

Biesboschstraat, which ends at the back of the Wolkenkrabber, functions as the axis of the Rivierenbuurt area. The hind façade of the Wolkenkrabber, with its flue and contiguous steel fire stairs, places extra emphasis on this symmetry. Vrijheidslaan (known as Amstellaan, up to 1946) leads straight from Berlagebrug to Victorieplein (known as Daniël Willinkplein up to 1946). The Wolkenkrabber (front side) is located on the Y crossing of Noorder Amstellaan, Zuider Amstellaan and Amstellaan, and is a central landmark in the Rivierenbuurt area.

According to *The Diaries*, Anne was always at the centre of attention. Hannah's mother used to say, 'God knows everything, but Anne knows best'.[10] Theo Coster characterised Anne as 'pert': she did not hesitate to speak before her turn in class. Hannah also related that Anne was at the centre of attention, yet Jacqueline van Maarsen (born in 1929) doubts whether there were as many boys courting Anne as she describes in her diaries.[11] Incidentally, Jacqueline also indicated Anne was not nice to Hannah.[12]

Eva Geiringer (born in Vienna in 1929) fled to Amsterdam in 1940 along with her mother Elfriede Geiringer (1905-1998, hereafter referred to as Fritzi), father Erich Geiringeren (1901-1945) and brother Heinz Geiringer (1926-1945). Jacqueline van Maarssen (born in 1929, hereafter referred to as Jacqueline) lived at 4 Hunzestraat, near Hermine 'Miep' Santruschitz (1909-2010, hereafter referred to as Miep) and Jan Gies (1905-1993, hereafter referred to as Jan), and claims the Franks and the Geiringers never met.[13] This, however, is not very probable: these families lived close to each other, were both Jewish, and Otto apparently liked Fritzi. The Jewish family lived at 46 Merwedeplein:[14] 'We lived across from the Franks, whom I liked to visit. Mister Frank was very nice. He always spoke German to me, because I did not understand Dutch very well yet.'[15]

Although Anne and Eva most probably knew each other by face and were of the same age, Eva Geiringer probably was not one of Anne's friends. Anne does not mention Eva[16] in her diaries.

Anne's green-brown eyes, lifelines, spirited nature, interested attitude and honesty went down well with not only her classmates but also her teachers. Anne enjoyed the limelight and loved to show her friends how, for instance, she could voluntarily dislocate her shoulder. They were impressed.

Although Anne liked to be around people, she also could keep herself amused by writing on her own. In 1940, Anne solved a local shop owner's riddle and won first prize.[17]

Anne regularly visited her friends and vice versa. Hannah 'Hanneli' Elisabeth Goslar (born in 1928, hereafter referred to as Hanneli) originally lived at 31 Merwedeplein, but relocated to a more spacious apartment on 16 Zuider Amstellaan later on. Anne thinks the place is a lively mess: 'And the kind of household the Goslars run; of the five rooms on Zuider Amstellaan one is rented out, Mrs. Goslar's parents live in the porch next to it but eat with the family, then there is a maid, the baby, the ever absent-minded and distracted Mr. Goslar, and the always nervous and irritable Mrs. Goslar, who is expecting again. Lies with her two left hands is as good as lost in this bear garden.'[18]

Susanna 'Sanne' Ledermann (1928-1943, hereafter referred to as Sanne) lived at 37-II Noorder Amstellaan and attended a different primary school to Anne, although their friendship remained close. Sanne, like many others, died in Auschwitz.

When Anne was young, there was still a lot of space for children to play outside. There were a lot of sandy plots around Rivierenlaan (renamed President Kennedylaan in 1964), especially at the current RAI area on Europaplein. These plots had been raised but had not as yet been built over because of the war. Towards Zuidelijke Wandelweg and Mirandalaan, the encircling dyke marked the border of Amsterdam at that time. Cows grazed on the polders and, in winter, the children would skate on the frozen over pools. Near to Mirandalaan, there were more raised sandy plots.

Anne and her friends also had plenty of space to play on Merwedeplein. Playing hide-and-seek, tag, hopscotch, balls, hula hoop, *slagbal* (similar to softball) and skipping were fashionable. They would play outside often. If any snow fell in winter, Anne would play with her little sledge.

From the 1950s, Amsterdam was expanding rapidly and new districts, such as Buitenveldert, and new neighbouring municipalities, such as Amstelveen, were thrown up. The area south of the ring road, Ringweg Zuid, has been built over completely. The green area south of Rivierenbuurt of Anne's times is no longer there.

In those days, people would be outside most of the time during summer. Adults had not yet been caught in the web of TV and computers. Front doors would stay open and families would chat with each other.

In Anne's days, there were many different shops on the not-yet asphalted Waalstraat and Rijnstraat: bakeries, butchers, greengrocers and bookshops, often family-owned companies of hard-working people—some of them Jewish—who thought highly of paying personal attention to customers.

Since there were not that many car fumes yet, Anne must have smelt the various aromas coming from the shops. There was not as much noise from hooting cars or smelly air pollution. However, children would have to watch out for horses and carriages.

After the war, the number of Jewish-owned shops had decreased dramatically. The current range of shops hardly compares to its pre-war variety. There is only one bookshop left in the entire Rivierenbuurt area: publisher and bookshop Jimmink B.V. on 62 Rooseveltlaan, formerly known as Boekhandel Blankevoort on 62 Zuider Amstellaan. Anne would pay regular visits to this shop.

The Wolkenkrabber and Merwedeplein still exude a 1930s atmosphere. Most of the buildings have been preserved, and there have been very few changes to the district's original urban design.

A 1941 photograph[19] displays Anne showing off her new coat. I noticed that the skyline of the houses in the back have remained the same, although their outlines are more difficult to distinguish now since the trees and shrubs have grown significantly over the years.[20] Some of the shrubberies have made way to playground equipment. The scene is blotted with a great number of cars and traffic signs. Some buildings are marred by plastic window frames, dormers or verandas at the front. In Anne's days, the streets and pavements were even. Nowadays, the roads are marked with signs all over: zebra crossings, give-way marks and directional lines—all on a vast base of asphalt.

In 1966, a statue of the urban designer of Plan Zuid was erected in the public garden in front of the Wolkenkrabber on Victorieplein: Hendrik Petrus Berlage (1856-1934, hereafter referred to as Berlage)[21] sculptured by Hildo Krop (1884-1970, hereafter referred to as Hildo).[22] The inscription on the pedestal reads, BERLAGE MASTER BUILDER 1856-1934. Berlage looks out on his only creation in Rivierenbuurt—a bridge named after him: the Berlagebrug.

Berlage designed the Berlagebrug in collaboration with the division 'Bridges' of the Amsterdam Public Works Department. The bridge was inaugurated on 28 May, 1932, and the festivities included swimmers diving off the bridge into the Amstel. The Berlagebrug connected Rivierenbuurt to Transvaalbuurt and Watergraafsmeer, and marked the end of the small ferry service that had provided the cross-river connection up to then. It was the remotest bridge from the city centre and the largest in Amsterdam at the time, measuring 80 metres long and 24 metres wide (approximately 260 by 80 feet). Berlage had directed much attention to the bridge's decorative finishing and symbolism.

The large tower on its city centre side bears an image of the Genius of Amsterdam rising from the water. This ceramic plate was designed by Hildo. The three green rings at the feet of the Genius of Amsterdam symbolise its ring of canals. The bridge's parapets have been drawn up in wrought iron with a brass top. Berlage used stones of various colours to construct the bridge: grey natural stone, yellow Bavarian granite, red bricks and green tiles. Anne would cross this bridge many times nine years later, biking her way to the Jewish Grammar school or *Joodsch Lyceum*.

On 8 May 1945, the Berlagebrug played a major part when the main forces of the Canadian army reached Amsterdam. The liberating troops crossed the Berlagebrug and were cheered on by a large number of Amsterdam's inhabitants. Looking back at the liberation with hindsight and our current knowledge, it has a bitter aftertaste: many Jewish children had become Holocaust victims and, during the war, political leaders had done very little to counter the mass murder on Jewish citizens.

I stood on the bridge, looking out on the Amstel. In this dynamic city, the river exudes a peaceful atmosphere. I saw a young man rowing a boat. Margot was a member of a rowing club; perhaps she, too, rowed under the Berlagebrug 70 years ago.

Before she arrived in Amsterdam, Anne stayed with her grandmother in Aachen. Edith regularly travelled from Aachen to Amsterdam in order to find a suitable home. Otto mainly focused on erecting an Opekta branch—an affiliate of Pomosin-Werke in Frankfurt am Main—and rented one or more rooms on the second floor of 24 Stadionkade.

On 16 August, 1933, Otto and Edith registered at the Amsterdam municipal registry offices. On 15 September, 1933, Otto registered his company with the Chamber of Commerce. His company was located at 120-126 Nieuwezijds Voorburgwal, in the Candida building.

Miep from Austria was Otto's assistant.

Opekta produced gelling agents—thickeners used in making jam—that were added to food products by manufacturers. These seasonal products were very popular. Reinier Saul (1910-1977)[23] designed Opekta's marketing material.[24]

It is likely that Otto travelled to work on tram 24 from Olympiaweg.[25] Otto lived close to the Olympic Stadium and rented a small office space with a kitchenette in the high-class Candida building.

The Candida building was designed in 1930 by architect F. A. Warners (1888-1952). In her memories, Miep notes: 'The building before me was the most modern on the street, practically a skyscraper. The beige-stone entrance was covered by a circular awning. Nine totally glass-enclosed storeys soared towards the cloud-filled sky, broken up by taupe-coloured stones. This unusual building was named, in black lettering on the street level 'Gebouw Candida'.'[26]

Warners was a pioneer of the 'storeyed building' in Amsterdam, and his office was at 13 Okeghemstraat. The designers did not opt for a steel frame, but chose a cheaper solution instead; a concrete frame consisting of a core of reinforced concrete on a foundation of Bavarian granite. The walls are not load-bearing and consist of warm-coloured bricks combined with a 'matter-of-fact' series of steel-framed windows. The seamlessly adjacent windows in two horizontal series allow plenty of light to enter the building. The floors are linked by a staircase or a so-called paternoster lift located in the centre of the building. The building has an inner courtyard from where you can see the fire stairs linking the balconies on the outside. The office block has a stately entrance and spacious staircase, and is located close to the Amsterdam Central Station.[27]

The Candida building now hosts various offices and companies, as well as a hotel. Its horizontal direction is dominated by the light floor linings and window sills, and the decorative brickwork in between. On the Nieuwezijds Voorburgwal side, the lining above the ground floor continues around a semi-circular canopy. The canopy highlights the entrance and acts as a floating support for the glass column of the full-length oriel above.

The main entrance was used by the directors of the various firms and their customers. Visitors would have to report to the porter seated in a glass cubicle immediately after the entrance. Staff would enter the building on the rear side, on Spuistraat. The porter's lodging and the bike cellar can also be reached from staff entrance at the rear. From the rear entrance, the staff would enter the central hall with its staircase and lifts.

The building keeps abreast of time. Its façades have recently been cleaned, and the steel windows have been replaced by synthetic ones. Some of the other buildings on Nieuwezijds Voorburgwal were important during the war as well.

The post office at 192 Nieuwezijds Voorburgwal played an indispensable role in international communications because it had telegraphic equipment and was therefore protected by sandbags against potential air raids. This stately neo-Gothic building now hosts the Magna Plaza shopping centre.[28] It is a national monument.

During the war, 292 Nieuwezijds Voorburgwal hosted a large telephone company operated by the Germans. During the present time, it still hosts various companies.

Amsterdam was full of German soldiers, army vehicles, roadblocks, checkpoints and advertising columns displaying propaganda posters. De Telegraaf, a Dutch national newspaper, and the *Deutsche Zeitung in den Niederlanden* (as of 1942), were located at 225 Nieuwezijds Voorburgwal[29] (currently Kas Bank NV and Amsterdam, BPG), whilst another national newspaper, the *Algemeen Handelsblad*, could be found at 232-240[30] (currently Clubcenter ECI Boekenclub Centrum).

The Frank family regularly went to the Amsterdam Central Station. The German entrepreneur Philip Holzman and Co. from Frankfurt am Main secured the tender for the Amsterdam Central

Station at 9 Stationsplein, which was constructed between 1881 and 1889 according to a design by the architects P. J. H. Cuypers (1827-1921, hereafter referred to as Cuypers) and A. L. van Gendt (1835-1901). The principals used Gothic and Renaissance architectural elements and sculptures.

Visitors enter the building at its palatial front through its midsection flanked by towers. The 360-metre-long building has been constructed on reclaimed islands in the IJ lake. L. J. Eijmer (1843-1889), civil engineer at the Dutch National Railway, designed the roof structure, which consists of 50 arched trusses spanning almost 45 metres.

Cuypers designed the truss decorations and the roof structure's head façade. In 1922, a second roof structure was added on the IJ side. Towards the end of the building period of this 'traveller's palace', its east wing named Koningspaviljoen (King's pavillion) was also completed. It had wide doors on each side, and was only to be used by dignitaries.

A grand stairway covered with ribbed arches leads from its entrance hall up to a landing. A frieze above the landing displays the four phases of human life: a child on leading strings, a student, an adult man immersed in his work, and a staring old man. Across the landing, one enters the abundantly decorated King's Hall—the royal family's waiting room. The main topics of the decorations and paintings are the royal house and authority.

In 2009, an information sign at the Amsterdam Central Station reminded passers-by of the barbed-wire roadblocks by the Germans in the city centre.

The Frank family moved to Merwedeplein on 5 December, 1933.[31] Like many of the apartments on Merwedeplein and the Noorder and Zuider Amstellaan, their apartment was owned by the Hilwis public limited construction and exploitation company (N.V. Bouw- en Exploitatiemaatschappij Hilwis).[32] When the Franks just moved in, construction was still going on but this came to a halt during the war. Children would play on the heaps of sand scattered around the neighbourhood.

Apparently Anne is also eager to join her family in Amsterdam. 'Rosa will have a hard time keeping the child there for a few more weeks [this would eventually become two months],' Edith wrote on 5 December 1933.[33]

Julius and Walter, Edith's two brothers, took Margot to Amsterdam. Anne wanted to go along, too, but she was made to stay with her grandmother a little longer.[34]

'In the Netherlands, after those experiences in Germany, it was as if our life was restored to us. In those days it was possible for us to start over and to feel free,' Otto said.[35] Compared to Germany, it was relatively quiet in the Netherlands, although the Dutch branch of the National-Socialist movement (NSB) was on the rise, and there were regular encounters between fascists and communists or those in favour of the NSB and its opponents in the streets of Amsterdam. On 30 March 1935, 16,000 people attended the NSB's third General National Gathering in the RAI Association building on Ferdinand Bolstraat.[36] A tobacco shop on Kalverstraat called *De Driehoek* sold the German anti-Semitic magazine *Der Stürmer*—even though the Dutch government prohibited its distribution.

Merwedeplein was still a peaceful oasis in an Amsterdam full of unrest. In those days, housing associations would still deliver the houses to their tenants in decent shape, meaning the Franks did not have to do any wallpapering: Edith furnished the house with their steel blue seatings, closets, her writing table, the Biedermeier pendulum, the library, and chests full of books, and all the other furnishings brought from Frankfurt am Main.

According to Edith, their apartment on Merwedeplein was smaller than their urban villa at 24 Ganghoferstrasse. Edith complained about not having a scullery or a cellar on Merwedeplein. She liked the fact that their home let in plenty of light (which I also noticed during my visit to the Frank family residence) and that she did not need a housekeeper and was able to handle everything herself. Edith apparently did not complain about the absence of a garden or a large balcony.

The furniture from Frankfurt am Main probably fitted well in their new apartment as she did not complain about this either. Edith did not understand that their home was spacious and cheap by Dutch standards. It was a comfortable place. The large bedrooms were equipped with sinks. It had central heating, a phone, a toilet, bathroom, and warm and cold running water. A French balcony could be accessed through the kitchen. Many of the Jews who came to Holland could not afford such places. Most Jews in Amsterdam lived in tiny, decrepit homes in the Jewish area around Waterlooplein in the city centre, sometimes with several families packed into one room. During the German occupation, this area was turned into a ghetto.

Some of the richer Jews looked down on the poor, working-class Jews who often acted as merchants on the market. They would mock them, calling them 'the orange Jews'. Whilst the Frank family was better off than the Jews on the market or the less skilled Jewish craftsmen, they certainly did not belong to the wealthy elite.

According to an advert in the Algemeen Handelsblad newspaper dated 26 February 1932, the heading of which proclaimed 'Wolkenkrabber on Daniël Willinkplein now completed',[37] the annual rent of an apartment in Wolkenkrabber was around 1,600 guilders, whilst the Franks paid about 75 guilders a month.

From the Wolkenkrabber, one would have a view of the entire city and the Zuiderzee (currently IJmeer, Markermeer and IJsselmeer). Every apartment was equipped with a refrigerator, which was a very modern convenience at the time.[38] The apartment in Wolkenkrabber had four bedrooms and a maid's room.

People more wealthy than the Franks also lived on Noorder Amstellaan, renamed Churchilllaan in 1946, and Waalstraat. On Beethovenlaan, along the Amstel west of the Rivierenbuurt area, there were luxurious urban villas owned by important lawyers and well-to-do entrepreneurs. The Franks would take advantage of the shops, butchers and fishmongers opening in their area.

The apartment seemed to please the family and the rent was affordable, meaning they stayed here until they went into hiding. Anne would lovingly call Merwedeplein 'the Merry'. Edith was still not fully able to get used to the new place: she missed her old surroundings in Germany, as well as her neighbours, acquaintances and friends. Otto already knew Amsterdam quite well and therefore easily adapted to his new environment. Children such as Anne were especially flexible and quickly felt at home in their new place. Anne and Margot rapidly learnt to speak Dutch (almost) without an accent.

I went up the stone stairway outside, which gives access to a deep landing with two doors. I felt excited knowing that Anne walked these stairs—I was walking in her track. The door on the left is the entrance to Anne's former residence. I rang and was kindly received by a foreign writer who was working there at the time. She asked me to wait a little while, since Mr. T. Perez of the Stichting Amsterdam Vluchtstad (Amsterdam City of Refugees Association), whom I was supposed to meet, had not yet arrived.

Following in the wake of Mr. Perez, I entered the apartment by a steep stairway that gives access to a central landing connecting the various rooms. The Franks' former residence has been refurnished in the style of the 1930s. The layout is (almost) the same as in Anne's time. The writer staying there at the time reminded me that this was Anne's former residence and, for privacy reasons, did not want me to visit her parents' former bedroom, which I respected.

I began setting up my camera and its equipment whilst the writer and Mr. Perez were seated at the table in the Frank family's former dining room. I tried to stay calm for I only had an hour to take the photographs.

The living room and dining room look out onto the street and are separated by sliding doors. The living room was furnished with a writing table like the one that Anne and Margot owned, as well as a grandfather clock from Frankfurt. The original built-in show glass cupboard is still there. Looking outside through an oriel window, I could see the square's central yard to the north. The chimney breast in the living room used to have a gas heater installed, in front of which Otto liked to sit.

In the hall, I saw the entrance door to the living room; Anne and Margot posed in front of this door with their guests in February

1934.[39] On 16 February 1934, Margot celebrated her 8th birthday. Anne was almost five, and some delicious smells penetrated the living room from the kitchen. Anne liked strawberry cake and Edith would spoil all their visiting playmates with various sweet snacks.

The south rooms were Otto and Edith's bedroom, the kitchen, and Anne and Margot's bedroom. In a letter to her family in Switzerland, Anne provides a detailed description of her bedroom: 'I am now at the writing desk, our room is very large. We have a chest of drawers, a sink, a closet and across the room mummy's writing desk [apparently moved from the living room] which we turned into this cute little writing table. Then there's Margot's foldaway bed and a side table, and the couch that I sleep on. And in the middle there is a small table with a large arm chair and all my paintings and photographs, just like Bernd did his.'[40]

A photograph[41] shows Anne writing at her desk. The photo must have been taken in the morning as direct sunlight enters the room.

Anne and Margot's bedroom has been reconstructed. The writing desk is placed against the wall, close to the window. It is a replica. Perhaps Anne's original writing desk is now in the possession of Miep's heirs.

An old sink was refitted in Anne's room. In the mirror over the sink, I could see the reflection of a historical picture of Anne. This photograph was probably taken by Otto or Margot. Anne smiles at the photographer. The photo is now on the desk Anne used for writing. There are spots of sunlight on the wallpaper; Anne will have seen those, too. It keeps her memory alive.

In the central hall, a winding stairway leads up to the attic with the extra (rented out) room. I climbed through the open attic window, like Anne used to do, and out onto the roof terrace. From this point, I could see the Wolkenkrabber to my left and the back of the Rooseveltlaan apartments (Zuider Amstellaan up to 1946). Perhaps Anne would have waved at her friends from this location.

One can see the small gardens from the roof terrace. The Franks celebrated the Friday night Purim festival[42] at the Goslar's, and all the children dressed up. Anne liked to act. During Sukkot, the festival of booths,[43] the Goslars and the Franks would build a booth together in the narrow corridor between the gardens of Merwedeplein and Zuider Amstellaan (renamed Rooseveltlaan in 1946).[44] There is no fence around the roof terrace, and the depth below me made me feel lightheaded when I looked out over the edge. The overgrowth in the enclosed gardens has increased greatly; there was hardly any growth in Anne's days.

The house I spotted from the roof terrace looks almost the same from the outside as in the old days. The green wooden laths under the windows and drainpipes are clearly visible. In Anne's days, the attic windows overlooking the roof terrace comprised two parts separated by a lath. Now, each window consists of a separate piece.

Anne liked to sit on the *platje* (the little platform) whenever the weather was nice. In an old photograph,[45] Anne sits on the roof in a garden chair with a hat on her lap. She seems relaxed and smiles at the photographer. This picture, too, was probably taken by Otto or Margot. Otto liked taking photos. Fortunately, Anne lived to experience these happy days. I took a photograph from the same perspective and felt the emptiness she left behind. Once, the photo was merely meant as a family picture; now, it is world heritage.

In May 1941,[46] Margot took a photograph of Anne from the French balcony. The photo shows the rear sides of the houses on Zuider Amstellaan (renamed Rooseveltlaan in 1946). The following is written on the front side of the photograph: 'Grandma had to have her picture taken, Margot took it and... while developing we discovered that grandma had just disappeared.'[47]

I climbed in through the same window and went to the roof terrace to the attic with its large storage. An old door gave way to a spacious room with an old sink, where the tenants of the Frank family must have lived. The floor creaked under my feet and I looked around the room. In my mind, I saw Anne walking around the house. If I would have been able to travel back in time with a time machine and meet her in real life, I wonder whether I would have been able to handle that emotionally.

The lamp in the attic is not the original one, but nonetheless it looks very similar. The original inhabitants have gone forever. What remains are mere memories revived by silent witnesses.

During the war, many of the Frank family possessions disappeared. Part of the furniture moved from Merwedeplein to the Secret Annex—the Franks' hiding place. Following the betrayal, the Puls moving company vacated the annex. Their house on Merwedeplein also probably would have been ransacked during the war. Otto was unable to claim their former residence on Merwedeplein after WWII because he had only paid the rent up to March 1943. After the war, several families lived in the apartment, unaware that this had been Anne's residence, and thus many of the original traces reminiscent of Anne have been lost forever. Because of all the attention focusing on *The Diaries*, no timely inventory was made of any physical reminders of Anne.

In 2004, the Ymere housing association bought the apartment at Merwedeplein and had it restored to its original state because it believed the apartment possessed historical as well as emotional value.

The reconstruction was completed in 2005 and was based on Anne's descriptions, old photographs, eyewitness accounts and computer animations.

Through the Amsterdam City of Refugees Association (Stichting Amsterdam Vluchtstad), foreign writers are lodged in the apartment. These writers appreciate a quiet working environment, and do not like to have coaches full of tourists in front of their house.[48] This is why there is no plate stating that Anne lived here from 1934 to 1942.

Although many of the original items have gone, I still experienced a glimpse of the 1930s atmosphere and the identity of the Frank family: green doors and yellow frames; bright colours that pleasantly contrast with the dark furniture; the chimney breast that gives the apartment a warm look and feel. I doubt whether the sofa and the lamp in the living room and the large table in the dining room actually belonged to the Franks.

Sunbeams entered through the window and warmed the apartment. The unobstructed view across the square was still there and made me feel peaceful. I can easily imagine Anne would have felt at home here.

In 1934, Otto's company Opekta moved into an office building at 400 Singel[49] in the centre of Amsterdam. Otto rented three floors in the building on one of the canals, as well as a storage room on the ground floor. It was located close to the flower market and looked out on one of the Singel corners.

One of the current inhabitants of 400 Singel allowed me to take pictures inside the building. An elegant lamp is suspended over the front door, and there is a small sculpture high on the ground floor wall. Anne's 80th birthday created quite an Anne Frank hype. On Singel, there was a billboard announcing a festival called *Dear Anne. A Symphonic Tribute to Anne Frank*, which was based on Anne's diaries.[50]

Business was not going well, and Otto felt extremely responsible for his family and company. Otto was going through a difficult period: he was not a born businessman and had to borrow money from his family. When his business had become relatively stable again, Anne arrived in the Netherlands on 16 February 1934. 'Margot went on to Holland in December, and I followed in February, and was put on Margot's table as a birthday present.'[51]

Eight-year-old Margot's welcome gifts included roller skates, with which she posed on Merwedeplein. Before long, their house was full of dolls and toys, colouring pencils and children's art work.

At 400 Singel, Miep, one of the people who would help the family during their stay at the Secret Annex, met the very young Anne, dressed in a little snow-white fur coat. Her hair was black and she had a fine-featured face, with keen eyes that would take in everything she saw. Anne liked watching the black typewriters in the office, and the trams, people on bikes, and pedestrians she could see passing by from the window. A historical photograph dated around 1935 shows Anne standing at the front door at 400 Singel, looking at her watch rather impatiently.[52]

Otto's company did not yield enough income to completely maintain his family. Therefore, he rented out their attic room. If no tenants were there, Anne and Margot liked to play in the attic. Although Otto was not exactly a rich man, Margot took skiing and tennis classes. Margot was a member of the Temminck Tennis Club at Zuidelijke Wandelweg and used to row (with classmates) at a club in Amsterdam. Their rowing team would also participate in competitions. In 1940, Margot and her friends won a medal in Zaandam. However, from 1941, Margot was prohibited from rowing at her regular club because she was Jewish. From then on, her friends refused to take part in any competitions. Anne used to go swimming and also played tennis. In *Delusions of Stardom*, Anne writes: 'In the afternoons I did my homework and played tennis.'[53]

Some of the Franks' neighbours ran a small business from their homes in order to supplement their income: Goslar & Dr Ledermann Consultancy at 31 Merwedeplein;[54] Jacob Kousen at 43 Merwedeplein;[55] and the magician Prof. Ben-Ali-Libi at 59 Merwedeplein.[56]

Michel Velleman (1895-1943, hereafter referred to as Velleman) was a Dutch magician and illusionist. During the 1920s, he moved to Amsterdam where he performed as a 'comedian-magician', Professor Ben-Ali-Libi. In 1924, the regional newspaper *Nieuwsblad van het Zuiden* reported: 'Ben Ali Libi is a handy magician who dumbfounds anyone present with his incredible tricks. All those tricks are naturally too numerous to mention, but he was very popular. No-one would be bored spending an entire evening with this magician.'[57]

He performed in front of Prince Hendrik (1876-1934, Hendrik Wladimir Albrecht Ernst) and in front of the German Emperor Wilhelm II (1859-1941, Frederik Wilhelm Victor Albert). He was arrested during a *razzia* in 1942 and died in Sobibor. Anne did not write about Velleman.

The German Jews in Rivierenbuurt were recent immigrants and did not mingle with other Jewish groups in Amsterdam. Some of these groups already had a long tradition in Amsterdam.

During the Thirty Years' War (1618-1648), many Jewish families from Catholic West Germany had settled in Amsterdam. In 1936, the *Hoogduitsch-Joodsche Gemeente te Amsterdam* (The High German Jewish Community in Amsterdam, a community of Ashkenazi Jews) celebrated the 300th anniversary of their arrival in Amsterdam.[58] From 1928 they used the Obrechtsjoel—a shul on the corner of Jacob Obrechtplein and Heinzestraat in the Oud-Zuid area. They grew into the largest group of Jews in Amsterdam and the Netherlands.

Following the war, Otto invested a great deal of effort into supporting the liberal synagogue on Jacob Soetendorpstraat. This building was demolished in 2008. On Zuidelijke Wandelweg, a new synagogue was built to replace it, which was inaugurated in 2010.

Most Jews in Amsterdam were poor. Many of them settled in the Oude Schans and Waterlooplein area around 1850—the latter of which had not yet been reclaimed. In Eastern Europe, Jews were a minority. The *Ostjuden*, who had settled in Amsterdam around 1900, had fled from the Russian and Polish anti-Semitists (clearly not a Nazi invention).

Many refugees from Eastern Europe settled in the Pijp and Transvaal areas. Some of them entered the diamond or tobacco industries around 1900. The poorest Jews who fled the terrors of Nazism in the 1930s ended up in refugee camps, such as Hooghalen, which later became the Westerbork concentration camp.

Amsterdam did not really have a close-knit Jewish community. German Jews, Portuguese Jews, Jews from Eastern Europe and other Jews did not mingle very often. *Ostjuden* highly valued their own culture, spoke Yiddish, and their community included not only orthodox religious people but also revolutionary anarchists and communists;[59] this is why they were not very popular with the Jewish immigrants from Germany, who mostly belonged to the middle classes. The Dutch Jews and the German Jews did not always get along, with many of the Dutch Jews regarding the Germans Jews as intruders.

Near Merwedeplein, various illegal organisations were active.[60] Jewish immigrants from Germany did not tend to be heroic members of the resistance. They would usually just bear the humiliations, hoping for better times. The *Reichsbürgergesetz* decree, which was proclaimed on 15 September 1935, turned Jews into foreigners in their native Germany, which put them into a life-threatening position. Emigrants were obliged to regularly report to the foreign police at the city hall, and they were expected to adapt to the Netherlands and maintain their family. One lapse and they were ordered to leave. Because parents in particular wanted to protect their family, they were not inclined to protest.[61]

There were, however, some mild, careful acts of resistance amongst the German Jews in Amsterdam. An order proclaimed, on 22 June 1942, that Jews were required to hand in their bikes. The Frank family resisted and did not heed the German order. 'Daddy has given Mummy's to a Christian family for safekeeping,' Anne noted.[62]

Jewish immigrants from Germany shared their social background, the problems they encountered when settling in the Netherlands, their worries about family members who were still in Germany, and the absence of their old friends and acquaintances. Families supported each other during these difficult, insecure times. Edith and Otto were in touch with other families who had fled Frankfurt am Main, such as the Wertheimers, and had befriended the Goslars and the Ledermanns. In 1934, around 4,200 Jewish refugees from Germany had settled in Amsterdam. Goslar & Dr Ledermann Consultancy was located at 31 Merwedeplein, as indicated above, and supported this group of refugees with advice.

Edith in particular sought the support of fellow refugees from Germany. In 1936, she visited her family in Frankfurt am Main, and Anne celebrated New Year's Eve 1935/1936 at her grandmother's home in Aachen. Travelling to Germany was not without hazard for Jews: by this time, the Nazis had opened their first prototype concentration camp in Dachau.

During the occupation, Jews were not permitted to hold meetings in synagogues or other public buildings, which is why they visited each other at home. Otto and Edith would invite people they trusted to visit them on Saturday afternoons and would discuss their personal difficulties and the problems in Germany and the Netherlands.

'During these Saturday afternoon gatherings, we would all sit around the large, dark mahogany table in the Franks' living room. The table would be filled with cups of coffee, cream jugs, Mrs. Frank's nicely polished silver and delicious home-made cheesecake or tea bread (...).[63] I particularly admired the high, elegant writing desk in nineteenth-century French style in between the two windows (...). In the background we could hear the soft ticking of a solemn grandfather's clock. It was an Ackerman, made in Frankfort [Frankfurt am Main],' Miep writes.[64]

Regular visitors of these Saturday afternoon gatherings were the Jewish German refugees Hermann van Pels (1898-1944, hereafter referred to as Herman) and his wife Auguste van Pels (1900-1945, hereafter referred to as Auguste), dentist Friedrich 'Fritz' Pfeffer (1889-1944, hereafter referred to as Fritz) and his non-Jewish girlfriend Charlotte Kaletta (1910-1985, hereafter referred to as Charlotte),[65] Miep and her fiancé Johannes or Jan, who lived at 12 Wielingenstraat and who was one of Otto's employees, and Kurt Baschwitz (1886-1968, hereafter referred to as Kurt) and his non-Jewish wife. After the war, Kurt became a professor of mass psychology in Amsterdam.[66]

Fritz lived at 23 Daniël Willinkplein (currently 23 Victorieplein)[67] and had fled Berlin. He was looked down upon by many because they disapproved of his living together with his girlfriend, Charlotte, even though they were not married. However, Anne wrote in her diary: '...Fritz Pfeffer. He lives with a much younger, nice Christian woman, to whom he is probably not married, but that doesn't matter.'[68]

Anne does not write about Miep and Jan, who were engaged and living together without being married at a landlady's place at 25 Hunzestraat.[69] They got married on 16 July 1941. The other future helpers during the Secret Annex period would probably also visit the Frank family: Johannes Hendrik Voskuijl (1892-1945, hereafter referred to as Johan), Elisabeth Voskuijl (1919-1983, hereafter referred to as Bep) and Victor Kugler (1900-1981, hereafter referred to as Victor). Johannes, Victor and Bep worked for Otto in his company at 400 Singel.

The Kahn family probably also attended these Saturday afternoon gatherings at the Franks. Richard Kahn (1889-1976, hereafter referred to as Richard) and Annelies Kahn (1925-1970) and their daughter Gabrielle (born 1927)[70] migrated to Amsterdam in 1935. Otto and Richard had been soldiers in the German army during WWI. After the war, Richard started to work for Deutsche Bank in Mannheim and helped Otto start a business. Anne visited the Kahn family on 59-I Michelangelostraat in the Amsterdam-Zuid area. In late-1941, this Jewish family fled to the United States.[71]

Rosel Wronker-Goldschmidt (born 1900, hereafter referred to as Rosel) also lived at 59-II Michelangelostraat in the Amsterdam-Zuid area.[72] She was the Frank family's domestic help from April 1936 through to October 1937. Paul Wronker (1903-1943),[73] hereafter referred to as Paul, rented a room with the Franks during 1940-1941, and Mr. Goldschmidt did so during 1942-1943. Rosel and Paul got married on 22 July 1942 in Amsterdam; at this time, Anne had been hiding for two weeks. The tenants and domestic help did not take part in the Saturday afternoon gatherings, but would have 'heard something'. Anne writes: 'Rosel and Wronker have been sent on to Poland.'[74] Rosel and Paul were murdered on 16 July 1943 in Sobibor. Mr. Goldschmidt survived the war.[75]

Anne and Margot were only children and did not participate in these gatherings. The neatly dressed sisters would greet the visitors courteously with a little nod and go to their room.

'In general people would discuss bad events as little as possible, especially in Jewish circles. Children were very much protected in those days, also before the war, and nasty things would generally be discussed by adults when the children were not there. I should think the same would be true for the Frank household,' writes Max C. van der Glas, a holocaust survivor.[76]

The Van Pels family lived at 34-II Zuider Amstellaan, close to the Franks and Anne is likely to have met Peter van Pels (1926-1945, hereafter referred to as Peter), if only briefly in the streets, before they went into hiding at the Secret Annex together.

Otto supported peace-loving Jewish organisations that became prohibited by the occupiers during the war. The *Comité voor Bijzondere Joodsche Belangen* (Committee for Special Jewish Interests) was founded on 21 March 1933 for the general purpose of promoting the interests of Jews in the Netherlands. In order to accommodate the needs of the many Jewish refugees entering the Netherlands, a sub-branch was founded, the *Comité voor Joodsche Vluchtelingen* (Committee for Jewish Refugees).[77] Otto supported the organisation by a monthly cash deposit.

On 19 September 1935, the Committee organised a protest meeting in the Apollohal at 1-5 Stadionweg (currently 4 Apollolaan, where Anne used to skate) against the racial acts of Nuremberg that had been passed six days earlier in Germany. These Acts formalised the Nazi political and ideological conviction that the white Aryan race, of which the Germanic race was supposed to constitute the elite, was superior to all other races.

The Nazis did not consider the Jews to be a religious community; they regarded them as the most impure race, contaminating other races. In *Mein Kampf*,[78] Hitler claims all Jews are *Untermenschen* or sub-humans.

The principles of the Nuremberg Racial Acts included the prohibition of marriages between Jews and non-Jews.[79] In 1936, The Committee for Special Jewish Interests wrote a letter to the Minister of Economic Affairs protesting against the extreme anti-Jew policy of the Nazis.

Jews were banned from participating in the 1936 Olympic Games in Nazi Germany, as well as from the fine arts competition that was held simultaneously. Photographer Cas Oorthuys (1908-1975) helped to build an anti-Fascist exhibition in Amsterdam entitled *De Olympiade onder Dictatuur* or DOOD ('The Olympics under Dictatorship'; the acronym means DEAD/DEATH). Barred and objecting artists sent in work that highlighted the Nazi-German terror: censorship, book burnings, persecution of the Jews, racial delusions, forced sterilisation, concentration camps and torture cellars. The German consul in Amsterdam was furious, and the German representative in The Hague wanted to intervene. The mayor of Amsterdam, Willem de Vlugt (1872-1945), used an article in municipal law to remove nineteen works, most of them by German immigrants. The German consul also felt the posters were insulting; however, the mayor did not find any grounds to prohibit these. They were, however, barred from municipal advertising columns.[80]

An example of an active Jewish organisation is the 'Jewish Central Information Office' (JCIO) headed by the German Arabist Alfred Wiener (1885-1964, hereafter referred to as Alfred),[81] who had fought for Germany in WWI—just like Otto Frank.

The JCIO office had been located on Sarphatistraat in the Amsterdam city centre since 1 February 1934. The JCIO was the first institute in Amsterdam and Europe that gathered information about the persecution of the Jews in Germany and fought Fascism and Nazism.

In 1938, a protest meeting attended by 25,000 people objecting to the maltreatment of Jews in Germany was held in the RAI conference venue.[82] I do not know whether Otto attended this meeting. In 1939, Alfred Wiener fled to London.[83] Otto and his family stayed in the Netherlands.

Anne did not take an interest in Jewish history neither before nor during her period in hiding. 'Following Daddy's good example [Otto regularly gave Anne books], Mummy has pressed her prayer book into my hand. For decency's sake I read some of the prayers in German, they are certainly beautiful, but they don't convey much to me. Why does she force me to be pious, just to oblige her?'[84]

Similarly, Otto did not take an interest in Jewish traditions, but he was concerned for the fate of Jews in general and, as such, visited the Jewish Invalid at 100 Nieuwe Achtergracht, a home for needy Jews run by an organisation by the same name, which had been founded in 1912. When Anne was a little older and had gone into hiding, she also became more interested in the hardships of Jews and the world around her.

Staal designed the 'Jewish Invalid'[85] building and used a great deal of glass and bricks in the construction. The organisation was founded by rabbi Meyer de Hond (1882-1943)[86] to provide disabled and elderly Jews with an occupation and care, and to educate younger Jews who wanted to emigrate to Palestine.[87] The Jewish Invalid did not receive any financial support from the government, and as such depended on private donations.[88] In 1938, the organisation moved into its new building on the corner of Nieuwe Achtergracht and Weesperplein. The Frank family's tenant, Mr. Goldsmith, worked at the Jewish Invalid.

On 1 March 1943, all patients and staff of the Jewish Invalid were deported. When the war was over, a memorial plaque was placed on the Weesperplein building, reading: 'Out of the iron of their chains the state of Israel was forged.' Today, the Jewish home for the elderly, Beth Shalom (House of Peace) has two buildings in the Amsterdam suburbs of Osdorp and Buitenveldert.[89]

At the corner where the river Amstel meets Zwanenburgwal stands the Jewish resistance monument: a metre-high black granite pillar incised with the Tablets of Stone. On the side, a text of the prophet Jeremiah laments in Dutch and Hebrew reads, 'Were my eyes fountains of tears then would I weep day and night for the fallen fighters of my beloved people'. The monument was an undertaking of the Comité Jewish Resistance Foundation 1940-1945, established in 1986. At this monument, the Night of Broken Glass (Kristallnacht) is commemorated annually.[90]

A ribbon of stone along the square in front of the current Opera House at 3 Amstel recalls the children and carers of the Jewish orphanage Megadlé Jetomim, demolished in 1977, who were deported to Sobibor by the Germans in 1943.[91]

Anne and Margot were from a liberal Jewish background and, as such, their parents chose a state-run public school—not a special Jewish one. In May 1934, Anne started attending pre-school at De Blauwe Distel (the Blue Thistle) on Dintelstraat, a preparatory class of the 6th Montessori School at 41 Niersstraat. Across from where the pre-school entrance used to be located, there is a small, square tile mosaic made by Willem Molin (1895-1959), which details flowers, fish, insects and various others creatures.

In 1934, this school had 350 pupils divided into nine classes, three of which were for pre-schoolers.[92] Dintelstraat lies east of the 6th Montessori School and at a straight angle with Niersstraat. Margot started attending the Vondelschool (currently the Robbeburg International Playgroup) at Jekerstraat in the Noorder Amstellaan (now Churchilllaan) area from 4 January 1934.[93] Anne was a very lively girl who would invest a lot of energy in the things that interested her. On the other hand, Margot was docile and kept things to herself. This is why the Montessori School fitted better with Anne than with Margot. 'Anne had a trait that was rather troublesome. She would constantly ask questions, not just when we were alone, but also when others were present. If we had visitors, it was rather difficult to get rid of her, because she was interested in everything and everyone. (...) It was good that Anne could attend a Montessori school, where all pupils were treated as individuals,' Otto writes.[94]

In Germany, education according to the Montessori system was strictly forbidden because it was not in line with Nazi ideology, in which there was no place for personal freedom. From 1934, Jews were not permitted to take part in state-run education in Aachen. There, as well as in Berlin and the rest of Germany, Montessori teachers were heavily persecuted.

In regard to their first day at school, Hanneli states: 'My mother took me to school, I didn't know the language yet and my mother was very apprehensive about how it would go, how I would react. But I came in and Anne was standing across from the door at the little bells and was ringing them. She turned and I threw myself into her arms and my mother went home feeling confident. I had abandoned my shyness and at the same time forgotten all about my mother. After pre-school, we attended the same school for six years, the 6th Montessori School (...).'[95]

One of their classmates at the Montessori pre-school was Sol Kim(m)el (born in 1928, hereafter referred to as Sol), who lived at 37 Zuider Amstellaan (37 Rooseveltlaan from 1946 onwards). Sally was

Anne's very first boyfriend and wanted to 'marry' her. Anne celebrated her fifth birthday at pre-school and after that at home, and received presents and mail from her family in Germany and Switzerland.[96]

The 6th Montessori School was located less than a mile's distance from Merwedeplein. Anne walked home from the Montessori School, most likely through Niersstraat, turning right into Maasstraat and left again into Zuider Amstellaan (renamed Rooseveltlaan in 1946). Whilst walking home, Anne passed a great number of shopping windows.

The 6th Montessori School building at 41 Niersstraat was part of the urban development plan *Plan Zuid*. The building had been designed by the Amsterdam Public Works Department and inspired by the American architect Frank Lloyd Wright (1867-1959).[97] The school building is situated on the corner of two streets and comprises two wings at a straight angle, linked by a lower square-shaped corner building. The Head of School's room was located in an oriel in the corner building.

Like the Frank family residence on Merwedeplein, the 6th Montessori School building is inspired (mainly) by New Objectivity. The varying sizes of the windows, wings and fasciae turn the building into a rhythmic structure.

Many authentic elements of the 6th Montessori School have been preserved. The central hall contains a circular mosaic, entitled *Levensweg* (Path of Life) by the artist Erik Thorn Leeson (1927-1970), who was educated at the Amsterdam academy of fine arts—the *Rijksacademie voor Beeldende Kunsten*. Another artist, Leo Visser (1880-1950) painted the large mural in the staircase in 1937, a panorama on plant and animal life. He was educated at the Amsterdam state school for art teachers, the *Rijksnormaalschool voor Teekenonderwijzers* from 1904 through to 1906. Resting on the cobalt-blue tiles of the handrail is a panther sculptured by Theo Vos (1887-1943).[98]

Anne's classroom has been preserved well. An old 1935 photograph shows Anne seated at the back of her class facing the teacher.[99] The school's room layout is virtually unchanged.

Children were responsible for clearing away their own materials. The pupils' storage spaces are still there to this day, and all pupils still have their own little table and chair. The blackboard was hung low so that the children could write and draw on it. The circular stove in the brick alcove also remains, although it is no longer in use, as is the white tiling of the kitchenette at the back of the classroom. The building also had rooms where the children could rest or wash.

The children took care of the plants in the classroom. Interchangeable pictures in frames and photographs decorated the walls. The classroom has large windows with low sills so that the children could see the school court well from their classroom. There were red flowers in earthen pots on the windowsills and a large tree in the courtyard.[100] When the weather was nice, the children would play or take their classes here or just eat their sandwiches. Every pupil had to take care of a small garden.[101] Anne did not develop an interest in household chores or her vegetable garden. Only during her period in hiding did Anne learn to appreciate nature.

Anne and Margot learnt Dutch quickly because they had plenty of contact with Dutch children and also because of the Dutch lessons in school. At the Montessori School, Anne developed her writing and acting talents. Anne was not a brilliant student, and arithmetic was particularly difficult for her. Anne loved music[102] but she had no talent for it, nor for drawing, and she did not play an instrument. She was, however, interested in history.

The teachers did not keep the children informed of the worrisome developments in Nazi Germany. Both the school board and the parents wanted the children to enjoy going to school. On 31 January 1938, Princess Beatrix was born and, in line with Dutch traditions surrounding births, the whole school ate rusk with aniseed comfits.

The window-side of the corridor leading to Anne's classroom still has the original coat hooks. Every hook has its own coloured tile with geometric shapes or an abstract picture of an animal, fruit or object.[103]

In the 6th form (6C), Anne's teacher was Mrs. Kuperus, the school head. Mrs. Kuperus (Riek de Rooij) was married to the well-known artist Sjoerd Kuperus (1893-1988). She did not have any children herself, suffered from depression, and never introduced the children to her husband.[104] She provided a fixed income so that her husband could become an artist.

On 12 June 1975, the (by then) late Anne's birthday, on behalf of the 6th Montessori School, Mrs. Kuperus was handed a portrait photograph of Anne by the then director of the Anne Frank Stichting.[105] Otto, Johannes and Miep were present for this occasion, at which the school was renamed Anne Frank School. The picture is still in the entrance hall.

At the Montessori School, Anne met Lutz Peter Schiff (1926-1945, hereafter referred to as Lutz), who lived at 37-III Amstellaan.[106] It was a summer romance. Only three and a half years later, on 7 January 1944, Lutz entered *The Diaries* for the first time. 'What a silly ass I am, I have quite forgotten that I have never told you the history of my great love,' wrote Anne, who had already been in hiding in the Secret Annex for a year and a half. Anne was also 'mad about his laugh'. 'I can still recall us walking hand in hand through the Zuider Amstellaan together,' she reminisced. Anne continued: 'Peter was a very good-looking boy, tall, handsome, and slim, with an earnest, calm, intelligent face. He had dark hair and wonderful brown eyes, ruddy cheeks and a pointed nose. When he laughed, a naughty glint came into his eye.'[107] When Lutz moved, their contact withered. Anne and Lutz last met at the Blankevoort Bookshop at 62 Zuider Amstellaan (currently Jimmink Publisher and Bookshop, 62 Rooseveltlaan) on 1 July 1942, shortly before Anne went into hiding. Lutz did not survive the war. In 2008, Lutz was given a face; one of Lutz' childhood friends donated to the Anne Frank Stichting a photo of Lutz from an old album.

The outside walls of the Anne Frank School display excerpts from *The Diaries*, created by the artist Harry Visser (born in 1929). The pupils work on projects about Anne and take care that the work of art is well-maintained and as impressive as at its unveiling in 1983 almost thirty years ago.

The wall with the diary excerpts stands in the shade of the trees. These were planted after Anne's time. Because they are located to the north of the building, they have not grown very strong over the years. The neighbouring children use the wall to play football. The street view is dominated by cars, bikes and parking metres—quite a contrast with the uninterrupted view of Anne's time.

Markedly, 81 out of 158 Jewish pupils forced to leave this school in 1941 did not survive the war. A plate in the school hall, unveiled in 2001, lists their names. The overview shows that most of these pupils perished in Auschwitz.

Of all pupils listed, only Anne died in Bergen-Belsen. Children who had to leave the school before 1941 are not listed on the plate.[108]

Everyone would go home during the lunch break from noon to 2 p.m. After school, the pupils of the 6th Montessori School liked to go swimming in the Zuiderbad at 26 Hobbemastraat,[109] a two-mile bike ride away. Its characteristic 1897 building with Jugendstil ornaments was designed by the architect Jonas Ingenohl (1855-1925) and was originally destined as Velox' indoor bicycle school. It is located opposite one of the corner wings of the Rijksmuseum. There is an elegant tympanum over the entrance.

When the bicycle school went bankrupt, the floor was fortified so that the building could be used as a showroom for heavy machinery. However, the showroom did not last for long either. The fortified foundation was convenient when the building was turned into a swimming pool: they 'only' had to add some extra piles to support the water basin's side walls. The Zuiderbad was inaugurated in 1912 and, at the time, was considered very modern. The raised roof construction, with glass on both sides, allowed sunlight to enter the building. The swimming pool could even be used in winter and when it was dark because of its central heating and electric lighting. Since the building was not originally constructed as a swimming pool, visitors had to walk up the stairs to enter the pool.

The Zuiderbad was renovated and the original interior was kept intact. The sand filter in the cellar is still there as well. Nowadays, a daily average of 700 visitors take a plunge in the Zuiderbad.[110]

The building at 160 Tolstraat (currently Bibliotheek Zuid, Cinetol)[111] was designed by Jan (Johannes Andreas) Brinkman (1902-1949) and Leendert Cornelis van der Vlugt (1894-1936) and was built in 1926 and 1927. It served as a temple for the Theosophical Society.

The building was modern for its times and was rather wide with a small square in front of its main entrance, which is rather different from the other buildings in the area. This concrete building has a rounded façade with a canopy above the modest entrance in the centre. Its green copper-clad roof is shaped like a quartered cone.

A committee that Otto and Walter Jacobsthal (1890-1944)[112] were a part of found some temporary space for the liberal Jewish community in Apollohal at 1-5 Stadionweg (currently 4 Apollolaan), the library at 16b Coöperatiehof (currently ARVH Marketing & Communication) and from 1926[113] in a house at 1 Waalstraat, corner Amstelkade (currently office space).[114]

From 1937, the liberal Jews used the synagogue at 160 Tolstraat.

The Montessori School board allowed children from orthodox families, such as Sally and Hanneli, to stay home from school during Shabbat.[115] Mary Bos (born 1928), one of Anne's classmates at the Montessori School, recalls: 'On Saturday we would go to school from nine to twelve. This was cleaning day and the [strict] Jewish children would go to the synagogue and not come to school (...).'[116] Anne was from a family of liberal Jews and went to school on Saturdays,[117] although she sometimes went to the synagogue. 'Saturday morning 27 June [1942] I was in the synagogue (...).'[118]

Anne probably visited the synagogue on High Festivals, when everyone put on their best clothes. Just like Anne, Otto did not feel a close connection with orthodox Judaism or Zionism,[119] was not very interested in Hebrew and had not undergone Bar Mitzvah, a festival celebrating the thirteenth birthday at which young Jews officially become part of the Jewish community. Otto did attend the Friday morning prayers at the liberal synagogue on Tolstraat.

In 1934, Ludwig Jakob Mehler (1907-1945)[120] became the rabbi of the Tolstraat synagogue.[121] Previously, he had been a rabbi in Frankfurt am Main, Anne's native city. He might have already known the Frank family in Frankfurt am Main. He died in Bergen-Belsen, like Anne, on 10 April 1945, and is commemorated on the Jewish Monument in Vijfhuizen. According to Melissa Müller, Anne did not want to go to religious classes[122] although she did attend Hebrew classes.[123] In this respect, Mrs. L. H. Isselman-Flatow (1921-2011) from The Hague writes: 'As one of the eldest members of the liberal Jewish community in Amsterdam, both in age and in seniority, I got to know every member in twelve years. I took classes from our first rabbi, L. J. Mehler, and the Frank family also sent their children to his religious classes, although I must say I had no personal connection with the Franks. First of all the girls were much younger than I. I was born in 1921. I did write a short versified play about the story Esther for Purim and directed it myself. Margot was Queen Esther (…).'[124]

Across the Tolstraat, at number 127, stands the monumental building of the Royal Asscher Diamond Association,[125] which Anne must have seen when going to the synagogue.

During the war, a cinema opened in the block, which closed down again in 1979. The neighbouring community protested against the intended demolition of the building. This had the desired effect. Currently, the building is a national monument and, since 1985, has housed a public library. The Theosophist headquarters and Cinetol community centre are on the same Tolstraat block.[126]

According to some authors,[127] the Frank family only visited the liberal synagogue on Tolstraat. However, Anne also visited the orthodox synagogue at 63 Lekstraat,[128] which is currently Arts & Antiques Group AAG and the Netherlands Israelite Head Synagogue Seminary, the only synagogue in Rivierenbuurt. Margot was a member of Maccabi Hatzair, a Zionist youth club.[129]

The synagogue at 63 Lekstraat was built in New Objectivity style, according to a design by the Jewish architect Abraham Elzas (1907-1995, hereafter referred to as Elzas)[130]. Hanneli scattered flowers at the synagogue's inauguration on 30 November 1937.[131]

Hidden behind the natural stone cladding of the building on Lekstraat is a reinforced concrete construction. The main synagogue is located in the largest block, on the Kinderdijkstraat corner. The adjacent building contained the secondary synagogue and had service rooms on the first floor and a service apartment with roof terrace on the second. Between the main and secondary building there was an entrance hall with a fountain, cloakroom and sanitary provisions behind a dividing wall. The entrance to the service apartment was situated at the side of the building. The two parts of the building are clearly separated in spite of their equal treatment. This clarity in form and layout is typical of Functionalist buildings.

The main synagogue was constructed using reinforced concrete with natural stone cladding on the outside. The side wing is more open in character with its roof terrace and rounded balcony. It is made of white enamelled brick and houses the service rooms, a meeting room, a staff residence on the top floor and a children's synagogue.

At ground floor level, light enters the building through simple, square window frames, and on the first floor there is an uninterrupted series of high windows on the long wall. The large area of blind wall above the entrance offers plenty of space for a Hebrew text from the Torah (I Kings 6: 13): 'And I will dwell amongst the children of Israel and I will not forsake my people Israel.'

From September 1943, when Anne had already gone into hiding at the Secret Annex, the occupier used the Lekstraat Synagogue to store furniture it had stolen from the Jews. Perhaps the furniture of the Frank family was stored here as well.

Remarkably, the Hebrew text above the main entrance was not removed during the war. Perhaps the Germans wanted to add to the humiliation of the Jews by making them pass through the entrance with the Hebrew text on their way to buying a Star of David. In Anne's days, the text was clearly visible. Now, however, a number of trees block the view of the main façade.

Following WWII, the number of Jews had decreased immensely and maintaining the synagogue became too expensive. During the 1970s, the building was put up for demolition. This plan was abolished and the Resistance Museum started using the building, whilst the former youth *shul* continued functioning as a synagogue. In 1999, the Resistance Museum moved to the Plancius building at 61 Plantage Kerklaan in Amsterdam. The large wing of the Lekstraat Synagogue is now being used as an auction house.

An elderly couple approached me whilst I was admiring the roses in Lekstraat. I told them that I was working on a photo project about Anne Frank. The elderly gentleman told me that he was born in 1929, just like Anne, and that he used to live 'around the corner' from where she lived.

Anne and Margot would go swimming in the Amstelparkbad, currently De Mirandabad at 9 Mirandalaan,[132] which, in Anne's time, was still a green area with plenty of trees. The swimming pool was considered very modern at the time, comprising a separate instruction pool and neat dressing cubicles. The Amstelparkbad swimming pool was later named after Monne de Miranda (1875-1942). He was a member of the Dutch Social Democratic Workers' Party (*Sociaal Democratische Arbeiders Partij*, SDAP).

In spite of Anne's frequent illnesses—Hanneli suspects Anne was suffering from rheumatic fever—[133] she liked to perform sports. In an undated letter to German friends, Edith writes: 'Anne enjoys learning how to swim. She seems much healthier this year. She must really have felt better, because she swam so well at the Amsterdam swimming pool that she won two medals.'[134]

There were several other bathing facilities in the vicinity of Merwedeplein. The public baths at 60 Diamantstraat, designed by Arend Jan Westerman (1884-1966) of the Amsterdam Public Works Department, opened in 1926.[135] At this public bath people could enjoy a few minutes' bathing in a shower for a modest amount of money or, for a few cents more, in a tub. At specific hours, young people could come and bathe for free. Aside from its hygienic function, a bathhouse would fulfil a social role as well. Anne did not use bathing facilities in working class areas.

After the war, most working-class residences were fitted with a bathroom, and public baths lost their social function.[136]

Generally, Anne did not look for contact with working-class children; she usually stuck to her own 'class'. Anne regularly visited the ice cream parlour Koco at 71 Rijnstraat (now DIY drycleaner Pamba, 71-73 Rijnstraat). The shops would be open from 5 a.m. until 8 p.m. on weekdays, and until 10 p.m. on Saturdays. Jewish shopkeepers and merchants would be active on Sundays as well, as was the Jewish market.

In 1936, the Jewish Max-Paul Josef Gallasch (1900-1948, hereafter referred to as Max) and his wife, who were also German refugees, opened the ice cream parlour Oase. It did not sell only ice cream, but also milk and other perishable products. It also contained a tea/coffee corner. The parlour would stay open during the weekend. The Gallasch family lived at 99 Roerstraat until 1939.

The Gallasches knew the Frank family. In 1943, when Anne was hiding in the annex, the Gallasch family was detained and deported to the Westerbork camp. In 1944, all four family members escaped from Camp Westerbork, went into hiding and survived the war. Max died from a heart attack in 1948.

Anne and her friends liked to visit the Oase ice cream parlour at 1 Geleenstraat (now a snack counter) as well. The Oase parlour employed Jewish staff. Anne mentions visiting this ice cream parlour three times before she went into hiding. 'We've quite given up scrounging for extra pocket money. Oase is usually full and among our large circle of friends we always manage to find some kindhearted gentleman or boy friend, who presents us with more ice cream than we could devour in a week.'[137]

Oase is still there now. It does not only sell ice cream and chips; it also sells donner meat and kebabs. The excerpt about the ice cream parlour from Anne's diary is on the wall. When I was at the parlour, a.k.a. snack counter, I met the owner's brother. He was very friendly and happily posed in front of the Oase. I was tired because I had walked a great distance in Amsterdam and sat down to rest over a coke and chips.

Anne also liked to get ice cream at Lunchroom Delphi at 1 Daniël Willinkplein 1 (currently Waarlé Grafic Design, 1 Victorieplein). In *The Secret Annex*, Anne wrote about this period:

'We 5 ping-pongers are very partial to an ice cream, especially in summer, when one gets warm at the game, so we usually finish up with a visit to the nearest ice cream shop, Oasis or Delphi, where Jews are allowed.'[138] The five girls of ping-pong club *Little Bear Minus 2* played ping-pong at Ilse Wagner's place (1929-1943, hereafter referred to as Ilse) at 11 Grevelingenstraat, over a mile from Lunchroom Delphi's. Their little ladies' club was inspired on the *Jopopinoloukicoclub* from the popular Dutch *Joop Terheul* series of books.[139]

When attending the ice cream parlours, Anne was probably troubled by odd looks from people who disliked Jews. Newspapers and magazines would regularly publish (anonymous) letters in which Jews were insulted:

A reader has written to us:[140]
My dear gentlemen, On 1 Daniël Willinkplein a Jew called Zilversmit runs a Yiddish lunchroom a.k.a. ice cream parlour. Even though it is already a very disagreeable sight to watch these stars slobber over their ice creams (they usually gobble them down in the street), the most scandalous thing is that the paper, and not too little of it, together with the spoons are thrown away right onto the street. Of course I know that this is just the Jew's habit, and that they feel at home in such an outright pigsty, but there is still the occasional goy living in the Zuid area as well. So he is forced to watch how the streets, which he has to pass along, too, are being defiled. Now don't think that Jew Zilversmit clears up his own mess. No, he'll let the goy take care of it. The goy is just a street sweeper, and apparently he enjoys his work because every time he cleans up the Jewish pigsty, he hops in and consumes a thing or two.

In spite of the fact that the parlour is a 'Jewish' parlour, and 'Accessible for Jews only'. What's more, Jew Zilversmit sold ice

creams to around thirty Christians on Whit Monday. Doesn't this give us plenty of cause to take forceful action?
Amsterdam, Hou Zee![141]
de J.[142]

Anne probably did not (or hardly ever) read any newspaper articles whilst living at Merwedeplein; she preferred having fun with her friends. In her short story *Riek*, Anne refers to two bakeries on the corner of a street. 'On the next corner lived another baker. In front of his window stood a little girl, eagerly looking at the displayed delicacies.'[143] Anne visited the Blommestein bakery on 26 Noorder Amstellaan (currently 26 Churchilllaan) who had been located on the corner of Noorder Amstellaan and Reggestraat since 1925.[144]

On the corner of Waalstraat and Zuider Amstellaan (renamed Rooseveltlaan in 1946) P. de Munk ran his shop[145] across from the Blankevoort bookshop on 62 Zuider Amstellaan (currently Jimmink Publishing House and Bookshop, 62 Rooseveltlaan). Anne and Hanneli would buy sweets and cake from P. de Munk.[146] On Monday 29 June, 1942, Hello Silberberg was introduced to Anne's parents. 'I had bought a cream cake, sweets, tea and fancy biscuits, quite a spread, but neither Hello nor I felt like sitting stiffly side by side indefinitely, so we went for a walk and it was already ten past eight when he brought me home. Daddy was very cross, and thought it was very wrong of me to be home so late [since the curfew prohibited (Jewish) people from going out after 8 p.m.] and I had to promise to be in at 10 to eight in future.'[147]

The Germans only allowed Jews to go to Jewish merchants' markets meant for Jewish customers only. From 3 November 1941 until 14 August 1943, a sign was put up at the children's playground on Gaaspstraat (which, according to Hanneli, was a meadow),[148] reading, 'only accessible by Jewish sellers, Jewish buyers and Jewish visitors'.[149]

The children's monument at 8 Gaaspstraat was designed by former member of the resistance Truus Menger (born in 1923) and was unveiled in 1986 by the then Mayor of Amsterdam Ed van Thijn (born in 1934). The monument is interpreted differently by different people. According to some, it commemorates the defenceless children who were murdered during WWII. Others are of the opinion that there is no monument to all (Jewish) children who became victims of the Nazi reign.[150]

A plaque at the Children's monument points out that 17,000 children lived in the Rivierenbuurt area, 13,000 of whom did not survive the mass murder. The number of Jews living in Rivierenbuurt who were killed was exceptionally high because this was the area to which German and Austrian Jews fled before 1940 in search of a safe haven. From 1942, Jews from across the Netherlands were forced to move to Amsterdam. The relative density of Jewish families in the Rivierenbuurt area made it easy for the Nazis to deport them to the east.

There is no memorial stone that lists the names of all Jews, members of the resistance and other residents of the area who were killed during the war.

Pupils of the Catharinaschool[151] lay a wreath at the Children's monument every year. Fortunately, children are able to play freely again here in the south of Amsterdam.

Anne was a busy bee: she liked to skate on the Apollohal artificial ice rink at 1-5 Stadionweg (currently 4 Apollolaan). In a letter to her family in Switzerland dated 13 January 1941, Anne writes: 'I am on the ice rink every free minute. Until now, I had my old ice skates that belonged to Margot before, they need to be adjusted with a small spanner while all my friends at the rink already had real figure skates that can be fastened to your shoes with nails [screws] and will never come off.'[152] Aside from the artificial ice rink, there was a real outside ice rink next to the Apollohal (in winter). There was another rink close to the Olympic Stadium, currently named IJsbaanpad [Ice Rink Path].[153]

Architect Albert Boeken (1891-1951), who was a member of the so-called Groep '32 club of rebellious architects, designed the Apollohal which was finished in 1932. Pieter Lodewijk Kramer's plan (1881-1961) to construct a festivity hall with villas in its stead did not gain much approval, nor did Berlage's plan to realise an artists' house here. Two rounded canopies made of steel and glass mark the entrances at the narrow Stadionweg side of the building.

The hall initially gave rise to a fair amount of protest from the neighbouring residents, because it was clearly visible from Boerenwetering as a solid glass and steel box resembling a factory. Six giant steel trusses span the 115 by 300 feet hall. Through the large glass façades, the trusses can be seen from outside the building. The roof consisted of hollow terracotta panels. The Apollohal has rectangular steel-framed glass panels, elegant rounded canopies and several circular windows. Its architecture is the odd one out in an area full of monumental buildings in the Amsterdam School architectural style.

The artificial ice rink and tennis courts, lighted by the sun at daytime through the glass walls above the brick façades and by a roof lantern, are no longer there.

The Apollohal was a multifunctional building with an exhibition hall and a director's residence with a roof terrace. Its restaurant looked out on the river Amstel, and could be reached by a steel and glass passage off Muzenplein. The restaurant has been extended and now also offers a modern hotel. The former Du Midi cinema made way to a gymnastics hall. Notably, since 2004, the Apollohal has been listed as a national monument.

On the way to Apollohal, Anne would bike across the bridge over the Amstel at Muzenplein. She could see the Amstel from this point, which branches off into five separate tributaries, all of which come together at this point. Anne must have seen the villa on 223 Churchilllaan, near Boerenwetering. G. J. Rutgers (1877-1962)[154] designed this villa in 1930. It has high, steep roofs, sharply pointed gables, canopies, a slender chimney and colourful accents around the rooftops.

There are other remarkable buildings in the vicinity of Apollohal, such as the former *Rijksverzekeringsbank* (National Insurance Bank), designed by D. Roosenburg (1887-1962).[155] It can be found diagonally opposite the Apollohal. The *Rijksverzekeringsbank* was founded in 1901 with the aim of taking care of the execution of the mandatory insurances for Old Age Pension (Algemene Ouderdomswet, AOW) and Widows' and Orphans' Pension (Algemene Weduwen- en Wezenwet, AWW) in cooperation with 22 Labour Boards. The *Rijksverzekeringsbank* building is a diamond-shaped complex with recessed entrances on its corners.

According to Hanneli, Anne skated on the Amsterdam canals.[156] This must have been in 1940 or before because, as of winter 1941-1942, Jews were no longer allowed to skate on the canals. Anne probably also skated on the Amstel and on Boerenwetering; many children from the area learned how to skate here; these were the skating locations closest to Merwedeplein.[157]

Anne never skated with her cousin Buddy. She regularly visited him in Basel and would send him postcards and letters in Switzerland. Anne hoped to become as good a skater as Buddy. According to Carol Anne Lee, Buddy practically worshipped Anne.[158] However, he never visited her in Amsterdam.[159] Buddy, whose mother was Otto's sister, lived at 11 Herbstgasse in Basel in 1933. His mother ran an antiques shop there, and therefore did not want to come to Amsterdam often. Buddy is currently the chairman of the Anne Frank Fonds in Switzerland.

The Franks kept in close touch with their family. During school breaks, family members from Aachen, Frankfurt am Main and Switzerland would visit the Frank family in Amsterdam. In 1935, Gertrud took Anne and Margot to Zandvoort.

During her period in hiding, Anne would often ease her loneliness by daydreaming about the children she considered her best friends. On 8 March, 1944, the artificial ice rink featured in a dream of the first-person persona in *The Secret Annex*. 'The night before last I was in our living room here, skating with that small boy from the Apollo Hall ice rink, who had come here with his little sister with-the-perpetually-blue dress-and-spindly-legs. I introduced myself to him in a very affected way as: Anne Frank and asked for his name, it was: Peter [Schiff]. In my dream I wondered how many Peters I now know!'[160]

In order to alleviate her loneliness, Anne also had the tendency to idealise people.

There are other buildings in Amsterdam that remind one of Anne. Jan Duiker (1890-1935) designed the Cineac Cinema at 31 Reguliersbreestraat, which was part of the French Cineac chain, in New Objectivity style. The visitors could continuously enter or leave the cinema. The façade contained a great deal of steel and glass just like, for instance, the Wolkenkrabber. The film hall was oval shaped, and its walls were sprayed with asbestos to ensure the proper acoustics. The elements on the outside façade kept warm those who were queuing to buy a ticket in winter. Hanneli and Anne watched child star Shirley Temple's films (born in 1928) in this Reguliersbreestraat cinema.[161] Anne also went to Cineac to watch the cinema world news, which included news about Hitler and Germany.[162] During WWII, films featuring Shirley Temple and other American productions were banned.

Anne mentions the Cineac cinema in her diary: 'Mr. Bunjes got sacked from Cineac because one evening he cut a film a bit short in order to catch the last tram, but they really did it because he is a quarter Jew, but doesn't count as one.'[163]

In her short story *Lodgers or Tenants*, Anne writes about a (fictional) tenant at their house: 'Every Sunday he would bring chocolates for the children, cigarettes for the adults and, more than once, took us all out to the cinema.'[164]

The Cineac cinema has been completely refurbished. Its exterior is still practically the same and is a protected monument. It is still being used as a cinema, as well as for some other purposes.

Cineac was not the only cinema on Reguliersbreestraat in Anne's days. The Theater Tuschinski cinema was located at numbers 26-28.[165] In 1935, members of the *Het Zwarte Front* (the Black Front) disrupted a screening in Tuschinski. Perhaps the Franks did not visit Tuschinski because it was a frequent stage to anti-Jewish riots. In November 1940, the occupier changed its Jewish name 'Tuschinski' into 'Tivoli'. As of 1941, the German occupier banned *Het Zwarte Front* because this anti-Jewish group wanted to create a separate,

Dutch movement. The façade now fortunately displays its original name again, Theater Tuschinski, in memory of Abraham Icek Tuschinski (1886-1942), the Jewish cinema owner who was killed in Auschwitz.

In January 1941, even before the Germans implemented such a ban, the opportunistic Dutch Cinema Association banned Jews from all cinemas in Amsterdam. From then onwards, German propaganda films were to be screened, including 'The Eternal Jew'.

The Rialto cinema on 338-340 Ceintuurbaan[166] was several miles closer to Merwedeplein than Cineac or Tuschinski. Rialto was built in Art Deco style and has a white façade with taut geometrical lines.

There was another cinema on 282-284 Ceintuurbaan that opened its doors to the public in 1921, just like Rialto.

During the war, cinemas were often disturbed by unrest. In the night of 25-26 October 1943, members of the Dutch resistance set fire to the Rembrandttheater on Rembrandtplein,[167] warning the general public to stay out of cinemas that screened Nazi propaganda. Cinemas were also frequently raided by the Nazis in order to arrest Jews and people who were trying to evade forced labour.

The Frank family probably dined at the Restaurant d' Vijff Vlieghen at 294-302 Spuistraat.[168] Nicolaas Kroese (1905-1971) opened this restaurant in 1939, which is still located in five interconnected 17th-century canal residences. Every chair in the restaurant on which a famous person had dinner, such as Walt Disney (1906-1966) or Danny Kaye (1913-1987), is marked with a copper name plate with the name of the VIP who once was seated on the chair. The oldest visitors' books date from 1946. I do not know where the Franks would have taken their seat.

During better times, perhaps Anne also visited the Amsterdam American Hotel (Hampshire Eden) on Leidseplein. Its building was constructed in Art Deco style and is listed as a national monument. During their miserable detainment in Bergen-Belsen, the Frank and Brilleslijper sisters would wistfully recall the food at 'American'.[169]

In her diary, on 17 November 1942, Anne mentions 'De Munt'. The Munt tower on Muntplein is clearly visible from Reguliersbreestraat and is located at the end of Kalverstraat.

The Frank family liked to go on outings and, in June 1938, possibly in connection with Anne's 9th birthday, they visited the very sunny country estate 'Amstelrust' at 319 Amsteldijk.[170] Otto took a photograph of Anne there. The young Anne smiles at the photographer, as usual. She wears a large white sun hat and is holding a rabbit.

According to Bob Polak, Anne and Hanneli would walk in (the vicinity of) Beatrixpark, then called Diepenbrockpark, with Hanneli's little sister Gabi Goslar (born in 1940) in a pram.[171] There were other parks in the area, such as the Sarphatipark in the De Pijp working-class area. According to Hanneli, she and Anne visited the Vondelpark.[172]

The peaceful protests of Jewish organisations against the Nazi threat did not have any effect. Neither individuals nor organisations that warned of Hitler received any support from the national government. On 12 March 1938, Germany invaded Austria. Miep recalls how 'the entire office staff [Singel 400] gathered around Mr. Frank's radio, listening to a dramatic voice announcing Hitler's triumphant entry into Vienna, the city of my youth.'[173] After the *Anschluss* or affiliation of Austria with Germany on 13 March 1938, many Jews fled from Austria to Amsterdam. Anne was staying in Villa Larêt in Sils Maria, Switzerland, with her grandmother, mother and Margot at the time. There were around 50,000 people living in the Rivierenbuurt area then, 32 per cent of whom were Jews.

Anne was still leading a carefree life at Merwedeplein. Anne does not describe any concrete memories of Switzerland in her diaries. Anne felt trapped during her period in hiding, and Switzerland was the backdrop on which she could project her dreams about freedom. Anne would dream about a film that would be screened in the Netherlands and Switzerland featuring her skating with her cousin Buddy.[174]

Following the *Kristallnacht* on 8-9 November 1938, even more Jews from Germany sought refuge in the Netherlands. Up until the beginning of the war, 10,000 German refugees were admitted; others entered the country illegally. The Dutch government did not want to spend any money on shelter; any initiatives taken were set up by private parties. The Dutch government's intention of setting up a central refugee camp in the Veluwe district was abandoned following protests by neighbours and the ANWB (The Royal Dutch Tourist Association). The protest by Queen Wilhelmina (1880-1962)—she did not want any refugees around her Het Loo palace in Apeldoorn—was particularly influential. Thus, the Dutch Cabinet decided that a refugee camp for Jews should be built in the province of Drenthe, funded by the Jewish community. The *Centraal Comité voor Bijzondere Joodsche Belangen* (Central Committee for Special Jewish Interests) and its subcommittee for Jewish refugees, *Comité voor Joodsche Vluchtelingen*, approved of the plan. In August 1939, construction workers on an unemployment relief scheme started building the barracks, and on 9 October 1939 the first Jewish refugees arrived at the *Centraal Vluchtelingenkamp* (Central Refugee Camp) in Westerbork.

Otto supported the Central Committee, but I am not aware of how he felt about the construction of this refugee camp. In any case, the Dutch government painted a brighter picture of the situation at the Westerbork Central Refugee Camp than it really was.[175]

Otto was very concerned about the violence against Jews. Rabbi David Schoenberger (1897-1989), who married Otto and Edith in the Promenadenstraße Synagoge in Aachen (now known as 23 Synagogenplatz), fled the country and survived the war. Many of the Jews in Aachen, however, were dragged out of their houses and deported to Buchenwald, Sachsenhausen or Dachau.[176]

The war came very close for the Franks when Julius and Walter, Edith's two brothers, were arrested as well. Julius had fought for Germany in WWI, and was therefore set free after a short period of time. Walter was released from Sachsenhausen on 1 December 1938, following his promise to leave Germany straight away. Walter ended up in a refugee camp in the Netherlands.

In 1939, Julius and Walter migrated to the United States.[177] Edith's mother was allowed to depart for the Netherlands in March 1939. On the card issued by the immigration department on 7 April 1939, her German nationality is registered, and she is said to be maintained by her son-in-law.

On 21 March 1939, Rosa Holländer moved from Aachen to Amsterdam.[178] Jews were declared outlaws in Germany. The residences on Adalbertstrasse and Theaterstrasse, less than half a mile from Rosa's house, were looted during *Kristallnacht*.[179] Rosa could not take any furniture or books with her. Her daughter, son-in-law and grandchildren on the Amsterdam Merwedeplein took her in. According to Bob Polak, Anne's grandmother had brought a special gift for her youngest granddaughter when she arrived from Aachen in the Netherlands in March 1939: a fountain pen in a red leather case.[180] However, Anne reports that her grandmother gave her the pen before, in February 1939. Anne was in bed with the flu, and a storm was raging outside. According to Anne, she received the pen in a parcel wrapped in cotton wool when she was nine years old; a 'sample without value' from her grandmother in Aachen.

Anne used her fountain pen to make the first notes for *The Secret Annex*. On 11 November 1943, she describes how her writing utility came to its end in her 'Ode to my Fountain Pen'.[181] Anne did not write about her grandmother being forced to leave Aachen. She would dream of her deceased grandmother whilst in hiding. As a young girl, however, she (as yet) led a carefree life and, on her 10th birthday, she and eight of her best friends posed together on Merwedeplein, all wearing their best dresses.

By this time, Germany had gathered a large army. On 18 August 1939, the Dutch government proclaimed general mobilisation. As a consequence, many men had to perform military services because of the war threat in Poland and Western Europe. Many people lived in fear; they were afraid that the Netherlands would also become involved in the war.

In an official statement on 31 August 1939, Hitler promised to respect the Netherlands' neutrality. On 1 September 1939, the German army invaded Poland. Great Britain and France supported Poland and declared war on Germany. WWII had begun.

The Dutch government informed its citizens of what to do during a potential bombing. In an empty storefront on Scheldestraat, scale models of houses and attics were on display, and it was indicated how one should quickly use a rake and spade to drop the fire bomb into a bucket of sand.

Residents of the Rivierenbuurt watched demonstrations of men in immensely heavy asbestos boiler suits disassembling fire bombs with a colander on their heads to protect against splinters. Everyone could try on a gas mask. There were samples of mustard gas and photographs showing the effects of all kinds of poisonous gasses.[182]

There were general blackout drills in Amsterdam. Cars and trams had to cover their head lights at night, and all curtains were to remain closed. Prince Bernard (1911-2004) watched a military plane demonstration from a towerlet on Berlagebrug.[183]

Apparently, German refugees were not particularly impressed, with most of them staying in the Netherlands. Otto could no longer hide the imminent dangers from Margot. In a letter dated 27 April 1940, the fourteen year old Margot writes to her pen pal in America: 'Because these are challenging times, we often listen to the radio. As a small country bordering Germany, we never feel safe.' Margot could no longer visit her family in Basel because Jews were no longer allowed to travel through Belgium and France. The ten year old Anne also wrote a letter to her pen pal in America, but there is no trace of worries about the war in hers.[184] I am not aware of whether Margot discussed her fears with her parents.

Otto declined an offer from his niece to take Anne and Margot to England;[185] similarly, the Frank family also chose not to flee to Switzerland or America,[186] with Otto and Edith instead remaining with their children in the Netherlands.[187] They probably did not involve the children in making these decisions. Otto, like many other people, hoped that the Netherlands would remain neutral, and he had invested a great deal of time and energy in setting up his business and did not like to become dependent on his family.

On 9 April 1940, Germany invaded the neutral countries Denmark and Norway. On 10 May 1940, the one thing everyone feared became a reality: the German army attacked the Netherlands. Queen Wilhelmina condemned the German violation of Dutch neutrality in sharp words. German bombers flew over the Rivierenbuurt area.

After the German invasion, some Jews committed suicide and other tried in vain to flee yet. On 13 May 1940, Queen Wilhelmina and her daughter Juliana (1909-2004), son-in-law Bernard (1911-2004) and granddaughters Beatrix (born in 1938) and Irene (born in 1939) fled from The Hague to London. At the same time, the entire Dutch cabinet fled to England, leaving behind their wives and children.

On 14 May 1940, the Dutch army surrendered following threats by the Germans to bomb the city of Utrecht. The Rotterdam city centre had already been destroyed completely. A member of the resistance, Geertruida 'Truus' Wijsmuller-Meijer (1896-1978), made sure 75 Jewish children were able to flee to England on a boat from IJmuiden on the day of the Dutch surrender; shortly afterwards, England closed its borders to refugees. From 15 May 1940, the Netherlands were occupied territory, and the Germans hermetically closed all ports. It was too late for the Franks to flee to a safer country.

During the German invasion, approximately 140,000 Jews lived in the Netherlands, 80,000 of whom lived in Amsterdam. Around 10,000 of these Jews did not have the Dutch nationality.[188]

Out of these 140,000 Jews, 102,000 would not survive the war.

'Now that the Germans rule the roost here we are in real trouble,' Anne writes in the Secret Annex.[189] When Anne had to go into hiding, she also experienced what is was like to be a victim of war.

In her speech on Radio Oranje, the queen in exile did not specifically mention the fate of the Jews in the Netherlands. Still, Queen Wilhelmina was very popular with the Dutch people because of her very explicit anti-Nazi statements. In *The Diaries*, Anne shows respect for Wilhelmina and the Dutch Royal House. Hanneli mentions that Anne collected pictures of the royal family.[190]

Whilst hiding, Anne felt supported by Wilhelmina's voice. Living on Merwedeplein, however, Anne did not mention the royal family—not even the marriage between Juliana and Prince Bernhard on 5 January 1937 in the The Hague Building for Arts and Sciences. During this marriage, German guests raised their right arm when the German anthem was played. The Building for Arts and Sciences staged plays, concerts and other events. It was located on the corner of Muzenstraat in The Hague and was inaugurated in 1874. It was destroyed by a fire in 1964.

The mood of the people around Merwedeplein hardened. The continuous air-raid alerts, announced by the hideous, deafening sound of sirens, kept everyone on edge. Children who had never experienced a war were frightened. During air-raid alerts, Anne and her friends would hide in the small entrance hall of an apartment block. The Germans imposed a curfew: no civilians were allowed on the streets from 8 o' clock in the evening.[191]

The streets were full of German soldiers. The Germans held military practice on the sandy area on Europaplein, the current location of the RAI conference centre. At the beginning of the occupation, there were no serious assaults on the Jews or large-scale *razzias* yet. The Germans were mostly polite and happy to spend their money in cafeterias and restaurants. The occupiers must have thought that honey catches more flies than vinegar.

The measures implemented by the occupiers were inconvenient but not (yet) life-threatening. From 4 July 1940 onwards, listening to 'enemy' radio stations, such as the BBC, Herrijzend Nederland and Radio Oranje, was prohibited. Violation led to severe punishment. I am not aware whether the Franks handed in their radio or kept it illegally.

On 16 July 1940, the Germans prohibited Jewish ritual slaughtering. All government officials had to state whether or not they were Jewish, and Jewish officials and teachers throughout the Netherlands were fired, as were any Jews who worked for the *Luchtbeschermingsdienst*—the air raid protection force. In autumn 1940, the occupying forces started to rule more forcefully. The Nazi ideology was imposed on the people, with several political parties banned.

It became illegal to display the Dutch flag. There was a prohibition on mentioning the names of the royal family members. Schools were closed and used as Germans military quarters. The beach was barricaded by the Germans. Anne would no longer be able to spend carefree days at the Zandvoort beach. The Allied Forces also became more active. On 8 October 1940, British planes bombed the Vechtstraat area and several houses were destroyed.[192] Many people were killed or badly injured, including children. One of the bombs hit the apartments on 56 Lekstraat. The forceful explosion and the ensuing blast of air pressure broke windows throughout the Rivierenbuurt area.[193]

Anne does not write about the bombings, the fights between Jewish and non-Jewish children, the German anti-aircraft guns and the screaming sirens in Rivierenbuurt. During her period in hiding, Anne would take the shelter of her father when she felt and heard the bombs strike around the Secret Annex.

A decree issued on 22 October 1940 obliged Jewish entrepreneurs to register with the *Wirtschaftsprüfstelle* (the business inspectorate). On 1 December 1940, Otto Frank moved his businesses, Opekta and Pectacon, from 400 Singel to 263 Prinsengracht.[194] He rented the building from a Jewish estate owner.

Otto formally withdrew from his companies because Jews were not allowed to own or run businesses under German rule and he wanted to prevent the companies and capital being seized by the Germans. 'Pectacon' became 'La Synthèse', and his non-Jewish helpers were in charge of the company (on paper). In 1941, the name of 'La Synthèse' changed to 'Gies & Co.', which used an image of the Westerkerk church as its letterhead. 'Daddy has been at home a lot lately, as there is nothing for him to do at business, it must be rotten to feel so superfluous. Mr. Kleiman has taken over Opekta and Mr. Kugler Gies en Co., which deals in (substitute) spices and was only founded in 1941.'[195]

Anne was not aware that Otto continued to run his companies in the background with the support of his faithful employees. Because they did not want to raise any suspicion with the Germans or with the German parent company, Opekta en Gies & Co. also supplied to the Germans.

263 Prinsengracht was an 18th-century canal-side house a stone's throw from the Westerkerk church. The four-storeyed building with its simple, dirty façade of red bricks was fairly inconspicuous between the other houses packed close together on the canal.

The offices and storage rooms were located in the front part of the building. The ground floor stockroom occupied the main building at the front of the house as well as the annex at its back. A narrow corridor connected the main building with the annex. Part of the annex was rented out to a Jewish pharmacist. The other rooms were still vacant.

Before they went into hiding, Otto would regularly take Anne along to the office on Sundays. Anne would play there with Hanneli or one of her other friends. They called each other on the internal telephone, used the typewriter and the various stamps to decorate papers with letters, or splashed water at the people below from the upstairs windows.[196] According to Buddy, Anne did not know about the annex before she went into hiding there.[197] Every fifteen minutes, the church clocks of the Westerkerk would sound. Anne really liked hearing these whilst she was in hiding.

The local government made a conscious effort to teach the children about the history of Amsterdam. Anne already knew about the inner city of Amsterdam from an early age, as can be deducted from a postcard she wrote to an American pen pal on 29 April 1940:

'This is a picture of one of the ancient canals of Amsterdam. But this is only one of them. There are large canals as well and all of them have bridges crossing over them. There are about 340 bridges in the city.'[198] During the Franks' Sunday afternoon strolls, Anne will have walked along Prinsengracht with her sister and parents.

Anne saw 17th-century bridges that have unfortunately disappeared during the 20th and 21st centuries. Amsterdam currently has 1,539 bridges, 252 of which are located in the inner city. This means that 88 bridges are no longer there. Old bridges are of great historical value and they adorn the cityscape. Amsterdam is still known as the Venice of the North, and since 2010 its ring of canals is on the UNESCO world heritage list.

The Franks probably also passed other monuments, such as Oudezijdse Kolk and Oude Schans. Anne mentions some of these locations, but it is difficult to tell whether she actually visited them. For example, Anne writes about 'Kaatje', who visits the Artis zoo in September 'when entry is only 25 cents'.[199]

Anne does not report the irregularities in the city. In 1940, supporters and opponents of Nazi Germany would regularly clash in Amsterdam. Members of the *Weerbaarheidsafdeling* (WA, militant wing) of the Dutch national-socialist movement (*Nationaal-Socialistische Beweging*, NSB) were violent, wore black uniforms and collaborated with the occupying forces. On 9 November 1940, the NSB commemorated Hitler's 1923 coup. The WA marched through the Jewish areas. The Jewish residents felt provoked and a came to blows with the WA. The Germans backed the WA and many opponents of the NSB ended up in labour camps.

The German occupiers made the Jews work for the *Heidemaatschappij*, the Dutch national association for structural engineering,[200] and the *Rijksdienst voor de Werkverruiming*, the Dutch government's unemployment relief service, who thus were ensured of cheap labour. In this way, the occupier could also ensure that no ready and able Jewish men would join the (Amsterdam) resistance.

The occupier instated a Jewish Council in 1941, which helped execute anti-Jewish measures. The Jewish Council would, for example, conduct medical examinations[201] and send workers' luggage to the labour camps. In 1943, after Anne had gone into hiding, a district office of the Jewish Council was located on 53 Merwedeplein.[202]

The people of Amsterdam started to show increasing opposition to the German occupation and the German misconduct that was particularly directed at Jews.

Otto kept his head and on 16 February 1941, Margot celebrated her 15th birthday with a smashing party. It was mainly working-class people and Jews from the surrounding areas who openly resisted the occupier. Many middle-class and upper-class citizens were too afraid and kept quiet.

As mentioned earlier, Anne liked to get ice cream from the Koco ice cream parlour at 71 Rijnstraat (currentl DIY drycleaner Pamba, 71 Rijnstraat). Koco's owners were Ernst Cahn (1889-1941)[203] and Alfred Kohn (1890-1945)[204] who also ran a branch on 149 Van Woustraat. Their parlours were popular with both Jews and non-Jews. Visitors would be indignant about the NSB provocations. In 1939, NSB members and Koco visitors clashed inside the parlour, as reported in *Het Vaderland* (25 May 1939): 'Knuckle-dusters and batons were used during yesterday [Wednesday] evening's clash in the ice cream parlour at Daniël Willinkplein [currently Victorieplein] in Amsterdam, where several were wounded, glasses were smashed and chairs and tables were turned over.' The police investigated whether 'this might have been an anti-Semitic riot because the ice cream parlour [71 Rijnstraat] is visited by many Jews and some witnesses made vague statements about anti-Jewish exclamations.'[205] A number of members of the NSB were convicted to six to eight months in prison, and the parlour's permit to stay open until late at night was withdrawn.

During the German occupation, riots broke out again on Waterlooplein and Amstelveld on 11 and 12 February 1941, respectively. A serious clash took place in the 149 Van Woustraat branch of the Koco parlour on 19 February 1941.[206] Its customers were becoming tired of the persistent NSB provocations and, as a precaution, had put a bottle of ammonia by the entrance. This time, the attackers met with splashes of the sharply scented caustic substance in their face. Alfred Kohn's son provides his own account of what happened: 'Mr. Kohn was wanted by the SS. When they learnt where Mr. Kohn was staying, they raided the Koco parlour. They entered the shop and started firing at random and hit one of the cooling system pipes with nitric acid and this spilled all over them. Following this incident, Mr. Kohn was arrested and put to death.'[207]

Incidentally, there were other bases from which Jewish assault groups operated, such as Café Nikkelsberg on Waterlooplein, which beat up NSB members on Rembrandtplein and Waterlooplein.

WA activist Hendrik Evert Koot (1898-1941) did not survive these street fights.[208] On 22 February 1941, as Jews were celebrating Shabbat at home, a German-led gang raided the enclosed Jewish area and entered the Tip Top Theatre at 27 Jodenbreestraat to arrest any Jews present.[209] Many non-Jewish residents of Amsterdam who visited the Sunday market in the Jewish area witnessed *razzias*.

Many people living in Amsterdam rose to the German terrorisation of the Jews. During 25-26 February 1941, hundreds of thousands of mainly working-class people went on a protest strike. The trams did not leave the Lekstraat depot. Anne does not write about the irregularities at Koco's, nor about the February strike; she details her friends, the carefree times and the ice creams.

Near the Lekstraat depot, the corners of the houses are decorated with sculptures characteristic of the Amsterdam School of architecture.

Shopkeepers and restaurant owners closed their doors and, at the docks, stations, newspaper offices and printing presses, the machines were shut down. On 27 February 1941, the *Wehrmacht* gathered 427 arrested Jewish men on Jonas Daniël Meijerplein. These men later died of exhaustion, torture or 'accidents' in the miserable stone pits of the Mauthausen concentration camp in Austria. 'The February Strike was the only massive, open protest against the persecution of the Jews throughout occupied Europe.'[210] Ernst Cahn was tortured at the Oranjehotel[211] in Scheveningen. He refused to give the name of the mechanic who installed the ammonia cooling system in his 149 Van Woustraat branch, and as a result was executed on 3 March 1941 on Waalsdorpervlakte[212]. Alfred Kohn did not survive the war, either; he was killed in Auschwitz.

A plaque on the 149 Van Woustraat façade commemorates the Amsterdam February strike. It is engraved with the following text:

'Wednesday 19 February 1941. This used to be ice cream parlour Koco. Its owners were the German Jewish refugees E. Cahn and A. Kohn. Together with their regular customers, they formed a mob which, on 19 February 1941, factually opposed the German occupier. Following this incident, Cahn was arrested and soon after became the first person to be executed in the Netherlands. This event was followed by large-scale *razzias* among the Jewish people of Amsterdam on 22 and 23 February. These led to the February Strike that broke out on 25 February 1941; a massive protest against the persecution of the Jews. Commemorate the fight against Nazism and Fascism!'

In 2008, bridge number 401 across the Amstelkanaal—which connects Van Woustraat and Rijnstraat—was renamed after Ernst Cahn and Alfred Kohn.

On Jonas Daniël Meijerplein, there is a sculpture called *De Dokwerker* (the dock worker), created by Mari(e) Silvester Andriessen (1897-1979). This robust, powerful image commemorating the February Strike was unveiled by Queen Juliana in 1952. Since 1968, there is Anne Frankstraat in Amsterdam as well, constructed following a traffic breakthrough in the former Jewish area around Jonas Daniël Meijerplein.

The February Strike could not prevent the mass murder of the Jews since many of the government officials collaborated with the Germans. The spring of 1941 was relatively quiet afterwards. Everyone feared German retaliation. The Franks kept their heads down. Many Dutch people assumed a passive attitude, and the Dutch authorities obeyed the occupier. Jews were incapable of freeing themselves from their precarious position.

After the Jews had been banned from leading positions, public institutions and the government, following their registration, the first riots and the initial deportations to labour and concentration camps, the occupying forces started to ban Jews from daily life. Children were not spared, nor were innocent citizens that did not want to have anything to do with this filthy war.

In the summer of 1941, Jews were banned from public baths, sports facilities, parks, sanatoriums and hotels. Anne was no longer allowed to swim in the Amstelparkbad (currently De Mirandabad at 9 Mirandalaan). In a letter to her grandmother in Switzerland dated 12 June 1941, shortly after her birthday, Anne writes: 'We don't have much chance of getting a tan, because we cannot go to the swimming pool anymore. A pity, but that's how it is.'[213] Apparently, Anne did not visit any of the baths designated as Jewish baths, such as those on 2 Nieuwe Uilenburgerstraat[214] and 28 Andreas Bonnstraat.[215] Perhaps Otto considered it too dangerous to let his daughters venture here.

Skating at the Apollohal also became a thing of the past, and similarly, Jews were not allowed to play any other sports either, such as football or tennis. Jews were no longer welcome at the large rowing course on Bosbaan.

Jews could no longer enter public buildings, such as the central station, without permission. Anne could not go to the beach in Zandvoort, even though in the summer of 1941 non-Jews were still allowed to buy tickets on Sundays to go to the Zandvoort beach. From September 1941 onwards, nobody was allowed on the beach. The Germans built bunkers and barricades. They laid down mine fields in the dunes and on the beaches, and many of the buildings, guest houses and hotels in the beach area were demolished.

Because the people were no longer permitted to go to the beach, elaborate beach life developed around the Parnassusweg bridge less than three miles from Merwedeplein.[216] There are no sources that suggest the Franks took part in this.

A decree issued on 7 November 1941 prohibit Jews from travelling across the border without permission. This meant the end of the Frank family trips to the Belgian beach in Middelkerk and to their family in Germany and Switzerland.

Anne attended Miep and Jan Gies' marriage on 16 July 1941 in the stately city hall on 197 Oudezijds Voorburgwal (currently Hotel the Grand). Otto was there, too. Apparently, they were allowed to be there (with the occupier's permission). Edith and Margot did not attend the wedding: Edith stayed home to take care of her mother and Margot was ill.

The city hall where Miep and Jan Gies got married was also called the Prinsenhof because Prince William of Orange (1533-1584) resided here. After a large fire in 1661, the building was given a beautiful new pilaster façade, inspired by the works of the architect Andrea di Pietro della Gondola (1508-1580). There is a sculpture of Neptune in the pediment, with a lion holding the High College's coat of arms and guarding the 'Garden of Holland'. Ferdinand Bol (1616-1680) supplied two chimney pieces to decorate the halls. When the city hall on Dam Square (147 Nieuwezijds Voorburgwal) had to be vacated on the order of Louis Napoléon Bonaparte (1778-1846) in 1808 because he wanted to use it as a royal palace, the Prinsenhof became the new city hall. In 1926, the city hall was extended in Amsterdam School style by municipal architect A. R. Hulshoff (1880-1958).[217] In the *Raadzaal* (council hall), three wooden figures depict the virgin city or *Stedenmaagd* created by John Raedecker (1885-1956),[218] and in the former marriage hall one can still admire the wall painting by Chris Lebeau (1878-1945).[219]

Following the ceremony at the city hall, Otto invited the guests to a celebratory reception at his Prinsengracht office. Twelve year old Anne, wearing a light-coloured dress with white socks[220] and with hair that had been brushed until it shone, gave Miep and Jan a silver dinner tray.[221]

A week later, Anne witnessed another wedding. The only film footage known of Anne was recorded on 22 July 1941.[222] It shows her watching from the apartment window as the bride and groom walk down the stairs between apartment numbers 37 and 39, get in a car and leave. The couple Anne was watching were Tiny Burger and dentist A. J. D. van Kalken, who had become engaged on 22 July 1939, as recorded in the *Algemeen Handelsblad* national newspaper (15 July 1939).[223]

The newspaper registers the groom's address as 55 Olympiaplein and the bride's as 39 Merwedeplein. According to Bob Polak, the bride's parents lived at number 39-II.[224]

Anne mentions Dam Square once in *The Diaries*, when she was in hiding in the Secret Annex: 'A newspaper seller in the Dam was crying: 'Turkey on England's side!' The newspapers were torn out of his hands. This is how the joyful report reached us too.'[225]

On 7 May 1945, when Anne had already died in Bergen-Belsen, there was another upheaval on Dam Square. A celebrating crowd had gathered on Dam Square to welcome the allied liberators. The party turned into a bloodbath when members of the German *Kriegsmarine* started firing away at the crowd from the balcony of *Sociëteit de Groote Club* at 27 Dam Square. People panicked and tried to find a safe spot. Bikes, bags, hats and bodies hit by bullets were left behind on the square. Deaths amounted to 22 people with dozens more wounded. A text on a plaque commemorates this tragic event.[226]

On 8 May 1945, the Canadian forces entered the city and the festival of liberation could truly begin.[227] The 1945 Wageningen Peace Agreement signed on 5 May 1945 marks the beginning of peace in the Netherlands, although a general surrender of the Germans only followed on 8 May 1945. Every year, the queen places a wreath at the National Monument that was erected in memory of the victims of WWII in 1956.

At the rear side of the monument, there are twelve coats of arms. These symbolise the eleven provinces of the Netherlands at that time, as well as the former Dutch East Indies colony, and contain urns with soil from the respective execution fields. Several important monuments are located on Dam Square, such as the Royal Palace, the Krasnapolsky Hotel and the Bijenkorf department store. In 1971, the Krasnapolsky Hotel bought the Amsterdam restaurant d'Vijff Vlieghen. Anne knew the Bijenkorf and, as mentioned earlier, dined at the restaurant.

Anne liked to act and loved the theatre, but I am not sure whether she visited any theatres or knew any actors. Actress Mary Dresselhuys (1907-2004), who was over 20 years older than Anne, lived at 29-III Merwedeplein. Her husband at that time was Cees Laseur (1899-1960), the artistic leader of the Centraal Theater on 14-18 Amstelstraat, close to the Jewish area.[228]

Theater Carré was located near the Joods Lyceum grammar school (currently Koninklijk Theater Carré at 115 Amstel). A poster from the beginning of the occupation period states: 'Al is niet alles pais en vree, kom toch eens lachen in Carré' ['Even though things are not all that well, do come and have a good laugh at Carré'].[229] Anne liked the theatre. She was fond of acting and, on her thirteenth birthday, her parents gave her the Variété board game consisting of various parts and a large, separate board. 'Variété, [...] is the latest party game for adults, something like Monopoly'.[230] Anne later bought 'a spare box for Variété' at the Blankevoort bookshop (currently Jimmink) on Zuider-Amstellaan.

Other popular family games at the time were Ludo, Rummy, Whist and pick-a-stick. I am not aware whether Anne played these family games with her sister and parents.

During the occupation, some theatres were meant for only Jews, such as the *Theater van de lach*, a comic stage at 4 Plantage Middenlaan.[231] There were Jewish bookshops as well, such as *Joachimsthal's Boekhandel N.V.* at 63 Joden Breestraat.[232] For fear of potential *razzias*, Jews would avoid visiting certain shops and recreational facilities.

Jews were banned from entering Carré from 15 September 1941. The Concertgebouw at 98 Van Baerlestraat[233] was also very popular in Amsterdam. The current main entrance of the Concertgebouw is located on Concertgebouwplein. *The Diaries* state that Bep Voskuijl went to a piano concert in the Concertgebouw.[234]

When the Jews were no longer permitted to use trams or other forms of public transport, as of July 1942, they were still able to use the ferry. 'We are allowed to go on the ferry and that is bout all, there is a little boat from the Jozef Iraëlskade, where the man took us at once when we asked him. It is not the Dutch people's fault that we are having such a miserable time.'[235]

As Anne indicates, she does not go on a large ferry. During the war she would take ferryman Cornelis Staal's rowing boat[236] that would take pedestrians (and bikers) across the Amstelkanaal, from Amstelkade to Jozef Israëlskade and back again. Because of the war, the occupier would not allow him to use a motor boat with a cable mechanism.[237] About 500 feet from the ferry was the Stadionweg bridge across the Amstel and the bridge connecting Scheldestraat to Ferdinand Bolstraat.

Pieter Lodewijk Kramer (1881-1961) designed the number 419 and 420 granite bridges across the Noorder- en Zuider Amstelkanaal on Muzenplein dating from 1931. Biking from Merwedeplein to Apollohal, Anne would pass Muzenplein and the series of sculptures on the wall connecting the two bridges. These include sculptures by Hildo Krop (hereafter referred to as Hildo, 1884-1970); they depict children holding a toy or pet: children with wavy hair holding a ball, a girl with a cat on her shoulder, another girl with her teddy and a bird, one with dolls, another one with a lamb, one with a snail house, one holding a little dog, and finally a child with a buffalo head.[238] The first and last sculptures are the wall's copestones. Anne will have taken for granted the decorations on the many bridges in Amsterdam, but they are of great artistic value now and remind us of the Amsterdam of the past.

From the ferry, Anne had a nice view of the Amstel which, at Boerenwetering, splits up into the Noorder Amstelkanaal and the Zuider Amstelkanaal. The Noorder Amstelkanaal bends west towards the Olympic Stadium—the area where Otto once lodged temporarily. The Zuider Amstelkanaal bends south and, like its northern counterpart, also finally passes the Olympic Stadium where the two canals are connected by the Stadiongracht waterway. Like the monumental residential blocks, the waterways are constructed in the architectural style of the Amsterdam School and the impressive lanes are amongst the most remarkable examples of urban development in the Plan Zuid area.

Anne regularly visited her dentist on Jan Luijkenstraat[239]; she wore braces. When Jews could no longer own bikes or use public transport, Anne had to walk to the dental practice. When they arrived, Anne and Hanneli, who sometimes accompanied her, would be offered a drink by his assistant.[240] Apparently, Anne did not always go straight back to school after her visit to the dentist; she once took the ferry to Amstelkade and most probably walked on to Merwedeplein.[241]

Anne sometimes relived painful moments; she associated a visit to the dentist with an incident that happened when she once went there with her mother and sister: 'Mummy and Margot were going to come with me and agreed that I should take my bicycle. When we had finished at the dentist, and we were outside again, Margot and Mummy told me the good news that they were going into the town now to look at something or buy something—I don't remember exactly what. I wanted to go too of course, but was not allowed to as I had my bicycle with me. Tears of rage sprang into my eyes and Mummy and Margot burst out laughing at me. Then I became so furious that I stuck my tongue out at them in the street just as an old woman happened to pass by, who looked very shocked! I rode home on my bicycle and I know I cried for a long time.'[242]

Anne would sometimes envy her sister. She was not as good a student as Margot and performed poorly in maths. In April 1942, Anne started taking extra classes in mathematics in Okeghemstraat. The architect of the Candida building had his office in the same street. Without bikes or public transport, Anne had to walk nearly four miles to get to Okeghemstraat. Jacqueline would accompany Anne on her way. To reach Okeghemstraat, they would probably walk along the Noorder Amstellaan (renamed Churchilllaan in 1946) and Muzenlaan, take the ferry to Jozef Israëlskade, and then follow Reynier Vinkelskade, Jan van Goyenkade and Peter Lastmanskade. Or, instead of taking the ferry, they walked along Apollolaan to Olympiaplein, crossed the Lyceumbrug and continued on Peter Lastmanskade until they reached Okeghemstraat. On Peter Lastmanskade they passed the *Amsterdams Lyceum* grammar school.

On 14 September 1941, Anne and her father, stayed at the Hotel Groot Warnsborn at 277 Bakenbergseweg in Arnhem. On a postcard to her grandmother in Basel, she writes: 'This is where we live! Isn't it wonderful! In the middle of the woods. Greetings from Anne.'[243]

Jews were still allowed to travel within the Netherlands, but within Amsterdam they could not enter any public places. The hotel management of this hotel, however, had no problems with Jews staying overnight.

When Anne stayed at the Hotel Groot Warnsborn, Willem Cornelis van Buuren (1905-1964), Groot Warnsborn's keeper and a member of the resistance, had already been arrested by the Germans. He was tortured in Camp Amersfoort but survived the war and devoted himself to reinstating the Warnsborn estate as a natural and recreational area.[244]

From January 1942, German officers started using the hotel to rest and regain their strength. The hotel burnt down in 1943. It was reconstructed during the period of 1950-1952, with the support of the Marshall Plan.[245] Nothing remains of the original hotel Anne stayed in. Other monuments, however, such as the nearby monastery, are still there. I can easily imagine Anne liked the beautiful surroundings. The forests and the sloping landscape are still the same.

Anne also went on other outings, one of which was her stay at the Op den Driest summer's house at 5 Koningsweg in Beekbergen, located near Apeldoorn.[246]

Rosa Holländer died of cancer on 29 January 1942. This was a great blow for Anne, who loved her grandmother very much. This was the first time she was confronted with death. Rosa was buried on the *Gan Hasjalom* Jewish cemetery in Hoofddorp.[247] Anne was now taking classes at the Jewish grammar school, as will be discussed later.

Even seventy years after her death, Rosa's grave, number E 08, still looks well taken care of. The text on the stela is clearly legible, and there are hardly any traces of decay. Close to her grave, a monument to the victims of the Holocaust has been erected. The upper side of the monument states: 'May God remember our dead, the martyrs who died during the years of persecution and whose grave nobody will know to this day. 1940-1945.' In the middle of the fifth row on the left, the names of Rosa's daughter and her two granddaughters are mentioned: Edith, Margot and Anne Frank.

In the Jewish weekly *Joodsche Weekblad* of 27 February 1942, there is an advertisement with a message from Otto and Edith: 'We would like to thank everyone for the numerous expressions of sympathy received following the demise of our dear mother, 3375 [ad number], Mrs. R. Holländer-Stern. Edith Frank-Holländer. Otto Frank. Amsterdam, Merwedeplein 37.'[248] Anne and Margot's names are not mentioned in the ad.

The German occupiers wanted to separate Jews from non-Jews, even at schools. In 1941, Otto tried in vain to migrate to the United States through Cuba, but it was too late. America was afraid of German spies and, following the destruction of their fleet at Pearl Harbor on 7 December 1941, made the decision to close its borders to German immigrants. Many German immigrants hoped their children would be safe if they continued to go to school.

Anne was due to spend an extra seventh year at the 6th Montessori School because she was behind in maths. As a Jew, however, she was no longer allowed to enter the public Montessori School and, after the 1941 summer break, she had to go to a Jewish school.

The Amsterdam municipality wrote all parents of Jewish children who attended public schools a note: 'According to our information, your child is Jewish in the sense of the aforementioned decree and, as of 1 September [1941], shall therefore no longer be admitted to the school it was attending (or was going to attend).'[249] Anne did not write about the forms she and other Jewish pupils of the Montessori School had to fill out by German orders shortly before the 1941 summer break. In one of her letters, Anne hints at things going downhill during the summer of 1941, but she does not specify this. Anne cried when she had to bid her old school farewell.[250] She was one of the 87 Jewish children who were expelled. Margot was forced to leave the Girls' Municipal Grammar School at 62 Reijnier Vinkeleskade in the Oud-Zuid area. The city of Amsterdam's Central Registration Office blindly followed the occupier's orders and reported 53,000 school children in Amsterdam in 1941, 7,000 of whom were Jewish. Out of those 7,000 Jewish children, 786 were attending grammar schools or higher professional education.[251]

Anne had to start attending the Jewish grammar school on 1 Voormalige Stadstimmertuinen, the *Joodsch Lyceum*. Because the school was not yet fully operational, classes did not start in September but on 15 October 1941. Until then, the Amstelschool, a public middle school, had been located here. Across from the *Joodsch Lyceum*, the Jewish school for higher professional education (HBS) was established. The city of Amsterdam collaborated with the occupying forces and managed the buildings. Jewish teachers were banned from working at public schools and the *Joodsche Weekblad*, its first issue having appeared on 11 April 1041, encouraged Jewish teachers to urgently report to the authorities: 'In order to get an overview of the available number of Jewish teachers for all branches of education in Amsterdam, the National Commissioner for Amsterdam invites those who are eligible to teach at schools with Jewish students only, to immediately report in writing to the Education Department, City Hall, stating their qualifications.'[252]

In September 1943, the occupier closed all Jewish schools and many of their students, teachers and members of the Jewish Council eventually ended up in concentration camps.

During the summer break, allied bombs fell near Merwedeplein and the Montessori School. On 14 August 1941, a bomb fell on Roerstraat. On 15 August 1941, fire bombs hit Niersstraat, Dintelstraat, Noorder Amstellaan, Zuider Amstellaan, Amsteldijk, Scheldestraat, Roerstraat and Maasstraat. A radio transmitter fell on the roof of 8 Merwedeplein.[253] Anne does not write about these bombings in her diary.

On 15 October 1941, Anne took her first classes at the *Joodsch Lyceum*. On 19 October 1941, the first Jews were deported to the concentration camps in the east from Frankfurt am Main, after they had been gathered at the Grossmarkthalle at 2-6 Rückertstrasse[254] On Theaterstrasse in Aachen, the Gestapo tortured Jews. In *My First Day at Grammar School*,[255] Anne describes having been to the *Joodsch Lyceum* registration day a week earlier. It was a rainy day so Anne took the tram. The two men in the corridor, described slightly mockingly by Anne, turn out to be the caretaker and the principal. 'In the corridor, I did see a chubby, friendly little man with red cheeks, who gave everyone a friendly nod, talking to another man of about the same height with glasses, a bit of fuzzy hair and a gentile face, but I had no idea the first one was the so-called *claviger* [caretaker] and the second one was the principal.'[256] The principal Anne described was Willem Salomon Hijman ('Puck') Elte (hereafter referred to as Elte, 1888-1983), who had been a maths and physics teacher in Zaandam.[257] In spite of Anne's maths deficiency—she had had to stay home often from the Montessori School due to various illnesses—she had been granted provisional admittance to the *Lyceum*. The principal considered the safety of the students more important than their school results and, under the circumstances of war, this was naturally in line with the concerns of the students' parents.

'(…) in my [Rector Elte's] opinion it is incorrect to think, that the deficiencies in knowledge [in Anne's case maths], resulting from their previous education or from their exclusion from schools in September/October 1941, have to be mended as soon as possible.'[258]

In late 1941, a small Jewish grammar school was established in the Okeghemstraat as well, but this was not the one Anne attended. This was the first time the Frank sisters went to the same school. Anne started in the first form of the *Joodsch Lyceum* at 1 Voormalige Stadstimmertuin and Margot started in the fourth form (4B2) of the HBS at 2 Voormalige Stadstimmertuin, in the other building.

On her first school day, Anne and her sister biked to the *Joodsch Lyceum* together. '[The older] Margot usually cycles really fast. After two minutes, I was so out of breath that I had to ask her to please slow down. After another two minutes, there was such a downpour that, remembereing those warm trousers, I got off my bike and struggled my way into the garment – taking care not to let it drag through the puddle – then got back on my bike and set off with new determination. It didn't take long for me to start lagging behind again, so that once more I had to ask Margot to go slower.

'She was a nervous wreck, and had already exclaimed the first time that she'd rather cycle by herself from now on. No doubt scared of being late! But we got to school in plenty of time. After putting our bikes in the racks, we started chatting again as we walked through the passageway to the Amstel River.'[259] Unlike her sister, Anne did not seem to have any apprehension about her first day at the new school. There were 350 students at school that first day.

Anne and Margot walked through the gate from the Amstel to the small square in front of the *Joodsch Lyceum*. I walked through the same gate in 2008, which was 'adorned' with recent graffiti. In 2010, I visited the *Joodsch Lyceum* again and the adornments had been removed from the gate's inside walls.

On the way back from school, Anne did not usually ride with Margot. On Amsteldijk, Anne rode behind Jacqueline after their first day at the *Joodsch Lyceum*. Jacqueline: 'A scrawny little girl with shiny black hair and a fine-featured face, quite out of breath, joined me on her bike.'[260] Anne saw the Nieuwe Amstelbrug[261] and the sparks of sunlight reflected in the water. The girls turned right onto the Amstelbrug (currently Berlagebrug) into Amstellaan (renamed Vrijheidslaan in 1956) on their way home. If the weather was bad, Anne would get on tram 8 at Daniël Willinkplein (Victorieplein since 1946) and get off at Weesperplein, just around the corner from the *Joodsch Lyceum*.

From June 1942, Jews were not allowed to travel on the tram anymore—that is, not voluntarily. Tram line 8, notoriously nicknamed the 'Jerusalem Express' during the war, was used for the deportations of Jews after the *razzia* on 15 July 1942. Following the war, there would be no tram line 8 in Amsterdam. Trams 13 and 17, which ran past 263 Prinsengracht during WWII, are still there.

Anne easily made contact with new students and teachers at the *Joodsch Lyceum*. There were twelve girls in Anne's class, including Hanneli, and eighteen boys. The *Joodsch Lyceum* had two floors and an attic. There were two paved playgrounds at the front and rear sides of the *Joodsch Lyceum*, where the children of the *Joodsch Lyceum* and HBS could play together. The playground behind the building is now closed off by a gate and grown over with weeds and bushes. If the large tree on this playground could speak, it would have a lot to say.

Anne kept in regular touch with Margot who was attending classes, including Hebrew, at the (orthodox) HBS. On Saturdays, Sundays and Jewish festival days, the *Lyceum* was closed, according to the wishes of the orthodox Jews. Liberal Jews like Anne complied. During its short-lived existence, this school brought together many of the Jews in Amsterdam from various neighbourhoods and locations across greater Amsterdam.

Students were required to strictly adhere to the rules so that they would remain inconspicuous to the Germans. During the break and after school, students were not allowed to linger on the streets. The streets were full of Germans, but there could also be a German behind every wall. Students should keep right on the stairs, hang their coats and be in their classroom before the bell sounded.

Anne writes remarkably little about the seven years she spent at the Montessori School. Her one year at the *Joodsch Lyceum* is treated elaborately, both in *The Secret Annex* and in *Tales from the Secret Annex*. 'Remember? Those are fine hours, when I can tell stories about school, teachers, adventures and boys. When we were still participating in normal life, everything was wonderful. I really enjoyed that one year at the *Lyceum*. The teachers, the many things I've learnt, the jokes, the esteem, the falling in love and the admirers.'[262]

Whilst in hiding, Anne probably longed more for the shelter of the *Joodsch Lyceum*. Both teachers and students were Jews and they were all in the same boat. Moreover, Anne was thirteen years old and started to develop sexual feelings; because of her going into hiding, she had no chance to experiment in this area.

According to Jacqueline, she sometimes discussed the hardships of the Jews with Anne at the *Joodsch Lyceum*.[263] Anne does not write about this. Anne did not write about being prohibited from having contact with non-Jewish children, either. Apparently, Anne wanted to keep away from the war and was not aware of the Nazi tactics to isolate Jews and then deport them.

At the Wannsee conference in Berlin on 20 January 1942, Nazi leaders discussed the *Endlösung der Judenfrage*. The presence of a gas chamber in Auschwitz II in November 1941 indicates the Germans were already planning on killing the Jews.[264] After they invaded Russia on 22 June 1941, SS paramilitary groups started murdering on a large scale behind the front line. However, the executioners deemed this method to be too labour-intensive and thus they continued the killing in a more industrial fashion.

Anne's biology teacher, Johanna Hermine Biegel (1889-1943), committed suicide on 1 June 1943 in Camp Westerbork.[265] Jakob Meijer (hereafter referred to as Jaap, 1912-1993) taught Anne history and survived Bergen-Belsen.[266] Jaap, who visited Anne's parents on Merwedeplein, clearly recalls Anne; her eyes made an impression on him, too. 'I can clearly envisage this last classroom on the right at the end of the ground floor corridor. Anne Frank was seated in the middle of the second bench. Her friendship with the daughter of the Goslars, my student from the same class, reinforced my attention to her. On several occasions, the girls accompanied me to my home on Amsteldijk, where we would sit and chat. Anne had a somewhat slow-sounding, penetrating voice, and remarkably warm, hypersensitive eyes. I can still clearly hear her slight German accent. I can vividly see her face, posture and bearings before me.'[267]

The total number of students at the *Joodsch Lyceum* was 490.[268] About half of the students at the Jewish HBS and *Joodsch Lyceum* survived the war. Many of its teachers and staff did not survive the concentration camps.

Out of the thirty students in Anne's class, twelve survived the genocide, 17 perished, and the fate of one remains unknown. If Anne would have been aware of this then, her relatively short life before she went into hiding would also have been hell.

The *Joodsch Lyceum* at 1 Voormalige Stadstimmertuin closed its doors after the last large-scale *razzia* on 29 September 1943, and has never been continued by a similar school with a community of mainly non-orthodox Jewish students and teachers. Looters and Germans emptied the building. A Perspex memorial plaque on the façade of the former *Joodsch Lyceum* bears witness to the building's 1941-1943 designation. A wrought Star of David designed by former student Ralph Prins (hereafter referred to as Ralph, born in 1926), is placed above the entrance of the school Anne used to attend. Ralph survived Theresienstadt and designed the Westerbork National Monument.

In 1948, the Jewish HBS at 2 Voormalige Stadstimmertuin reopened its doors and changed its name to *Joods Lyceum Maimonides*. The school is now located at 15-17 Noordbrabantstraat.[269] The mosaic text 'Joods Lyceum Maimonides' above the entrance thus dates from after WWII.

To compensate for their exclusion from public cultural life, teachers at the *Joodsch Lyceum* paid attention to arts and culture, and Jewish families organised home recitals. The Franks visited theatre and musical performances at Jewish friends' houses. Otto thought Anne was too young to go to reading circles where the classics were read. From 1941, all German Jews that migrated to the Netherlands after 1 January 1933 had to register, during which they were given the first name Israel (for males) or Sara (for females). Registration enabled the Nazis to track down Jews more easily. A 'J' was stamped onto their proof of identity. Practically all Dutch government officials collaborated on the exclusion of Jews.

From 1 May 1942, Jews were obliged to attach to their clothes a star with the word 'Jew' written on it. Through these measures, the occupier subjected Jews to extreme stigmatisation and humiliation. These yellow, six-pointed stars with 'Jew' written on them in black letters that imitated the Hebrew alphabet had to be sown tightly to the upper piece of clothing, whether a coat, suit or dress, but not just in any place: they had to be clearly visible, attached at breast height and on the left side only. Otto probably bought the starts at the Tolstraat synagogue. Everyone who could show the 'J' in their identity papers could buy four stars. They cost four cents per piece, in addition to part of one's textile coupon. This meant that Anne had to start wearing the yellow star when she went to the *Joodsch Lyceum*. Some Dutch people started being extra friendly to their Jewish fellow citizens. Some, especially students, put on a yellow star themselves. The illegal paper *De Vonk* printed pamphlets proclaiming 'Jews and non-Jews are equal', and spread thousands of these amongst the general population. The Germans deported Dutch non-Jews wearing a star to camps.[270]

Anne celebrated her thirteenth birthday at the *Joodsch Lyceum*. She treated her friends to homemade cookies during the break and, at gymnastics, she chose volleyball as a present to her classmates. Anne could not take part in this because one of her arms or legs could dislocate during the game. Her classmates danced around her and sang 'happy birthday'. Knowing what we know now, this has an awkward ring to it. After school on Friday, Anne celebrated her birthday at home with Sanne, Ilse, Hanneli and Jacqueline.

For Anne's birthday, her parents gave her a diary. Anne was excited: 'But of course I was not allowed to get up at that hour, so I had to control my curiosity until a quarter to seven. Then I could bear it no longer, and went to the dining room, where I received a warm welcome from Moortje (the cat). I closed the communicating doors of course. Soon after seven I went to Mummy and Daddy and then to the sitting room to undo my presents, the first to greet me was you, possibly the nicest of all.'[271] On the day of her birthday, Anne wrote in her diary: 'I hope I shall be able to confide in you completely, as I have never been able to do in anyone before, and I hope you will be a great support and comfort to me.'[272]

The small, square-shaped book is bound with a course checked fabric in red and soft green. Officially it was a friendship book but it was also very suitable as an intimate diary. On the back there was a linen lip with a narrow metal catch that fitted into the small lock on the front cover which Anne could easily reopen by pulling a tiny pin on its side.

Anne might have confided in her diary because she could not discuss any intimate topics with her sister or parents and, as a thirteen year old teenager, was confronted with her own maturing body and sensuality, and the fears and insecurities that accompany this age. Within German Jewish families such things were not usually discussed.[273]

Anne was aware of the fact that she was rather close-mouthed: 'I can never bring myself to talk of anything outside the common round or we don't seem to be able to get any closer, that is the root of the trouble.'[274]

From 20 June 1942 onwards, Anne addresses *The Diaries* to her imaginary friend 'Kitty'. She probably derived this name from Kitty

Francken, the main character's friend in the popular series of Joop Ter Heul books by Cissy van Marxveldt, pseudonym of Setske de Haan (1889-1948).[275] Anne knew the Amsterdam-Zuid area Joop ter Heul grew up in well, and the stories will have appealed to her. Anne and Cissy are similar in many respects: they both had the ambition to publish a book, suffered from health problems, had a vivid imagination and a sense of humour, included autobiographic elements in their stories, disliked housekeeping chores and shared the will to choose their own direction in life. This influenced Anne's style of writing. Anne and Margot often acted out scenes from the Joop ter Heul series.

One of Anne's friends, who lived in the Wolkenkrabber on 45 Daniël Willinkplein (currently Victorieplein), was also called Käthe 'Kitty' Egyedie. It is also possible Anne named her alter ego after this girl.

On a Sunday afternoon on 14 June 1942, Anne celebrated her birthday and Otto played a Rin-Tin-Tin video.[276] Jews were no longer permitted to visit public cinemas. Otto also played a promotional video about making pectin. Anne does not mention that this is her first birthday with only Jewish children.[277] Jews and non-Jews were no longer allowed to visit each other.

Nanette 'Nanny' Konig gave Anne a bookmark. Anne was spoiled on her birthday. In spite of all the presents they gave her, ungrateful Anne criticised her classmates three days later: 'E. S. [Nanette Konig] is a girl whose dreadful tittle-tattle is beyond a joke. When she asks you something she is always fingering your hair or fiddling with your buttons. They say that E. can't stand me, but I can manage to put up with that all right since I don't think she's all that likeable either.' And about Ilse: 'Ilse Wagner is a nice, cheerful girl, but she is very fussy and goes on and on about something for hours.' She even has a go at Jacqueline: 'Jacqueline van Maarsen, considered to be my best friend, but I've never had a real friend (…).'[278]

Ilse's father died on 22 October 1942 in Auschwitz.[279] In January 1943, Ilse was put on a transport to the Westerbork camp. On 2 April 1943, she was gassed in Sobibor with her mother and grandmother.[280]

Anne's father bought the diary they gave her as a birthday present around the corner, at bookshop Blankevoort at 62 Zuider Amstellaan (currently Jimmink Publishing House and Bookshop, 62 Rooseveltlaan).

According to Hanneli, Anne and herself would buy school books and stationery at the Blankevoort bookshop.[281] Bookshop Blankevoort is also mentioned in Anne's works. In her short story *Lodgers or Tenants*,[282] 'a neat ad is put up in window of the bookshop on the corner' for a week. The story is about 'renting out our large back room'.[283] In real life, the Franks rented out the large attic room to various consecutive tenants.

The occupier changed the name of the *Hollandsche Schouwburg* (Dutch theatre) into *Joodsche Schouwburg* (Jewish theatre) and, as of October 1941, only Jewish musicians and artists were allowed to perform here for a Jews-only audience.

On 3 July 1942, the 'promotion' of the *Joodsch Lyceum* took place in the *Hollandsche Schouwburg* at 24 Plantage Middenlaan. Before the reports were handed out and the students were promoted to the next form, a Jewish orchestra performed and principal Elte made a speech. Anne was not unsatisfied with her first Easter report at the *Joodsch Lyceum*; only her maths was unsatisfactory. Apparently, the extra maths classes did not suffice. Notably, Anne thought her parents did not worry about her report all that much:

'They were certainly pleased at home, although over the question of marks my parents are quite different from most. They don't care a bit whether my reports are good or bad as long as I'm well and happy (...)'.[284] Anne does not notice that parents and teachers are mainly concerned with guaranteeing the children's safety and does not speak a word about the students in higher classes who stop their teachers on the day of the promotions to tell them that they have been called to report for *Arbeidseinsatz*—forced labour.[285] As if nothing was the matter, Anne visited the Oase ice cream parlour on Saturday 4 July 1942.

In August 1942, Walter Süskind (1906-1943)[286] was appointed director of the *Hollandsche Schouwburg* by the Jewish Council.

Thanks to him, many Jews were able to escape from the theatre and the preschool connected with it across the street at 31-33 Plantage Middenlaan.

On 29 September, the last large-scale *razzias* were held in Amsterdam. A huge 10,000 individuals were arrested, including the members of the Jewish Council. The Süskind family was deported to the Westerbork camp. In Auschwitz, his wife, daughter and mother were gassed immediately upon arrival. When Russian troops were approaching Berlin and the concentration camps in 1944, Walter Süskind was driven West by foot, together with thousands of surviving prisoners. Walter Süskind died on 28 February 1945 during a so-called death march.

As of 29 September 1943, there were no Jews left in the Netherlands according to (official) Nazi accounts. Most Jews had been deported to and killed in concentration camps, with the exception of a small group of mixed-marriage Jews, i.e. Jews who had married a non-Jewish partner. And, of course, there were the people in hiding.

After the last large-scale deportation on 19 November 1943, the Hollandsche Schouwburg was not used as a depot for Jews; in 1943 and 1944 there were only a few deportations from the various prisons, namely the *Huis van Bewaring I* (Weteringschans), *II* (Havenstraat 6) and *III* (Oostelijke Handelskade 12, Koninklijke Hollandsche Lloyd).

The *Hollandsche Schouwburg* was listed as a war monument 1962. On the wall close to the eternal flame is an engraved list of 6,700 family names of the Jews who were deported from Holland and subsequently killed. These names symbolise the 104,000 Jewish victims from the Netherlands.

There are more references to the war around the *Hollandsche Schouwburg*, such as the Anne Frankstraat in the former Jewish area.

There was a selling point for Stars of David at 9 Plantage Parklaan.[287]

During the war, a preschool was located at 31-33 Plantage Middenlaan (currently Rob van Erven, Deli Products). Its staff rescued over 500 Jewish children. A bronze plaque on the building reads: 'To all who helped preserve Jewish children from deportation during the German occupation. 1940-1945.'

Slightly north of the *Hollandsche Schouwburg*, in the Wertheimpark, there is a Monument of Mirrors. The Auschwitz remembrance is held here annually since 1993. The monument consists of broken mirrors reflecting the sky. According to its creator, writer and visual artist Jan Wolkers (1925-2007), the broken mirrors symbolise that, 'after Auschwitz, the heavens will be fragmented forever'.[288] These monuments bridge the gap between past and present.

[1] http://www.verbond.eu/ (Dutch only, English version under construction at http://www.verbond.eu/en).
[2] http://www.nik.nl/ (Dutch only).
[3] Carol Ann Lee, *Anne Frank. Het leven van een jong meisje* [The Life of a Young Girl. The Definitive Biography] (Amsterdam, 2009), p. 53.
[4] http://www.freebase.com/view/en/matthew_j_perry.
[5] *The Diaries*, 24 June 1942.
[6] http://www.freebase.com/view/en/eefje_de_jong.
[7] Bob Polak. *Naar buiten, lucht en lachen! Een literaire wandeling door het Amsterdam van Anne Frank* [Outside: fresh air and laughter! A literary walk through Anne Frank's Amsterdam] (Amsterdam, 2006), p. 44.
[8] http://www.architectenweb.nl/aweb/archipedia/archipedia.asp?ID=829 (Dutch only).
[9] 'De verdooping van straten hier ter stede gaat voort. Nu heeft de gemeenteraad Woensdag 8 mei l.l. [jongstleden] weer besloten den naam van de Amstellaan te veranderen in Stalinlaan, dien van de Noorder Amstellaan in Churchilllaan, dien van de Zuider Amstellaan in Rooseveltlaan en dien van het Daniël Willinkplein in Victorieplein.' [The renaming of streets in this city is being continued. The city council has decided on Wednesday 8 May, to change the name of Amstellaan into Stalinlaan and that of Noorder Amstellaan in Churchilllaan, Zuider Amstellaan has become Rooseveltlaan and Daniël Willinkplein is now Victorieplein.] *Amstelodamum* (Amsterdam, 1946).
[10] Willy Lindwer, *De laatste zeven maanden van Anne Frank. Het ongeschreven laatste hoofdstuk van het Dagboek* (Hilversum, 2008), p. 34. English edition: *The Last Seven Months of Anne Frank. The Stories of Six Women who Knew Anne Frank.* (Macmillan, 2004).
[11] Theo Coster, *Klasgenoten van Anne Frank* (Amsterdam, 2009), p. 84. English editon: *We All Wore Stars: Memories of Anne Frank from Her Classmates* (Macmillan, 2011).
[12] Jacqueline van Maarsen, email dated 12 January 2011.
[13] Jacqueline van Maarsen, *De erflaters. Herinneringen van de jeugdvriendin van Anne Frank* (Amsterdam, 2004), p. 78, 85. English edition: *Inheriting Anne Frank.* Arcadia books, 2010. 'Eva Schloss (…) never knew Anne, nor Anne's friends (…)'. (Jacqueline van Maarsen, email dated 21 December 2010).
[14] Eva Geiringer, email dated 29 April 2011.
[15] http://www.verzetsmuseum.org/tweede-wereldoorlog/nl/themas/evaverhaal,amsterdam (Dutch only).
[16] Not to be confused with Eva Gold, whom Anne does mention in her diaries.
[17] As referred to earlier in this book. The periodical's title is *The Consumer* ('De consument. Officieel orgaan op verkoopgebied verspreid door winkeliers aangesloten bij de Vakvereniging E.M.M.') dated 11 January 1940. Page 7 lists the winners of puzzle 77 and 78. Anne Frank, 37 Merwedeplein won a photo album in group B (to be collected from shopkeeper J. v. Zalingen). In addition to a children's

page, the periodical contained recipes, a serial and advertisements. Mrs. S. L. L. Fransen presented the periodical as a gift to the Anne Frank Stichting in 1996. (Email from the Anne Frank Stichting, dated 15 December 2011).

[18] *The Diaries*, 5 July 1942.

[19] http://www.gettyimages.nl/detail/news-photo/full-length-portrait-of-anne-frank-wearing-a-hat-and-coat-news-photo/3229102.

[20] According to Hannah Goslar, there were no trees on Merwedeplein in Anne's days (interview by phone on 6 January 2011). However, photographs do show newly planted trees (Collection Amsterdam City Archives, inventory no. B00000023690) and shrubbery in the central area on Merwedeplein (Collection Amsterdam City Archives, inventory no. B00000023691).

[21] http://www.freebase.com/view/en/hendrik_petrus_berlage.

[22] http://www.freebase.com/view/en/hildo_krop.

[23] http://www.zuidelijkewandelweg.nl/actueel/reiniersaul.htm (Dutch only).

[24] http://www.zuidelijkewandelweg.nl/actueel/reiniersaul.htm.

[25] http://www.amsterdamsetrams.nl/lijnen/lijn24.htm (Dutch only).

[26] Miep Gies, *Herinneringen aan Anne Frank. Het verhaal van Miep Gies, de steun en toeverlaat van de familie Frank in het Achterhuis* (Amsterdam, 1987), pp. 23-24. English edition: *Anne Frank Remembered: The Story of the Woman Who Helped to Hide the Frank Family* (Simon and Schuster, 2011).

[27] http://zoeken.nai.nl/CIS/project/28186 (Dutch only).

[28] http://www.magnaplaza.nl/en/history.

[29] http://hetgrachtenhuis.nl/?lang=en#!page/37/p_100065.

[30] http://grachtenboek.hetgrachtenhuis.nl/objecten.php?id=6799.

[31] Following a request by the Stichting Amsterdam Vluchtstad (email dated 20 August 2009), I do not mention the Franks' exact address in my books.

[32] http://www.zuidelijkewandelweg.nl/architectuur/wolkenkrabberarchieven/index.htm (Dutch only).

[33] Melissa Müller, *Anne Frank. De biografie* (Amsterdam, 1998) p. 47. Original German title: *Das Mädchen Anne Frank. Die Biographie*. English edition: *Anne Frank: The Biography* (Macmillan 2013).

[34] http://www.annefrank.org/en/Anne-Frank/Emigrating-to-the-Netherlands/A-new-start/.

[35] http://www.annefrank.org/en/Anne-Frank/Emigrating-to-the-Netherlands/A-new-start/.

[36] http://www.raivereniging.nl/about-us/rai-vereniging/geschiedenis.aspx (Dutch only).

[37] http://www.zuidelijkewandelweg.nl/architectuur/wolkenkrabber75.htm (Dutch only).

[38] http://www.geheugenvanplanzuid.nl/architectuur/wolkenkrabber75.htm (Dutch only).

[39] http://www.gettyimages.nl/detail/news-photo/full-length-portrait-of-anne-frank-her-sister-margot-frank-news-photo/3208599. The Frank family apartment is not on

the cultural heritage list: (http://monumentenregister.cultureelerfgoed.nl/php/main.php).

[40] http://www.trouw.nl/tr/nl/4324/nieuws/archief/article/detail/1708863/2005/10/27/Het-andere-huis-van-Anne-Frank-is-hersteld.dhtml (Dutch only).

[41] http://www.gettyimages.nl/detail/82657583/Premium-Archive. According to Hannah Goslar (interview over the phone on 6 January 2011), Anne used a children's writing table. Anne describes her room and writes that she uses her mother's writing table. On the 1941 photo, Anne is seated behind her mother's writing desk on a cushion with a pen in her hand.

[42] During Purim, the Jews commemorate the fact that the Jewish people, who were forced to live in exile in the Persian realm in the 5th century before Christ, survived because of the intervention of the Jewish Esther. During Purim, the Megillah is read in the synagogue, the parchment scroll that records this narrative, children make lots of noise with their graggers, songs are sung, the children dress up, there is a feast and charity is given to the poor. (http://www.chabad.org/holidays/purim/article_cdo/aid/648312/jewish/Purim-2014-Guide.htm).

[43] The festival of booths, 'Sukkot' in Hebrew, commemorates the Jew's 40-year journey through the desert between leaving Egypt in 1312 B.C. (6 Sivan 2448 on the Jewish calendar) and arriving at the Promised Land. The harvest is also celebrated during the festival of booths.

[44] Bob Polak. *Naar buiten, lucht en lachen! Een literaire wandeling door het Amsterdam van Anne Frank* (Amsterdam, 2006), p. 38.

[45] http://www.gettyimages.nl/detail/news-photo/portrait-of-anne-frank-sunbathing-on-her-familys-roof-taken-news-photo/3208586.

[46] http://www.gettyimages.nl/detail/3229115/Premium-Archive.

[47] http://www.gettyimages.nl/detail/3229115/Premium-Archive.

[48] 'I see touring cars full of tourists at the 'Merwedeplein' who all want to get a glimpse, at the outside, of the house she used to live in and where, in the park in front, a little statue is placed in memory of her and where tourists quickly are taking a snapshot, before they go back into the bus, to show their relatives and friends back home how cultural they have been during their trip.' (Max C. van der Glas, email dated 23 December 2010).

[49] Carol Ann Lee's assertion that Otto's company was located on Singelgracht is incorrect. The 400 Singel building is on the Dutch national heritage list (http://monumentenregister.cultureelerfgoed.nl/php/main.php, Dutch only).

[50] http://www.hyves.nl/agenda/14621503/Premiere_Dear_Anne_A_Symphonic_Tribute_To_Anne_Frank_in_Amsterdam_Tuschinski/ (Dutch only, but with links to English pages).

[51] *The Diaries*, 20 June 1942.

[52] http://www.gettyimages.nl/detail/news-photo/anne-frank-wearing-a-coat-a-hat-and-gloves-looking-at-her-news-photo/3208600.

[53] Anne Frank, *Verhaaltjes, en gebeurtenissen uit het Achterhuis. Met de roman in wording Cady's leven* (Amsterdam, 2005), p. 71. English edition: *Tales from the Secret Annex. Including her Unfinished Novel Cady's Live* (Halban Publishers, 2010).
[54] Regional newspaper *Dagblad van het Noorden* 4 May 1936 (Dutch only), http://kranten.kb.nl/.
[55] http://kranten.kb.nl/view/article/id/ddd%3A010318315%3Ampeg21%3Ap012%3Aa0050.
[56] http://kranten.kb.nl/view/article/id/ddd%3A010318321%3Ampeg21%3Ap007%3Aa0041.
[57] http://www.joodsmonument.nl/person/452294/en.
[58] Amstelodamum (Amsterdam, 1936).
[59] Philo Bregstein, *Herinnering aan joods Amsterdam* (Amsterdam, 1999), p. 249 English edition: *Remembering Jewish Amsterdam* (Holmes & Meier Pub, 2004).
[60] An important stronghold of the resistance movement was located at 178 Lekstraat in Rivierenbuurt, which stood up for the Jews and printed and distributed the illegal paper *De Waarheid* (The Truth).
[61] Philo Bregstein, *Herinnering aan joods Amsterdam* (Amsterdam, 1999), p. 265.
[62] *The Diaries*, 24 June 1942.
[63] Miep Gies, *Herinneringen aan Anne Frank. Het verhaal van Miep Gies, de steun en toeverlaat van de familie Frank in het Achterhuis* (Amsterdam, 1987), p. 46.
[64] Miep Gies, *Herinneringen aan Anne Frank. Het verhaal van Miep Gies, de steun en toeverlaat van de familie Frank in het Achterhuis* (Amsterdam, 1987), pp. 35-36.
[65] http://www.freebase.com/view/en/charlotta_kaletta.
[66] http://www.freebase.com/view/en/kurt_baschwitz.
[67] South of the Wolkenkrabber continued from Zuider Amstellaan.
[68] *The Diaries*, 10 November 1942.
[69] Mr. Andre Holten lived close to Miep Gies (email dated 20 January 2011) at 33 Hunzestraat.
[70] http://www.freebase.com/view/en/old_phoebe_halliwell.
[71] http://www.freebase.com/view/m/0h2t9ky.
[72] http://www.joodsmonument.nl/person/510358/en.
[73] http://www.joodsmonument.nl/person/529156/en.
[74] *The Diaries*, 20 October 1942.
[75] Bob Polak, *Naar buiten, lucht en lachen! Een literaire wandeling door het Amsterdam van Anne Frank* (Amsterdam, 2006), p. 158 (Dutch only).
[76] Max C. van der Glas, email 22 December 2010.
[77] http://archievenwo2.nl/archieven/archief-blok/comit-voor-bijzondere-joodsche-belangen/nederlands-instituut-voor-oorlogsdocumentatie-niod (Dutch only).
[78] Published in the Netherlands as: Adolf Hitler, Mijn Kamp (Ridderkerk, 1982), no post-war English editions have been published.

[79] http://www.annefrank.org/nl/Subsites/Amsterdam/Tijdlijn/#!/en/Subsites/Annes-Amsterdam/Timeline/Before-the-war/1935/1935/Protests-in-the-Apollohal-against-the-Nuremburg-Laws/?viewtype=Contextual&subjectId=11773.

[80] http://www.annefrank.org/nl/Subsites/Amsterdam/Tijdlijn/#!/en/Subsites/Annes-Amsterdam/Timeline/Before-the-war/6/1936/Cas-Oorthuys---Mayor-tries-to-forbid-criticism-of-Nazi-Germany/?viewtype=Contextual&subjectId=11773.

[81] http://www.jmberlin.de/main/EN/03-Collection-and-Research/02-Read_and_Research/03-wienerlibrary.php.

[82] http://www.annefrank.org/nl/Subsites/Amsterdam/Tijdlijn/#!/en/Subsites/Annes-Amsterdam/Timeline/Before-the-war/1933/1933/Protest-meeting-held-in-the-RAI-against-the-persecution-of-the-Jews-in-Germany/?viewtype=Contextual&subjectId=11773.

[83] http://www.dbnl.org/tekst/kris004gesc01_01/kris004gesc01_01_0002.php (Dutch only).

[84] *The Diaries*, 29 October 1942.

[85] http://stadsarchief.amsterdam.nl/english/archives_database/overzicht/1213.en.html (Dutch only).

[86] http://www.jhm.nl/cultuur-en-geschiedenis/personen/h/hond,+meijer+de (Dutch only).

[87] Philo Bregstein, *Herinnering aan joods Amsterdam* (Amsterdam, 1999), p. 269.

[88] http://www.jhm.nl/culture-and-history/amsterdam/the-jewish-home,-joodse-invalide.

[89] http://www.jhm.nl/culture-and-history/amsterdam/the-jewish-home,-joodse-invalide.

[90] http://www.jhm.nl/culture-and-history/amsterdam/monument-to-/jewish-resistance.

[91] http://www.joodsmonument.nl/page/537470.

[92] *6ᵉ Montessorischool Anne Frank 1932-2007. 75 jaar en springlevend!* [6th Montessori School 'Anne Frank', 75 Years and Alive] (Amsterdam, 2008), p. 37 (Dutch only).

[93] Letter Edith, dated 5 December 1933 (Melissa Müller, *Anne Frank. De biografie* (Amsterdam 1998) p. 47).

[94] http://www.annefrank.org/en/Anne-Frank/Emigrating-to-the-Netherlands/At-Home-in-Amsterdam/.

[95] Willy Lindwer, *De laatste zeven maanden van Anne Frank. Het ongeschreven laatste hoofdstuk van het Dagboek* (Hilversum, 2008), p. 31.

[96] Carol Ann Lee, *Anne Frank. Het leven van een jong meisje* [The Life of a Young Girl. The Definitive Biography] (Amsterdam, 2009), p. 86.

[97] http://www.architectenweb.nl/aweb/archipedia/archipedia.asp?ID=4448

[98] 6th Montessori School. *Anne Frank. 75 Jaar en springlevend!* (Amsterdam, 2008), p. 55.

[99] http://www.gettyimages.nl/detail/news-photo/portrait-of-anne-franks-montessori-school-class-with-her-news-photo/3229496.

[100] Hannah Goslar does not recall this tree (telephone interview, 6 January 2011).

[101] 6th Montessori School. *Anne Frank. 75 Jaar en springlevend!* (Amsterdam, 2008), p. 27.
[102] *The Diaries*, 9 June 1944.
[103] 6th Montessori School. *Anne Frank. 75 Jaar en springlevend!* (Amsterdam, 2008), p. 54.
[104] http://nostalgisch.koudum.nl/SjoerdKuperus-01.html (Dutch only).
[105] 6th Montessori School. *Anne Frank. 75 Jaar en springlevend!* (Amsterdam, 2008), p. 48.
[106] http://www.joodsmonument.nl/person/533337/en.
[107] *The Diaries*, 7 January 1944.
[108] www.joodsmonument.nl lists the names of Montessori School pupils who died during the war but are not mentioned on the plate.
[109] http://rijksmonumenten.nl/monument/505901/velox++zuiderbad/amsterdam/ (Dutch only).
[110] http://www.iamsterdam.com/en-GB/Ndtrc/Zuiderbad.
[111] Gerrit Vermeer, Ben Rebel en Vladimir Stissi, *D'Ailly's Historische gids van Amsterdam. De stadsuitbreidingen 1860-1935* [D'Ailly's Historical Guide to Amsterdam: City Extensions 1860-1935] (Amsterdam, 2010), pp. 69-70.
[112] Walter Jacobsthal and his wife were gassed in Auschwitz on 21 October 1944. http://www.joodsmonument.nl/person/492308/en.
[113] Max C. van der Glas, email dated 23 December 2010.
[114] http://zoeken.nai.nl/CIS/project/7120 (Dutch only).
[115] Shabbat is a weekly Jewish festival day emphasizing the importance of the seventh day of Creation. It starts on Friday after sunset and lasts until Saturday after sunset. Many of the Jews who were merchants on the market or shopkeepers could not afford to close their businesses on Saturday.
[116] Carol Ann Lee. *Anne Frank. Het leven van een jong meisje* [The Life of a Young Girl. The Definitive Biography] (Amsterdam, 2009), p. 112.
[117] Willy Lindwer, *De laatste zeven maanden van Anne Frank. Het ongeschreven laatste hoofdstuk van het Dagboek* (Hilversum, 2008), p. 31.
[118] *The Diaries*, 30 June 1942.
[119] Zionists strived for an independent Jewish state.
[120] http://www.joodsmonument.nl/page/563859.
[121] Liberal Jewish Community, email dated 14 December 2011.
[122] Melissa Müller, *Anne Frank. De biografie* (Amsterdam 1998) p. 94.
[123] According to Hannah Goslar (telephone interview, 6 January 2011) Anne took Hebrew classes.
[124] Letter by L.H. Isselman dated 8 February 2011.
[125] http://stadsarchief.amsterdam.nl/onderwijs/buurt_en_stad/zuid/depijp/tolstraat/koninklijke_asscher/ (Dutch only).
[126] http://stadsarchief.amsterdam.nl/onderwijs/buurt_en_stad/zuid/depijp/tolstraat/koninklijke_asscher/ (Dutch only).

[127] Gerrit Vermeer, Ben Rebel and Vladimir Stissi, *D'Ailly's Historische gids van Amsterdam. De stadsuitbreidingen 1860-1935* (Amsterdam, 2010), p. 204; Bob Polak, *Naar buiten, lucht en lachen! Een literaire wandeling door het Amsterdam van Anne Frank* (Amsterdam, 2006), p. 77.

[128] Carol Ann Lee. *Anne Frank. Het leven van een jong meisje* [The Life of a Young Girl. The Definitive Biography] (Amsterdam, 2009), p. 91. Carol makes this claim based on Frank family documents; however, she does not publish these in her book. Buddy Elias, in an email dated 30 December 2010, states that he is not sure 'if ever she visited the liberal Synagogue'. According to Ruth Wiener (1927-2010) who knew Anne because they had both attended the Joods Lyceum grammar school, Anne visited both synagogues—the one on Tolstraat as well as the one on Lekstraat. (Dienke Hondius, *Absent. Herinneringen aan het Joods Lyceum Amsterdam 1941-1943* [Absent: Memories of the Jewish Lyceum in Amsterdam] (Amsterdam, 2001), p. 211 (Dutch only)).

[129] http://www.annefrank.org/en/Museum/Exhibitions/Margot-Frank-items/Margot-what-does-he-enjoy-doing/.

[130] http://en.nai.nl/collection/view_the_collection/item/_rp_kolom2-1_elementId/1_102927.

[131] Hannah Goslar (telephone interview, 6 January 2011).

[132] During WWII, Mirandalaan had not been constructed yet. (E. Lambrechtsen, Amsterdam City Archives, email dated 3 October 2008).

[133] http://o.elobot.eu/artikel/reumatische-koorts.

[134] Bob Polak, *Naar buiten, lucht en lachen! Een literaire wandeling door het Amsterdam van Anne Frank* (Amsterdam, 2006), p. 81.

[135] Gerrit Vermeer, Ben Rebel en Vladimir Stissi, *D'Ailly's Historische gids van Amsterdam. De stadsuitbreidingen 1860-1935* (Amsterdam, 2010), p. 184.

[136] Gerrit Vermeer, Ben Rebel en Vladimir Stissi, *D'Ailly's Historische gids van Amsterdam. De stadsuitbreidingen 1860-1935* (Amsterdam, 2010), p. 184.

[137] *The Diaries*, 20 June 1942.

[138] *The Diaries*, 20 June 1942.

[139] http://www.leestafel.info/cissy-van-marxveldt (Dutch only)

[140] http://www.annefrank.org/en/Subsites/Annes-Amsterdam/Timeline/Occupation/1942/1942/Anti-Semitic-complaints-about-an-ice-cream-parlour/#!/en/Subsites/Annes-Amsterdam/Timeline/Occupation/1942/1942/Anti-Semitic-complaints-about-an-ice-cream-parlour/.

[141] Hou Zee: 'Hooray' or 'Keep steering the right course', the Dutch National-Socialist greeting, equivalent to 'Heil Hitler'.

[142] Translated from: *De Misthoorn*, 6 June 1942.

[143] Anne Frank, *Verhaaltjes, en gebeurtenissen uit het Achterhuis* (Amsterdam, 2005), p. 117.

[144] According to Mrs F. Bachra (born in 1932) pupils from the Vondelschool on 84 Jekerstraat visited the Blommestein bakery (email dated 11 February 2011). This was one of 17 Jewish public schools that all 'public' Jewish children had to attend as of September 1941.

[145] Willie van Oijen owned the, P. de Munk bakery. Later on, her son Emiel took over the shop (email from Willie van Oijen dated 20 July 2011).
[146] Hannah Goslar (telephone interview, 6 January 2011). These shops are not listed on http://buurtwinkels.amsterdammuseum.nl/.
[147] *The Diaries*, 30 June 1942.
[148] Hannah Goslar (telephone interview, 6 January 2011).
[149] http://www.geheugenvanplanzuid.nl/tijdtijn/planzuidendejoden.htm (Dutch only).
[150] Email from Max van der Glas dated 22 December 2010.
[151] http://www.catharinaschool.nl/ (Dutch only).
[152] Anne Frank Stichting, *Anne Frank. Haar leven in brieven* [Her Life in Letters] (Amsterdam, 2006), p. 22.
[153] *Amstelodamum* (Amsterdam, 1941).
[154] http://www.zuidelijkewandelweg.nl/architectuur/architecten.htm (Dutch only).
[155] http://www.architectenweb.nl/aweb/archipedia/archipedia.asp?ID=4345 (Dutch only).
[156] Hannah Goslar (telephone interview, 6 January 2011).
[157] Max C. van der Glas, email dated 22 December 2010.
[158] Carol Ann Lee. *Anne Frank. Het leven van een jong meisje* [The Life of a Young Girl. The Definitive Biography] (Amsterdam, 2009), p. 98.
[159] Buddy Elias, email 30 December 2010.
[160] *The Diaries*, 8 March 1944.
[161] Hannah Goslar (telephone interview 6 January 2011); Jacqueline van Maarsen writes: 'I doubt whether Anne went the [the Cineac cinema], because she doesn't write about it in her diary.' (Jacqueline van Maarsen, email dated 9 March 2009).
[162] Hannah Goslar (telephone interview, 6 January 2011).
[163] *The Diaries*, 30 September 1942.
[164] Anne Frank, *Verhaaltjes, en gebeurtenissen uit het Achterhuis* (Amsterdam, 2005), p. 62.
[165] http://beeldbank.amsterdam.nl/beeldbank/weergave/record/?id=010107002067.
[166] . http://nl.wikipedia.org/wiki/Rialto_(filmtheater)
[167] http://www.annefrank.org/en/Subsites/Annes-Amsterdam/Timeline/Occupation/1943/1943/The-Rembrandt-Theatre-is-set-on-fire/#!/en/Subsites/Annes-Amsterdam/Timeline/Occupation/1943/1943/The-Rembrandt-Theatre-is-set-on-fire/.
[168] Email from 'Mapope' in response to my advertisement in the *Echo* local newspaper, *Zuid* edition, dated 7 February 2011.
[169] Carol Ann Lee. *Anne Frank. Het leven van een jong meisje* [The Life of a Young Girl. The Definitive Biography] (Amsterdam, 2009), p. 23.
[170] http://www.gettyimages.com/detail/3229076/Premium-Archive; http://www.gettyimages.com/detail/3229111/Premium-Archive.
[171] Bob Polak, *Naar buiten, lucht en lachen! Een literaire wandeling door het Amsterdam van Anne Frank* (Amsterdam, 2006), p. 59.
[172] Hannah Goslar (telephone interview, 6 January 2011).

[173] Carol Ann Lee, *Anne Frank. Het leven van een jong meisje* [The Life of a Young Girl. The Definitive Biography] (Amsterdam, 2009), p. 101.
[174] *The Diaries*, 15 October 1942.
[175] http://www.kampwesterbork.nl/geschiedenis/vluchtelingenkamp/bouw/ (Dutch only).
[176] Manfred Bierganz and Annelie Kreutz, *Juden in Aachen* [Jews in Aachen] (Aachen, 1988), p. 70 (German only).
[177] http://www.annefrankguide.net/en-us/bronnenbank.asp?aid=37867.
[178] Email from the Aachen Stadtarchiv dated 23 November 2010.
[179] Manfred Bierganz and Annelie Kreutz, *Juden in Aachen* (Aachen, 1988), p. 68 (German only).
[180] Bob Polak, *Naar buiten, lucht en lachen! Een literaire wandeling door het Amsterdam van Anne Frank* (Amsterdam, 2006), p. 33.
[181] *The Diaries*, 11 November 1943.
[182] http://www.zuidelijkewandelweg.nl/ingezonden/eppooomkens.htm (Dutch only).
[183] http://www.zuidelijkewandelweg.nl/ingezonden/eppooomkens.htm (Dutch only).
[184] http://www.traces.org/anne.html.
[185] Anne never went to England or America (Buddy Elias, email dated 30 December 2010).
[186] 'Our family was also moving to New York. My father had already arranged all the documents. But my mother backed out at the last moment.' (translation of a Dutch email from Francien Bachra, 8 January 2010).
[187] Melissa Müller, *Anne Frank. De biografie* (Amsterdam, 1998), pp. 100-101.
[188] Philo Bregstein, *Herinnering aan joods Amsterdam* (Amsterdam, 1999), p. 11. English edition: *Remembering Jewish Amsterdam* (Holmes & Meier Pub, 2004).
[189] *The Diaries*, 16 July 1942. Anne speaks about 'Germans', not about occupiers or Nazis.
[190] Willy Lindwer, *De laatste zeven maanden van Anne Frank. Het ongeschreven laatste hoofdstuk van het Dagboek* (Hilversum, 2008), p. 34.
[191] Carol Ann Lee mentions the curfew started at midnight. Carol Ann Lee, *Anne Frank. Het leven van een jong meisje* [The Life of a Young Girl. The Definitive Biography] (Amsterdam, 2009), p. 134.
[192] http://beeldbank.amsterdam.nl/beeldbank/weergave/search/layout/result/indeling/detail?q_searchfield=010003042760.
[193] http://www.geheugenvanplanzuid.nl/tijdtijn/bommen.htm (Dutch only).
[194] According to Hannah Goslar (telephone interview dated 6 January 2011), Otto's company was already located at 263 Prinsengracht in 1933; Otto may have obtained extra storage space when the piano roll manufacturer left the premises in 1939 or 1940.
[195] *The Diaries*, 5 July 1942.
[196] Hanneli and Anne would also spill water from the window of the Franks' apartment on Merwedeplein (Hannah Goslar, telephone interview dated 6 January 2011).

[197] Buddy Elias: 'No, Anne did not know the hiding place before the family moved in.' (email dated 30 December 2010).
[198] Carol Ann Lee, Anne Frank 1929-1945. Het leven van een jong meisje [The Life of a Young Girl. The Definitive Biography] (Amsterdam, 2009), p. 304.
[199] Anne Frank, *Verhaaltjes, en gebeurtenissen uit het Achterhuis* (Amsterdam, 2005), p. 46.
[200] In 1972, its commercial branch ARCADIS became a separate organisation from the idealistic KNHM association. 'KNMH currently functions as an independent association with an idealistic objective, i.e. contributing to an enhanced living environment.' Their website does not mention this black page in their history during WWII (http://www.knhm.nl/hoofdmenu/over-knhm/historie-knhm, Dutch only).
[201] http://www.geheugenvanplanzuid.nl/tijdtijn/razzia's.htm#10 January 1942 (Dutch only).
[202] *Het Joodsche Weekblad* (23 July 1943), National Library of the Netherlands, inventory number 9158 A7.
[203] http://www.joodsmonument.nl/person/546360/en.
[204] http://www.joodsmonument.nl/person/546359/en.
[205] http://kranten.kb.nl/view/paper/id/ddd%3A010018451%3Ampeg21%3Ap001%3Aa0021/layout/fullscreen (Dutch only).
[206] There are differing accounts of what happened at the Koco parlour. Please refer to http://www.zuidelijkewandelweg.nl/tijdtijn/koco.htm and http://www.zuidelijkewandelweg.nl/ingezonden/rdscohen.htm (Dutch only).
[207] http://www.zuidelijkewandelweg.nl/ingezonden/rdscohen.htm. According to Carol Ann Lee (*Anne Frank. Het leven van een jong meisje* [The Life of a Young Girl. The Definitive Biography] (Amsterdam, 2009), p. 134) customers sprayed the attackers with ammonia.
[208] Philo Bregstein, *Herinnering aan joods Amsterdam* (Amsterdam, 1999), p. 312.
[209] http://buurtwinkels.amsterdammuseum.nl/page/3434/nl (Dutch only).
[210] http://www.joodsmonument.nl/page/274192/nl?lang=en.
[211] http://www.oranjehotel.org/ (Dutch only).
[212] http://www.dodenakkers.nl/oorlog/algemeen/23-waalsdorpervlakte.html (Dutch only).
[213] Bob Polak, *Naar buiten, lucht en lachen! Een literaire wandeling door het Amsterdam van Anne Frank* (Amsterdam, 2006), p. 81.
[214] http://beeldbank.amsterdam.nl/beeldbank/weergave/search/layout/result/indeling/detail?q_searchfield=Nieuwe%20Uilenburgerstraat%202&q_search_straat=Nieuwe%20Uilenburgerstraat%20&q_search_huisnummer=2.
[215] J. Presser, *Ondergang. De vervolging en verdelging van het Nederlandse Jodendom 1940-1945* I [Desctruction. The persecution and extermination of Dutch Judaism 1940-1945] (The Hague, 1965), p. 121; http://m.iamsterdam.com/explore_locations/view/213.

[216] Paul Arnoldussen en Alice van Diepen, *Bibliotheek van Amsterdamse herinneringen 02: Nieuw-Zuid* [Library of Amsterdam Memories 02: The New 'Zuid' District] (Amsterdam 2003), p. 25.
[217] http://www.architectuurgids.nl/project/list_projects_of_typeofbuilding/typ_id/19/prj_id/2657
[218] http://www.nieuwsbank.nl/inp/2005/02/09/R200.htm (Dutch only).
[219] http://www.iisg.nl/bwsa/bios/lebeau.html (Dutch only).
[220] http://www.gettyimages.nl/detail/3229102/Premium-Archive.
[221] Melissa Müller, *Anne Frank. De biografie* (Amsterdam 1998) p. 119.
[222] http://www.annefrank.org/en/subsites/annes-amsterdam/timeline/occupation/1941/1941/repudo---14-anne-filmed/#!/en/subsites/annes-amsterdam/timeline/occupation/1941/1941/repudo---14-anne-filmed/.
[223] http://kranten.kb.nl/view/article/id/ddd%3A010664973%3Ampeg21%3Ap008%3Aa0087 (Dutch only).
[224] Bob Polak, *Naar buiten, lucht en lachen! Een literaire wandeling door het Amsterdam van Anne Frank* (Amsterdam, 2006), p. 35. In Anne's days, addresses would be stated without indicating the relevant floor.
[225] *The Diaries*, 19 March 1943.
[226] http://www.4en5mei.nl/oorlogsmonumenten/zoeken/monument-detail/_rp_main_elementId/1_11442 (Dutch only).
[227] http://deoorlog.nps.nl/page/mappen/784083/Bevrijding+Amsterdam?afl=6&d=784082 (Dutch only).
[228] http://www.eenlevenlangtheater.nl/mary%20dresselhuys/biografie/137.html (Dutch only).
[229] http://www.carre.nl/nl/over-carre/carr-istorie (Dutch only).
[230] *The Diaries*, 12 July 1942.
[231] http://kranten.kb.nl/view/article/id/ddd%3A010318315%3Ampeg21%3Ap011%3Aa0042 (Dutch only).
[232] http://kranten.kb.nl/view/article/id/ddd%3A010318166%3Ampeg21%3Ap012%3Aa0036/layout/fullscreen (Dutch only).
[233] *De Amsterdamse Gids* [The Amsterdam Guide] (Amsterdam, 1930).
[234] *The Diaries*, 15 March 1944.
[235] *The Diaries*, 24 June 1942.
[236] http://www.geheugenvanplanzuid.nl/tijdtijn/kaartAnneFrank.htm (Dutch only).
[237] http://www.zuidelijkewandelweg.nl/tijdtijn/pontje.htm (Dutch only).
[238] http://www.zuidelijkewandelweg.nl/archief/architectuur/beeldentuinalmstraat.htm (Dutch only).
[239] His exact address is unknown. Hannah Goslar (telephone interview, 6 January 2011).

[240] Hannah Goslar (telephone interview, 6 January 2011).
[241] *The Diaries*, 24 June 1942.
[242] *The Diaries*, 6 January 1944.
[243] http://www.grootwarnsborn.nl/show/en/pagina/,.php
[244] http://home.kpn.nl/witie/Willem%20van%20Buuren.htm (Dutch only).
[245] Lammert de Vries, managing director Hotel & Restaurant Groot Warnsborn, email dated 5 August 2011.
[246] Mellisa Müller's note that it was 5 Koninginneweg is a mistake (*Anne Frank. De biografie* (Amsterdam 1998) p. 120).
[247] http://www.dodenakkers.nl/beroemd/algemeen/28-hollander.html.
[248] *Het Joodsche Weekblad*, 23 July 1943, National Library of the Netherlands, inventory number 9158 A7.
[249] Dienke Hondius, *Absent. Herinneringen aan het Joods Lyceum Amsterdam 1941-1943* [Absent: Memories of the Jewish Lyceum in Amsterdam] (Amsterdam, 2001), p. 40 (Dutch only).
[250] *The Diaries*, 20 June 1942.
[251] Dienke Hondius, *Absent. Herinneringen aan het Joods Lyceum Amsterdam 1941-1943* (Amsterdam, 2001), p. 37 (Dutch only).
[252] *Het Joodsche Weekblad*, 23 July 1943, National Library of the Netherlands, inventory number 9158 A7.
[253] http://www.geheugenvanplanzuid.nl/tijdtijn/bommen.htm (Dutch only).
[254] Rachel Heuberger and Helgo Krohn, *Hinaus aus dem ghetto…Juden in Frankfurt am Main 1800-1950* [Out of the Ghetto: Jews in Frankfurt am Main 1800-1950] (Frankfurt am Main, 1988), p. 189-190, http://www.frankfurt.de/sixcms/detail.php?id=3793411&_ffmpar%5B_id_inhalt%5D=32561 (German only).
[255] Anne Frank, *Verhaaltjes, en gebeurtenissen uit het Achterhuis* (Amsterdam, 2005), pp. 49-50.
[256] Anne Frank, *Verhaaltjes, en gebeurtenissen uit het Achterhuis* (Amsterdam, 2005), pp. 49-50.
[257] http://www.joodsmonumentzaanstreek.nl/pagina-1092-Elte-Willem.htm, http://www.joodsbw.nl/cgi/b/bib/bib-idx?type=boolean;lang=nl;c=jbw;rgn1=entirerecordexcl;q1=Willem;op1=And;q2=Salomon;op2=And;rgn2=entirerecordexcl;q3=Hijman;op3=And;rgn3=entirerecordexcl;cc=jbw;view=reslist;sort=naam;fmt=long;page=reslist;start=1;size=1 (Dutch only).
[258] Dienke Hondius, *Absent. Herinneringen aan het Joods Lyceum Amsterdam 1941-1943* (Amsterdam, 2001), p. 109 (Dutch only).
[259] Anne Frank, *Verhaaltjes, en gebeurtenissen uit het Achterhuis* (Amsterdam, 2005), p. 50.
[260] Jacqueline 'Jopie' van Maarsen, *Anne en Jopie. Leven met Anne Frank* [Anne and Jopie. Living with Anne Frank] (Amsterdam, 1990), p. 15.
[261] http://m.iamsterdam.com/explore_locations/view/195.
[262] Anne Frank, *Verhaaltjes, en gebeurtenissen uit het Achterhuis* (Amsterdam, 2005), p. 22.

[263] Dienke Hondius, *Absent. Herinneringen aan het Joods Lyceum Amsterdam 1941-1943* [Absent: Memories of the Jewish Lyceum in Amsterdam] (Amsterdam, 2001), p. 120 (Dutch only).
[264] The *NRC* national newspaper, 10 November 2008.
[265] http://www.communityjoodsmonument.nl/person/197932/nl?lang=en.
[266] http://openlibrary.org/authors/OL1054939A/Jakob_Meijer (Dtuch only).
[267] Dienke Hondius, *Absent. Herinneringen aan het Joods Lyceum Amsterdam 1941-1943* (Amsterdam, 2001), pp. 170-171 (Dutch only).
[268] Theo Coster, *Klasgenoten van Anne Frank* (Amsterdam, 2009), p. 84 24. English editon: *We All Wore Stars: Memories of Anne Frank from Her Classmates* (Macmillan, 2011).
[269] http://www.jbo.nl/index.php?id=197 (Dutch only).
[270] Melissa Müller, *Anne Frank. De biografie* (Amsterdam, 1998), p. 129. Original German title: *Das Mädchen Anne Frank. Die Biographie*. English edition: *Anne Frank. The Biography* (Macmillan, 2013).
[271] *The Diaries*, 14 June 1942.
[272] *The Diaries*, 12 June 1942.
[273] 'German parents raised their children more strictly than Dutch ones. The Dutch did not involve their children in their worries. If there was a serious or disturbing conversation going on, children were often sent to the other room. You would mostly get your information from friends who were a little older. (Francien Bachra, email dated 8 January 2010).
[274] *The Diaries*, 20 June 1942.
[275] Bob Polak, *Naar buiten, lucht en lachen! Een literaire wandeling door het Amsterdam van Anne Frank* (Amsterdam, 2006), p. 29.
[276] *The Diaries*, 15 June 1942.
[277] According to Mary Bos (born in 1928) Käthe 'Kitty' Egyedie was Anne's best friend (Carol Ann Lee, *Anne Frank. Het leven van een jong meisje* [The Life of a Young Girl. The Definitive Biography] (Amsterdam, 2009), p. 224. Kitty, who was not a Jew, was present when Anne celebrated her tenth birthday.
[278] *The Diaries*, 15 June 1942.
[279] http://www.joodsmonument.nl/person/522479?lang=en
[280] http://www.joodsmonument.nl/person/522477?lang=en
[281] Hannah Goslar (telephone interview, 6 January 2011).
[282] Anne Frank, *Verhaaltjes, en gebeurtenissen uit het Achterhuis* (Amsterdam, 2005), p. 62.
[283] Anne Frank, *Verhaaltjes, en gebeurtenissen uit het Achterhuis* (Amsterdam, 2005), p. 61.
[284] *The Diaries*, 5 July 1942.
[285] Dienke Hondius, *Absent. Herinneringen aan het Joods Lyceum Amsterdam 1941-1943* (Amsterdam, 2001), p. 129 (Dutch only).
[286] http://www.joodsamsterdam.nl/perssuskind.htm (Dutch only).
[287] *Vervolging en verzet in Amsterdam. Herinneringen aan de Tweede Wereldoorlog. Een wandeling van het Anne Frank Huis naar het Verzetsmuseum*

[Persecution and resistance in Amsterdam. Reminders of the Second World War. A walk from the Anne Frank House to the Resistance Museum] (Amsterdam, 2006).
[288] http://www.auschwitz.nl/en-nac/memorial/history.

THE SECRET ANNEX

I stayed overnight in Bennekom and took the 6:11 a.m. train from Ede-Wageningen to Amsterdam Central Station on 8 May 2008. It was still quiet in Amsterdam, and I was welcomed by a yawning construction worker. I walked through the Raadhuisstraat, past the Westerkerk with its remarkable crowned peak. I received a warm welcome at the Anne Frank Stichting office at 10 Westermarkt and took photographs of the Secret Annex from 8:00-9:00 a.m. I was not allowed to photograph the open (allegedly) original diary with its chequered cover, even though I was not using a flash.

However, I was allowed to photograph the (now late) chestnut tree from the roof of the Anne Frank Stichting office. On 18 December 2009, I explored the Secret Annex without a camera. Since there were no visitors yet, there was no distracting noise. The people in hiding had to be as quiet as a mouse when the stockroom assistants were at work. The annex was deserted, but I did not see Anne.

After an hour, I simply left the annex. Anne could not leave: she was trapped there for two years without much privacy or elbow room. It was still relatively chilly inside. It must have warmed up when the visitors started radiating their bodily warmth in the course of the morning. I had gone by the time they entered. The steps on the stairs were rather worn out. I felt excited knowing that Anne had walked here, too. The edge of the carpet was wearing thin because of the many footsteps of the visitors. Fingerprints were visible on the bookshelves. Had any traces of Anne's DNA been found here, perhaps on the bookshelves?

Whilst Anne was at home on Sunday afternoon, 5 July 1942, her sixteen-year-old sister Margot received a summons: she was to report to the Germans for work.

'On Sunday morning Hello and I lay on our balcony [rear side of the roof terrace] in the sun, on Sunday afternoon he was going to come back but at about three o'clock a policeman arrived and called from the door downstairs Miss Margot Frank, Mummy went down and the policeman gave her a card which said that Margot Frank has to report to the S.S.'[1]

All summons for boys and girls aged fifteen to eighteen drawn up by the *Zentralstelle für jüdische Auswanderung*, the Central Office for Jewish Emigration at 1 Adama van Scheltemaplein (currently a supermarket), were delivered by the Dutch national mail provider PTT.

Anne wanted to lead a carefree life and not concern herself with the war. The summons, striking like a bolt from the blue, made Anne panic and cry: all of a sudden, the war seemed very close. Looking back on this moment from the Secret Annex, she wrote: 'It was a great shock to me, a summons; everyone knows what that means, I picture concentration camps and lonely cells.'[2] Anne knew about Camp Westerbork when she was living on Merwedeplein; however, as of 5 July 1942, I do not think she yet knew of the extermination camps in Eastern Europe.

Otto had started making preparations for going into hiding—even before Margot received her summons; he wanted to protect his family from the terrors of Nazism. In spite of the fact that Jews were forced to hand in their radios on 15 March 1941, Otto had heard BBC broadcasts about Jews being gassed. News that arrived from his home country was also very disconcerting: on 22 March 1942, Jews from Aachen were deported to Theresienstadt.[3]

A truck owned by Hermann van Pels' brother moved the Franks' furniture to their future hiding place at 263 Prinsengracht. This was an extremely risky undertaking since Jews were not allowed to move their furniture. Smaller items, such as linen, canned food and clothing, were easier to move without attracting any unwanted attention. Anne's friends apparently did not notice any furniture missing from the Franks' apartment. Even before their period in hiding, all windows facing the annex were painted blue, and those on the landing where the bookcase would later be placed were covered with cellophane.

Otto and Edith could no longer hide the war from their children: Anne learned that they were going into hiding before, not on, 5 July 1942,[4] and on 8 July 1942, Otto told Anne the exact address. 'When we walked across our little square together a few days ago, Daddy began to talk of us going into hiding, he is very worried that it will be very difficult for us to live completely cut off from the world. I asked why on earth he was beginning to talk of that already. "Yes Anne," he said "you know we have been taking food, clothes, furniture to other people for more than a year now, we don't want our belongings to be seized by the Germans,[5] but we most certainly don't want to fall into their clutches ourselves. So we shall disappear of our own accord and not wait until they come and fetch us." "But Daddy, when would it be?" He spoke so seriously that I grew very anxious.'[6] Anne has a keen memory, and meticulously describes events in her works.

Why 263 Prinsengracht? Probably because Otto knew helpers there that he could trust. Moreover, the building had enough space for his own family, as well as for the Van Pels family. In this stage of the war, it had become very difficult to find a place to hide an entire family anywhere.[7] Otto and Edith wanted to stay with their children.

Because Margot had received her summons,[8] Otto wanted to take his family into hiding earlier than planned. Hello rang Anne's doorbell on the afternoon of 5 July 1942, but nobody was there. Margot and Anne were already packing their personal belongings. 'Margot and I began to pack some of our most vital belongings into a school satchel, the first thing I put in was this diary, then hair curlers, handkerchiefs, schoolbooks, a comb, old letters; I put in the craziest things with the idea we were going into hiding. But I am not sorry, memories mean more to me than dresses.'[9] Otto had already taken some of Anne's other belongings, such as her diary and her collection of film star pictures and postcards, to Prinsengracht.

Otto left a note behind, giving the impression that the Frank family had fled to Switzerland. Apparently, Otto also believed the German police would believe this and therefore would not immediately raid Otto's work address.

Anne loved her cat Moortje very much and left their tenant written instructions on how to take care of it.

On 6 July 1942, Anne's parents woke her up at 4:30 am. It was raining. 'All four of us put on heaps of clothes as if we were going to the North Pole ....[10] No Jew in our situation would have dared to go out with a suitcase full of clothing. I had on two vests, three pairs of pants, a dress, on top of that a skirt, jacket, summer coat, two pairs of stockings, lace-up shoes, woolly cap, scarf, and still much more; I was nearly stifled before we started but no one inquired about that.'[11] Margot biked to their hiding place at 6:00 a.m. with Miep. She had removed the Star of David from her coat because Jews were not allowed to ride bikes. Moreover, Jews were not permitted to travel on a tram or by car either.[12] Margot probably rode her mother's bike. They had not turned this in, in spite of the decree issued on 22 June 1942 to that effect.

According to Miep, they took 'The busy streets: from Merwedeplein to Waalstraat, then left onto Noorder Amstellaan [renamed Churchilllaan in 1946], [right onto Scheldestraat] and on to the Ferdinand Bolstraat [the Pijp area], on the Vijzelstraat to Rokin, Dam Square and Raadhuisstraat and finally onto Prinsengracht.' The shorter route would have taken them straight into Prinsengracht from Vijzelstraat.

Otto, Edith and Anne left at 7:30 a.m. Whilst walking there, Otto told Anne where they were going to hide, and advised that the Van Pels family would also come into hiding with them, including Peter's cat.[13] Despite the fact that she had had to leave her own cat behind, Anne apparently did not get angry.

Walking to their hiding place, they probably crossed the 19th-century working-class Pijp district. Anne notes: 'So we walked through the pouring rain, Daddy, Mummy and I, each with a school satchel and shopping bag filled to the brim with all kinds of things thrown together anyhow. We got sympathetic looks from people on their way to work. you could see by their faces how sorry they were they couldn't offer us a lift, the gaudy yellow star spoke for itself.'[14]

The national newspaper *Het Parool* published an interview with Jet Schepp, an artist born in 1940,[15] about her plan to place a sculpture of Anne on Merwedeplein. Through a petition, she succeeded at realising her ambition. A design by Jeroen Krabbé (born 1944), who in 1985 played Otto in a play inspired by *The Diaries*, did not pass the selection.

Former Mayor of Amsterdam Job Cohen (born in 1947) unveiled the bronze statue on 9 July 2005.[16] Pupils of the Anne Frank School (then the 6th Montessori School at 41 Niersstraat) recited poems, and a Jewish and a Muslim pupil both gave a lecture related to their 'Second World War in Perspective' project.[17]

The sculpture shows a proud Anne looking back at her home before leaving for the Secret Annex. Many consider this an image of hope. In *The Diaries*, Anne condemns violence in general and hostility against Jews in particular. In November 2005, the sculpture and the entrance to Anne's apartment on Merwedeplein were smeared with paint.[18]

On 5 May, the Dutch Liberation Day is not only celebrated at Dam Square but also on Merwedeplein, where residents put out the Dutch flag. There are flowers on and around the statue of Anne and little flags fly in the wind.

On Monday, 6 July 1942 at 8:30 am, Anne and her parents arrived at 263 Prinsengracht after over an hour's walk. Miep and Margot had already arrived earlier. They entered the main building through a door on the left. According to Anne, she and her father immediately started tidying.

'When we arrived at 263 Prinsengracht, Miep led us quickly through the long passage, up the wooden stairs, straight to the "Secret Annex". She closed the door behind us and we were alone. Margot was already waiting for us, having arrived much more quickly on her bicycle. Our living room and all the other rooms were chock-full of rubbish, indescribably so. All the cardboard boxes which had been sent to the office in the previous months lay piled on the floor and the beds; the little room [probably Peter's] was filled to the ceiling with bed clothes. We had to start clearing up immediately, if we wished to sleep in decent beds that night. Mummy and Margot were not in a fit state to take part; they were tired and lay down on their unmade beds, they were wretched, and lots more besides, but the two "clearers-up" of the family, Daddy and myself, wanted to start at once. The whole day long we unpacked boxes, filled cupboards, hammered and tidied, until we were dead beat. We sank into clean beds that night. We hadn't had a bit of anything warm all day, but we didn't care; Mummy and Margot were too tired and keyed up to eat, and Daddy and I were too busy.'[19]

Anne wrote that they arrived at 8:30 a.m., which would be the time that the stockroom assistants also started work. This is why Miep quickly took them upstairs: they probably arrived just before the stock assistants. Therefore, I presume Anne and Otto only started tidying in the evening.

Some safety precautions were taken: the windows on the first floor were blacked out with pieces of cloth that were sewn together.[20] Since they went into hiding earlier than planned, they apparently had not had time to hang curtains beforehand. The linoleum floor in Edith and Otto's room muffled the sound.

The Secret Annex was one of a long row of annexes. The main building at 263 Prinsengracht was one of many houses and, architecturally speaking, it was not a very conspicuous one.

There were many more artisans and small family enterprises on Prinsengracht. It was an industrious area.

Neighbouring 263 Prinsengracht on the right was the C. (Cornelis) Keg Firm from Zaandam, a tea wholesaler that also roasted coffee,[21] and on the left at 265 Prinsengracht was a furniture workshop. The canal houses at 267-275 were still standing proud. Diagonally across from 263 Prinsengracht, at 180 Prinsengracht, was the coffee- and tea-trading company Keijzer. A herring trader called A. Koot had his business on the corner of Prinsengracht and Laurierstraat in the Jordaan area between 1916 and 1961.[22] A dairy shop, 'Nieuw Leven' (New Life), had been founded in 1930 and was located at 392 Prinsengracht. These were nothing like modern-day supermarkets; they were family businesses that valued the social and business contact with their customers.

Many of the canal buildings dated from the 17th century and their past was still reflected clearly in their gable stones depicting ancient crafts.

Importantly, 263 Prinsengracht is now famous as Anne's hiding place; however, the building has a long history preceding the Second World War. Both 263 and 265 Prinsengracht were constructed in 1635. René Descartes (1596-1650), the exiled French philosopher, lived at 6 Westermarkt in 1634 and witnessed the construction of the premises at 263 Prinsengracht. The Secret Annex was built in 1740, and in 1840 the pointed gable was replaced by a straight cornice. During the 19th century, the chemical firm A. d'Ailly was based here, and from 1928 until late-1939, Euterpe produced its piano rolls here.

The building has a very complicated layout. Anne elaborately described the main building and the annex at 263 Prinsengracht in the B version of her diary, intended for publication following the war. Apparently, Anne thought it important that posterity would explicitly note all the details of her hiding place. The premises were not very conspicuous, yet were visible from all sides, including the houses that looked onto the back of the annex. The stockroom on the ground floor could be accessed through the two doors in the centre of the façade that were often open if the weather was nice or if there were activities going on inside. The stockroom ran under the annex all the way through to the back garden. The glass sun room could be accessed from the stockroom, and through a door in the sun room, one could access the back garden. 'I will describe the building, there is a large warehouse on the ground floor which is used as a store and that is subdivided into various little compartments, such as the milling room, where cinnamon, clove and substitute pepper were ground up, the stockroom and the veranda.'[23] The second door on the left of the façade was the official entrance to 263 Prinsengracht with two name plates of Otto's companies. After passing through this door, there was a landing. The door on the right led to the stockroom. The door on the left side of the ground floor landing opened onto a stairway that led to a landing on the first floor and the door that gave entry to the hallway, which led to the front office of the first floor of the main building: the office of Miep Gies, Jo Kleiman and Bep Voskuijl. 'The front door to the house is next to the warehouse door, and inside the front door is a second doorway which leads to a staircase. There is another door at the top of the stairs with a frosted glass window in it, which has "Office" written in black letters across it. This is the large main office, very big, very light, and very full.'[24] A door at the back of the front office opened onto the landing (which Anne referred to as the 'cabinet') where a door on the opposite side gave access to Otto's office. 'Bep, Miep and Mr. Kleiman work there in the daytime, a small dark room containing the safe, a wardrobe and a large cupboard, leads to a small, stuffy, dark director's office.'[25] At the end of the first-floor corridor in the main building, a door on the right also gave access to Otto's office. 'One can reach Kugler's office from the passage, but only via a glass door which can be opened from the inside but not easily from the outside.'[26] The corridor on the first floor of the main building that could be reached through 'the regular front door' then led to the area between the main building and the annex and, through a door and a small stairway of four steps, to Otto's private office and the Secret Annex's kitchen.

'... a long passage goes past the coal store, up four steps and leads to the showroom of the whole building, the private office. Dark, dignified furniture, linoleum and carpets on the floor, radio, smart lamp, everything first class, next door there is a roomy kitchen with a hot-water faucet and a gas stove and next door the WC. That is the first floor.'[27] The canal house had no central heating; hardly anyone had central heating at home or at work in those days. Anne also described the landing on the second floor that connected the main building and the Secret Annex. 'A wooden staircase leads from the downstairs passage to the next floor. There is a small landing at the top. There is a door to the right and left of the landing, the left one leading to the front of the house, with spice room, corridor room, a front room, and to the attics. One of those really steep Dutch staircases runs from the side to the other door opening on to the street.'[28] These were the stairs that the people in hiding would use to leave the annex and access the office spaces on the first floor of the main building in the evenings and during the weekends. Anne and Margot sometimes went to the front attic, which contained many chests.

'To the right of the landing lies our "Secret Annexe". No one would ever guess that there would be so many rooms hidden behind that plain door painted gray. There's a little step in front of the door and then you are inside.'[29] After their first month in hiding, the people in the annex decided that the door to their hiding place should be camouflaged. The step was removed and the access door to the annex was lowered. Stockroom supervisor Voskuijl built a bookcase. 'The entrance to our hiding place has now been properly concealed. Mr Kugler thought it would be better to put a cupboard in front of our door.'[30] A further paragraph details, 'There is a steep staircase immediately opposite the entrance. ON the left a tiny passage brings you into a room, this room was to become the Frank family's bed-sitting-room, next door an even smaller room, study and bedroom for the two young ladies of the family.'[31]

Anne and Margot's room contained two divan beds and three wall cabinets, whilst their parents' room held two divan beds and a storage cupboard with canned food. Following the arrival of dentist Fritz Pfeffer in November 1942, Margot moved into her parents' room, and Anne had to share hers with the dentist. Otto kept track of the girls' height by marking the wallpaper in their room. Miep Gies and her husband once stayed at the Secret Annex, and Anne and Margot spent the night in their parents' room. 'Margot and I went in Mummy and Daddy's room for the night so that the Gieses could have our room.'[32]

To the right of the little hallway was a door to the washroom. 'On the right a little room without windows, containing the washbasin and small WC compartment, with another door leading to Margot's and my room.'[33]

The stairs led up from the hallway to Peter and his parents' room on the third floor of the Secret Annex. 'If you go up the next flight of stairs and open the door, you are simply amazed that there could be such a big light room in such an old house by the canal. There is a stove in this room (thanks to the fact that it was used before as Kugler's laboratory) and a sink. This is now the kitchen as well as bedroom for the v.P. couple, besides being general living room, dining room and scullery. A tiny little corridor room will become Peter v.P.'s apartment. Then just as on the lower landing there is a large attic. So there you are I have introduced you to the whole of our beautiful "Secret Annexe!"[34]

In her *Tales*, Anne gives an elaborate description[35] of Peter's room. To practice writing, Anne had a fictional interview with Peter. 'Early in the evening when you knock on his door and hear his soft-spoken "come in", you can be sure that when you open the door, he'll be looking at you through the steps of the ladder to the attic, and that most of the time he'll utter an inviting, "So there you are!"

'His room is actually a... hmm, I'm not sure what it is. I think it's a kind of landing going up to the attic. It's very small, very dark and very damp, but... he's managed to turn it into a real room.

'When he's sitting to the left of the ladder, there's only about three feet between it and the wall. This is where he has his table, which is usually strewn with books like ours is (the steps also get the overflow), and a chair. On the other side of the ladder is his bicycle, suspended from the ceiling. This now useless form of transportation has been wrapped in brown paper, and a long extension cord dangles merrily from one of the pedals. To add the finishing touch to the interviewee's work space, the light bulb above his head has been covered with the latest trend in lamp shades: cardboard decorated with strips of paper.

'From where I'm standing in the doorway, I look to the opposite side of the room. Against the wall, i.e. across from Peter, behind the table, there's a divan with a flowery blue counterpane; the bedding has been tucked behind the backrest. There's a lamp hanging above it, much like the one two feet away, as well as a hand mirror, and a bit further away, a bookcase filled from top to bottom with books that have been covered – with a boy's typical disregard of elegance – with brown paper. To spruce things up even more (or because the owner has no other place to put it), there's also a tool-box, where you're sure to find whatever you're looking for. Though it admittedly happened quite a while ago, I once found my favourite knife, which had long been missing, in the bottom of this very tool-box, and it wasn't the first thing to find its way there.

'Next to the bookcase is a wooden shelf, covered with paper that used to be white. Actually, this shelf was supposed to be for milk bottles and other kitchen items. But the youthful occupant's treasury of books has expanded so rapidly that the shelf has been taken over by these learned tomes, and the various milk bottles have been relegated on the floor.

'The third wall also has a small cabinet (a former cherry crate), where you can find a delightful collection of such things as a shaving brush, a razor, tape, laxatives, etc., etc. Beside it is the crowning glory of the Van Daan family's ingenuity: a cupboard made almost entirely out of cardboard, held together by only two or three support posts made of stronger material. This cupboard, which is filled with suits, coats, shoes, socks and so forth, has a really lovely curtain hanging in front of it, which peter finally managed to get hold of after weeks of begging his mother. So much stuff is piled on top of the cupboard that I've never worked out exactly what's there.

'The rugs of Mr Van Daan Junior are also worthy of note. Not only because his room has two large genuine Persian carpets and one small one, but because the colours are so striking that everyone who enters the room notices them right away. So the floorboards, which have to be negotiated with care since they're rather loose and uneven, are adorned with these precious rugs.

Two of the walls above have been covered in green burlap, while the other two have been lavishly plastered with film stars – some beautiful, others less so – and advertisements. You need to overlook the grease and burn marks, since, after one and a half years of living with so much junk, things are bound to get dirty.

'The attic, hardly the height of comfort either, is like all the others round here, with old-fashioned beams, and since the roof leaks down via the attic into Peter's room, several sheets of cardboard have been put up to keep out the rain. The many water stains show that it's not the least bit effective.

'I think I've been round the entire room now and have only forgotten the two chairs: number one is a brown chair with a perforated seat and number two is an old white kitchen chair. Peter wanted to repaint it last year, but noticed when he was scraping off the old layer that it wasn't such a good idea. So now the chair, with its partially stripped paint, its one and only rung (the other was used as a poker) and its more-black-than-white colour scheme, is not exactly presentable. But as I've already said, the room is dark, so the chair hardly sticks out. The door to the kitchen is festooned with aprons, and there are also a few hooks for the dusters and cleaning brush.'

The second and third floors of the main building contained extra storage space. On the fourth floor of the main building, at the same height as the common room of the Secret Annex, there was a pulley.

Only while she was in hiding did Anne realise that she had also become a victim of war, and that her carefree life (at Merwedeplein) had come to an end. Later, Anne would look back in her diary: 'My happy-go-lucky, carefree school days are gone forever.'[36] As always, Otto and Edith did their very best to help their children through this difficult period.

Before she went into hiding, Anne enjoyed her freedom just like any other child in the Netherlands. Edith van Hessen (born in 1925, hereafter referred to as Edith van H.)[37] started keeping a diary in 1938. She was thirteen at the time. She described her life in The Hague—school, parties, boys—without a trace of worry. Just like Anne, she kept the war at a distance. Unlike Anne, however, Edith van H. was from an intellectual family and was an excellent student. She was cheerful and optimistic, and did not give up easily—characteristics she shared with Anne. In 1941, Edith van H. was also confronted with signs reading 'Prohibited to Jews' on the beach, and was forced to attend a Jewish secondary school (at 135 Fisherstraat in The Hague). When deportations started in July 1941, Edith van H. and her family went into hiding. Edith van H. found a place in Breda and survived the war, but many of her family members did not. Anne did not survive the war either: of all the people hiding in the annex, only her father lived to see the end of the war. Edith has been living in the United States for several decades now, where she published her wartime diary in 1997. The Jewish grammar school in The Hague was open from 15 October 1941-15 April 1943. Notably, 267 students attended this school; at least 161 were killed. Of the 43 teachers, 15 would not survive the war. Five out of eight members of the auxiliary staff perished. Clearly, Anne's life had much in common with the lives of other young Holocaust victims. These children could in no way defend themselves against the terrors of the Nazis. Coincidence, fortune and random circumstances determined these people's fate. Anne became famous posthumously because of the publication of *The Diaries*.

Anne slept in the same room as Margot, right next to that of her parents. Before long, Anne started decorating her wall with pictures of film stars to make it more homely. 'Our little room looked very bare at first with nothing on the walls; but thanks to Daddy who had brought my film-star collection and picture postcards on beforehand, and with the aid of paste pot and brush, I have transformed the walls into on gigantic picture. This makes it look much more cheerful'[38] Anne regularly rearranged these pictures: 'Yesterday I put up some more film stars in my room, but this time with photo corners, so that I can take them down again.'[39] I wonder what Margot thought of Anne's decorating activities.

Approximately a week before the Franks went into hiding, on 14 July 1942, a large-scale raid was held in Amsterdam. This raid was preceded by a number of events. Margot was not the only one who did not obey the summons by the Germans, and the *Sicherheitspolizei* (Security Police) threatened to deport all Jews if less than 4,000 reported for labour in the German camps. On 11 July 1942, churches in the Netherlands had already put on a protest against the announced deportation of Jews.[40] Jews who were detained at that time were transferred to the *Hollandsche Schouwburg*—where Anne had received her grammar school report only a week earlier—to be deported from there via Amsterdam Central Station or Muiderpoort Station to Camp Westerbork. On 16 July 1942, the first train with Jews left the Westerbork Camp for Auschwitz.[41] Just a day before the big raid of 13 July 1942, the Van Pels family arrived at the Secret Annex.

The people hiding in the annex lived in great fear of being caught. 'Evening after evening the green and grey army lorries trundle past and ring at every front door to inquire if there are any Jews living in the house: if there are, then the whole family has to go at once. If they don't find any they go on to the next house. No one has a chance of evading them, unless one goes into hiding. Often they go round with lists, and only ring when they know they can get a good haul. Sometimes they let them off for a ransom–so much per head.[42] It seems like the slave hunts of olden times... I get frightened when I think of close friends who have now been delivered into the hands of the cruellest brutes the world has ever seen. And all because they are Jews,'[43] Anne Frank wrote.

Every unexpected noise in the building or outside, as well as the break-ins in the warehouses, caused great panic amongst those in hiding. A number of examples can be seen: 'Peter forgot to unbolt the front door. The result was that Kraler and the men could not get into the house, so he had to go to Keg and force open the kitchen window. What can they be thinking?' Two days later, Anne wrote, 'It all turned out all right with the forgotten bolt, Kugler was incredibly inventive; he has knocked together a piece of wood out of the broken window frame. Just think, the manager of Keg's had already fetched a ladder to climb through Pf.'s open window. Kugler was only able to stop him in time because the ladder was fortunately too short.'[44] Supposedly, in his panic, Kugler had forgotten to enter in a less conspicuous way through the sun-room door.

On 25 May 1944, their greengrocer delivery man Hendrik van Hoeve was arrested for hiding two Jewish people in his home: '... This morning v. Hoeven was picked up for having two Jews in his house. It is a great blow to us, not only that those poor Jews are balancing on the edge of an abyss, it's terrible for v. Hoeven ... Bep can't and isn't allowed to haul along our share of potatoes ... We're going to be hungry, but nothing is worse than being discovered.'[45]

Van Hoeve survived internment in several camps, but during transport acquired injuries to his legs due to freezing. The Jewish couple he had hidden were deported and did not survive the war. Van

Hoeve played himself in *The Diary of Anne Frank*—a 1959 American film.

The stockroom assistants had not been told about the people in hiding. Only the warehouse supervisor, Johan, Bep's father,[46] knew about the people in hiding. This does not detract from the fact that those in hiding had to be careful they were not discovered.

Those in hiding, as well as their helpers, made up safety rules as they went along, but not an escape plan. When Amsterdam Noord was heavily bombed on 25 July 1943, Anne wrote: 'I clasped my "escape-bag" close to me, more because I wanted to have something to hold, than with an idea of escaping, because there's nowhere we can go and if the worst came to the worst the street would be just as dangerous as an air raid.'[47]

Anne's so-called 'escape bag' was not a bag that Anne would take along if the family would have to escape. Many of those in hiding had a suitcase or rucksack ready to take along in case of emergency. During a *razzia*, there was often no chance to gather things together to take along; one had to go directly outside and enter the raid vans that were waiting in the streets.[48]

Friends from Merwedeplein and the *Joodsch Lyceum* grammar school wondered where Anne was. Jacqueline and Hanneli visited the residence to see if Anne's diary was still there, but the book was gone. 'I've heard meanwhile that Hanneli and Jacque (at least I think it was them) were in our house to look at my diary, they wanted to get hold of Daddy's mysterious letter of course.'[49] Anne had to leave her books and games behind. Jacqueline and Hanneli took only Anne's swimming medallions with them, although it was strictly forbidden to remove items from an abandoned Jewish house.

Jetteke Frijda (born 1925) was a friend of Margot, and together they attended the Meisjeslyceum (girls' school) and later the Joods Lyceum school.

'On a summer's day Margot Frank had suddenly disappeared. I went to their house on the Merwedeplein straightaway because I wanted to know what had happened. I heard from a neighbour that the Franks had fled to Switzerland. The door was slightly open and all their things were still there. I went into Margot's room and looked around. I took a book from the shelf to remember her by. It was a book about Dutch poets. Margot and I were both very interested in literature. Then I left quickly because what I had done was dangerous. I was wearing a Star of David and I was looking around the house of a Jewish family that had fled.'[50]

The departure of the Frank family was cause for much gossip. 'One family from the Merwedeplein had seen all four of us pass on bicycles very early in the morning and another lady knew quite definitely that we were fetched by a military car in the middle of the night.'[51]

All kinds of thoughts went through Anne's mind as well: Anne thought that their sub-lessee Goldschmidt had stolen items from their house[52] and given some of them to the Jewish Council. A month later, Anne retracted this: it was her mother who thought that Goldschmidt had misappropriated everything, but Anne did not want to be so mistrustful.[53] It was not Goldschmidt who had ransacked their house. Hilwis Building and Operating Company recounted the damages it had suffered due to the destruction by Jews when forced to leave their houses and due to the loss of rental income from Jewish funds that had been repossessed by Lippmann, Rosenthal & Co.

Otto paid the rent until 1 July 1943.[54] Most likely, it was the moving company A. Puls that emptied the Frank family's house under the orders of the Germans. Before going into hiding, Otto had entrusted items to one of his representatives, possibly including the writing table that Anne had used, which ended up at Miep's house after the war. In the autumn of 1943, there were new tenants at 37 Merwedeplein.

Anne became very agitated about her family's furnishings at Merwedeplein—the Van Pels' furnishings left her indifferent. After the Van Pels' residence was emptied, Anne wrote: 'We haven't told Mrs. v.P. yet. She's "all nerves" already, and we don't feel like listening to another moan over all the lovely china and beautiful chairs that she left at home. We had to leave almost all our nice things behind, so what's the good of grumbling about it now?'[55]

Anne missed her familiar surroundings and her friends. Anne also soon missed Moortje, as well as the personal things—including her red shoes—she was forced to leave behind.

Those in hiding killed time by reading, writing and performing household chores. The helpers assisted them at the risk of their own lives and those of their family members. Jan arranged for rations on the black market. Miep got food for those in hiding from befriended store owners and books from the city library (Bibliotheek, 42 Stadhouderskade; now: depot Rijksmuseum).[56] Jan Gies got books for them at the Como bookstore at 227 Rijnstraat (now: Evy Kinderdagverblij (Evy Day-Care Centre)). Anne was cut off from the outside world, and the helpers informed those in hiding about what was going on outside of the Secret Annex. They also got information from radio messages and newspapers. The Germans decided that no one was allowed to possess a radio anymore. Otto removed the radio from his private office, and in the common room they listened illegally to a self-made radio. 'Kleiman has a clandestine little baby set at home, which he will let us have to take the place of our big Philips ... We shall of course have the little radio upstairs.'[57]

When the stockroom assistants worked or there were visits from business relations, mechanics, the maid and such, it had to be quiet. For the young high-spirited Anne, this was difficult: she was locked up with a number of grown-ups with whom she clashed; Anne could not walk outside to escape the pressure; the lack of daylight and good food impaired her health; and the air raids and her fears did not help her to sleep well.

As 1943 progressed, Anne became more and more bothered about being locked up. 'I wander from one room to another, downstairs and up again, feeling like a songbird who has had his wings clipped and who is hurling himself in utter darkness against the bars of his cage.'[58] Anne missed nature, being outside, freedom, and fresh air: 'I remember very well that, before, the bright blue sky, chirping birds, moonlight or blossoming flowers could not hold my attention for long. That has changed here.'[59] Being forced to hide sabotaged her plans for the future. Anne became homesick for Merwedeplein. 'But most of all

I long for a home of our own, to be able to move freely and to have some help with my work again at last, in other words-back to school!'[60]

During the course of 1944, Anne increasingly sought support from God, whom she saw especially in nature and not in the religious (Jewish) actions. 'You see, once I was alone with nature I realized, without actually being aware of it, that fear does not help anything or anyone and that everyone who is as fearful as I was then, should look at Nature and see that God is much closer than most people think. From that moment on, though countless bombs fell close by, I was never truly afraid again.'[61] Anne experienced the lack of fresh air, being outside, and her freedom—things that seemed so matter of course at Merwedeplein. Peter and Anne loved to retreat to the attic in the annex and enjoy the view from the window over the roofs of Amsterdam. Margot was always somewhere else: 'Both of us [Peter and Anne] looked at the glorious blue of the sky [from the garret window], the bare chestnut tree on those branches little raindrops shone [apparently early in this Wednesday morning], at the seagulls and the other birds that looked like silver in the sun and all these things moved and thrilled the two of us so much that we could not speak.'[62]

The window in the garret also offered a beautiful view. 'At half past twelve, we [Peter and Anne] went up to the loft [stock assistants on break], during the quarter of an hour he [Peter] was chopping wood we remained silent. I watched him and saw that he was so obviously doing his best to show off his strength. But I looked out of the open window [in the afternoon] too, over a large piece of Amsterdam, over all the roofs and on to the far distance, fading into purple [C version: pale blue]. As long as this exists, I thought, and I may live to see it, this sunshine, the cloudless skies, while this lasts, I cannot be unhappy.'[63] The attic window was not blacked out and therefore offered Anne the opportunity to enjoy the view, which elicited reflections of nature and God. Anne found it increasingly difficult to rest in her own room, especially when sharing her room with Fritz.

Anne began to suffer from mood swings and lived between hope and fear. She called herself the 'Secret Annexe's bundle of nerves',[64] stating, 'I swallow valerian pills every day against worry and depression, but it doesn't prevent me from being even more miserable the next day.'[65] Absolute trust in the goodness of humans was something Anne lacked.

In her loneliness, Anne sought comfort with Peter. However, Peter lacked her sensitivity and intellectual capacities. She sought protection by her father; during air raids she would hide with him. Anne expressed her deepest emotions and thoughts only in her diary.

Otto was often seen to adopt the role of a referee during mealtimes when tensions amongst those in hiding erupted once again. Apparently, this also became too much for Otto from time to time: '... I felt lonely but hardly ever in despair! I have never been in such a state as Daddy, who once ran out onto the street with a knife in his hand to put an end to it all.'[66][67] Otto's dramatic reaction was very likely caused by a hurtful letter from Anne to her parents, a kind of 'declaration of independence', written on 5 May 1944. The letter stemmed from the fact that Otto did not want Anne to have intimate contact with Peter. Anne become furious and handed her father the letter, in which she asks him to 'leave me alone, if you do not want me to lose faith in you forever'. The letter did not, as Otto told Anne, get burned in the stove but was saved.

Going into hiding was very traumatic. 'Not much attention was invested in this afterwards. But it meant a loss of identity, of occupation, of your own context, of your family, of taking your own space for granted, of social networks, of books, properties. It meant losing everything. In most cases it meant making oneself dependent on benevolent or less benevolent helpers ... And all from one day to the next and motivated by the fact that anything would beat the fate that the Germans would have in store for you. All in all a great trauma, which could last for years and to which people would adapt—but it is still a fact that the meaning of this has very much been underestimated,' said Bloeme Emden (born 1926),[68] whom Anne had met in the Westerbork Camp.

It was impossible to retreat from the influence of the Germans. Anne read not only 'innocent' fairytales but also poets and literature. Victor bought *Cinema & Theater* for Anne each week.[69] The popular magazine directed much attention to entertainment, popular actors, comedians, shows, movie stars, and sex symbols from 1924-1944. Before World War II, it dedicated considerable attention to Pola Negri (1897-1987)[70]—a Polish actress who had fled Germany in 1938. The magazine also paid attention to the film adaptation of Erich Maria Remarque's book *All Quiet on the Western Front*.[71] In 1936, the film journal reported that Hitler banned the movie *Modern Times*, written and directed by the world-famous Charley Chaplin (1889-1977), in Germany.

In 1937, the magazine devoted considerable attention to the fledgling film star Shirley Temple (born 1928),[72] who was very popular with Anne. In 1938, the magazine wrote about the movie *Olympia* by Lenie Riefenstahl (1902-2003),[73] which was commissioned by the International Olympic Committee, and thus not made for the Nazis.

During the war, the Germans dictated the contents of the magazine, which was published by *De Amsterdamse Keurkamer* (993 Prinsengracht). The National Socialist Movement held the leadership in the editing department. The Chief Editor opened the 1 January 1944 issue with an attack on the actors who refused to perform[74] for the Germans. During the war, the magazine paid a great deal of attention to Nazi propaganda films, such as *Triump des Willens* by the same Leni Riefenstahl mentioned earlier.[75] Anne was especially interested in the film stars' appearances and dreamed of becoming an American actress.[76]

Radio traffic was also largely dominated by the Germans. All the same, on Saturday nights, Anne would listen to '*Een bonte avond*' (a variety show),[77] and on Sundays those in hiding would listen to '*unsterbliche Musik Deutscher Meister*' (immortal music by German masters)[78] to relax.

Victor Kugler sometimes took the NSDAP's weekly newspaper *Das Reich* (The Empire) along for them.[79] Anne was also aware of the resistance newspapers, such as *Vrij Nederland* (The Free Netherlands).[80]

By reading between the lines, those in hiding could get news from these sources that were supplemented by information from illegal radio senders, such as Radio Oranje (Radio Orange) and the BBC. During the war, almost all media sources were tainted by the Germans.

Anne had found a means to relax. When she walked from the Merwedeplein to the annex, she passed by the Westerkerk. Even before the period of hiding, Anne would hear the bells of the Westerkerk. During her period of hiding, Anne found the sound of the Westerkerk carillon ringing very peaceful. The bells rang every quarter of an hour. Sometimes, the carillon was played for a longer time in order to calm the population. 'By order of the mayor of Amsterdam ... as of 5 January 1942, every Monday afternoon from 12 to 1 o'clock, a city carillon will be played manually ... *2 Februari Oudekerkstoren, carilloneur Frans Hasselaar, 9 Februari Westertoren, carilloneur P.J. Vincent ...*'[81] (Quote *Amstelodamum*).

'We already know the Monday afternoon performances, always from 12 to 1 o'clock, alternating from the Oudetoren, the Zuidertoren, and the Westertoren .... In addition there will be sentimental summer evening performances .... To the satisfaction of many lovers of the 'heavenly bell music' ... during the months of August and September the carilloneurs climbed into all three of the city towers at the same time and played the carillons from 12 to 1 o'clock.'[82] (Quote *Amstelodamum*).

The carillon was temporarily out of order. 'For the last week we've all been in a bit of a muddle about time, because our dear and beloved Westertoren clock bell has apparently been taken away for war purposes, so that neither by day nor night do we ever know the exact time. I still have some hope that they will think up a substitute (tin, copper or some such thing) so that the neighbourhood gets reminded of the clock.'[83] (Quote Anne Frank).

The Westerkerk was designed by Hendrick de Keyser (1565-1621) and built between 1620 and 1631. The 58-metre-high church tower is still the highest in Amsterdam, and was built in the Renaissance style, adopting the shape of a double cross. The building itself is rectangular: it is 48 metres long, 28 metres wide and 27.5 metres high up to the wooden barrel vaulting in the nave. The sunlight enters through the 36 large windows on all sides—the church is completely detached. This 'light effect' is enhanced by the white inner walls of the church.

The sounds of the Westertoren were a pleasant way for Anne to keep contact with the outside world. Anne was justifiably concerned about the fate of her friends and family, with whom she could have no contact during the period of hiding. Apparently, this period taught her the value of her contacts. Anne was afraid that she would not see her friends again and she regretted things she had said to them. As an example, three weeks before she went into hiding, she had made a condescending comment about Betty Bloemendal (hierna: Betty, 1929-1942). 'Betty Bloemendaal looks rather poor, but that's what she is I think, she lives in Jan Klasenstraat in West [Amsterdam] and none of us knows where that is. She is very clever at school, but that's because she works so hard, since her cleverness isn't all it seems.'[84] A good three months later, she wrote about Betty: 'Now and then we have news of other Jews, unfortunately things are going badly for them. For instance, a girl I know from my class has been carried off with her family.'[85] Betty Bloemendal[86] was gassed in Auschwitz on 1 October 1942. Her mother and only brother died on the same day in Auschwitz. Her father died in 1944.

On 21 February 1943, the churches in the Netherlands protested against German terror by means of a pastoral letter. Anne wrote in her diary: 'Jan brought a copy of the bishop's letter to churchgoers for us to read; it was very fine and inspiring. "Do not rest, people of the Netherlands, everyone is fighting with his own weapons to free the country, the people and their religion. Give help, be generous and do not dismay!" is what they cry from the pulpit—just like that. Will it help? It won't help the people of our religion.'[87]

Before she went into hiding, Anne never wrote about protest and resistance activities by the churches. On 27 October 1940, the

Reformed Church of the Netherlands protested against the so-called declaration of Aryan origin. On 23 March 1941, all reformed churches disassociated themselves from the totalitarian state (including the German one) and called for mercy for all races. Nor does Anne mention the churches' protest on 11 July 1942—Anne had already gone into hiding for a number of days—against the announced deportations of Jews.

Anne was probably witness to the rounding up of people: '… in the evenings when it's dark, I often see rows of good, innocent people accompanied by crying children, walking on and on, in the charge of a couple of these chaps, bullied and knocked about until they almost drop. Nobody is spared, old people, children, babies, expectant mothers, the sick each and all join in the march of death.'[88] Anne could never have actually seen this herself simply because, according to David Barnouw, there were no raids on the Prinsengracht.[89] It is possible that Anne was describing not one of the infamous raids on the Prinsengracht but rather a 'torture march'—or perhaps Anne saw a group of people who had wanted to avoid the work duty and had been picked up during one of the smaller *razzias*.[90] For that matter, there were also round-ups of resistance heroes and others.

It is clear that Anne had deep respect for the helpers, and she knew that they risked imprisonment and their lives by (unconditionally) helping those in hiding. She wrote: 'Our helpers are a very good example, they have pulled us through up till now and we hope they will bring us safely to dry land. Otherwise they would have to share the same fate as the many others who are being searched for, never have we heard one word of the burden which we certainly must be to them, never has one of them complained about all the trouble we cause.'[91]

Anne also had great respect for the illegal resistance in general and the help offered to those in hiding: 'Thousands and thousands of identity and ration cards are being provided, sometimes for nothing and sometimes for money. Goodness knows how many false identity cards are in circulation. Jewish acquaintances are going about under ordinary Christian names and there are certainly not many people in hiding like ourselves who have no identity cards and never go out.'[92]

The resistance in the Netherlands led to acts of vengeance by the Germans. By going into hiding, the Frank family avoided the raids in the Rivierenbuurt. The date of 6 August 1942 is known as 'Black Thursday' as there were raids until late at night in Amsterdam. Many Jews committed suicide after this. Under the command of Sybren Tulp (1891-1942), a Dutch police battalion rounded up 2,000 Jews in Amsterdam. After this, 2 October 1942 became known as 'Black Friday' as a result of German and Dutch police, NSB and SS carrying out huge raids.

'This morning Miep told us that last night they were dragging Jews from house after house again in South Amsterdam. Horrible. God knows which of our acquaintances are left.'[93]

Apparently, many of those arrested ended up in the Gestapo Headquarters (99 Euterpestraat, now: Scholengemeenschap Gerrit van der Veen, 99 Gerrit van der Veenstraat). The *Judenreferat* (IV B4) and the *Zentralstelle für jüdische Auswanderung* (Central Office for Jewish Emigration, now a supermarket) were located at 1 Adama van Scheltemaplein. This annex stood across from the main building of the Gestapo at 99 Euterpestraat.

On 6 October 1942, in her diary, Anne refers to this location: 'Every night people are being picked up without warning and that is awful particularly for old and sick people, they treat them just like slaves in the olden days. The poor old people are taken outside at night and then they have to walk for instance as far as A.v. Scheltemaplein in a whole procession with children and everything. Then when they arrive at A.v. Scheltemaplein they are sent to Ferdinand Bolstraat and from there back again to A.v. Scheltemaplein and that's how they plague these poor people.'[94]

The rest of the country was also in turmoil. 'This, however, is not the end of my bad news. Have you ever heard of hostages? That's the latest thing in penalties for sabotage. Can you imagine anything so dreadful? Prominent citizens—innocent people—are thrown into prison to await their fate. If the saboteur can't be traced the Green police simply put about five hostages against the wall. Announcements of their deaths appear in the papers frequently. These outrages are described as "fatal accidents". Nice people, the Germans, and to think that I am really one of them too! But no, Hitler took away our nationality long ago, in fact Germans and Jews are the greatest enemies in the world.'[95] On 16 October 1942, the daily papers announced that fifteen hostages had been executed by a German firing squad in retaliation for a number of sabotage activities in Twente.

At this time, Anne was certainly aware of what was going on in the world around her: '… because it's a fact that in Poland and Russia millions and millions of people have been murdered and gassed.'[96] Anne was also very worried about her life and those of the other people in hiding.

In 1943, Germany was losing the war, and the Allied Forces had bombed German cities, causing many civilian casualties. On their way to Germany, the Allied aeroplanes flew over Amsterdam. German positions in Amsterdam were bombed by the Allies as well, which often were not precision bombings. Here, too, innocent victims fell. 'The Carlton-hotel is smashed to bits. Two British planes loaded with incendiary bombs fell right on top of the *Offizierenheim*. The whole Vijzelstraat-Singel corner is burnt down.'[97]

On 27 April 1943, a burning Allied plane, shot down by German anti-aircraft artillery, crashed in the Reguliersdwarsstraat behind the Carlton Hotel (now: NH Carlton Amsterdam, 4 Vijzelstraat). Houses and a part of the hotel went up in flames. At the time, German officers were staying in the hotel. A month earlier, on 27 March 1943, there had been an enormous fire in Amsterdam; the resistance, under the command of Gerrit van der Veen (1902-1944), had attacked the building of the Population Register (34 Plantage Kerklaan).

Almost all of the attackers were betrayed and put to death. The monument Gerrit van der Veen—*Monument voor het kunstenaarsverzet* (Monument to the Artists' Resistance) by Carel Kneulman (1915-2008) was commissioned by the Stichting Kunstenaarsverzet 1942-1945 (Artists' Resistance 1942-1945

Foundation) and is located at the crossing of the Plantage Middenlaan and the Plantage Westermanlaan.[98]

On 17 May 1943, the English Allies bombed two large dams in Germany. 'I witnessed a terrific air battle between German and British planes. Unfortunately a couple of the Allies had to jump from their burning machine. Our milkman, who lives in Halfweg, saw four Canadians sitting by the roadside, one of them spoke fluent Dutch. He asked the milkman to give him a light for his cigarette and told him that the crew had consisted of 6 men. The pilot was burnt to death and their 5th man had hidden himself somewhere. The German police came and fetched the four perfectly fit men.'[99] (Quote Anne Frank).

In the Fokker factories, the Germans made Bücker-Bestmann aeroplanes and parts for Junkers 'Ju 52' transport aeroplanes.

'North Amsterdam was very heavily bombed on Sunday. The destruction seems to be terrible, whole streets lie in ruins, and it will take a long time until all the people are dug out. Up till now there are two hundred dead and countless wounded; the hospitals are crammed. You hear of children lost in the smoldering ruins, looking for their parents. I shudder when I recall the dull, droning rumble in the distance, which for us marked the approaching destruction.'[100] The bombs missed the Fokker factories, resulting in more than 150 dead and many more wounded (Quote Anne Frank).

A week later, on 25 July 1943, the Fokker factories were successfully bombed. 'We had the first warning siren while we were at breakfast, but we don't give a hoot about that, it only means that the planes are crossing the coast.' At about 2:30 p.m., the bombing began. 'And yes, the house rumbled and shook, and down came the bombs.'[101] At about 3:00 p.m., the noise stopped and Anne saw the 'columns of smoke above the IJ'. 'Before long you could smell burning and outside it looked as if a thick mist hung everywhere.'[102] (Quote Anne Frank).

On 23 March 1944, Anne wrote: 'A pilot crashed near here yesterday; the occupants were able to jump out in time by parachute. The machine crashed onto a school, but there were no children there at the time. The result was a small fire and two people killed. The

Germans shot at the airmen terribly as they were coming down. The Amsterdammers who saw it nearly burst with rage and indignation at the cowardliness of such a deed.'[103] German anti-aircraft guns had hit the English bomber. One of the pilots of the English bomber parachuted onto a residence in the Bremstraat. The other pilot landed on the ground in one piece despite being shot at. The aeroplane bored its way into the top floor of the R.K. Sint Alfonsusschool (Roman Catholic St Alfonsus Primary School, 63 Westzaanstraat). The parsonage of the Roman Catholic church (11 Spaarndammerstraat) was hit directly as well. There were three dead and five seriously injured. The two pilots and the other eight crew members later ended up in the prisoners of war camp Luft 1 in Barth near Peenemünde. They were liberated in May 1945 by the Russian army and half a year later the complete crew of the crashed bomber was home again.[104]

According to Anne, the English aeroplane passed the *Markthallen* (covered market)[105] on 22 March 1944. In 1934, the complex *De Centrale Markthallen* (The Central Covered Market, now: Food Center Amsterdam, Jan van Galenstraat) was opened, partly due to the politician Monne de Miranda (1875-1942). At the site, there is a monument by Hildo Krop that reminds us of the many Jewish merchants killed during World War II. Since 2007, the complex has become a national monument because of its cultural historical and architectural value.

A few days later, it was hit again. On Sunday 26 March 1944, the Allies bombed IJmuiden harbour, approximately 25 kilometres away from Prinsengracht. 'How scared the ladies are during the air raids. For instance on Sunday when 350 British planes dropped ½ million kilos of bombs on IJmuiden, how the houses trembled like a wisp of grass in the wind …'[106]

The specific target of the bombardment on 26 March 1944 was the German bunker at the head of the Haringhaven, where the so-called S-boats were moored. These torpedo boats placed mines in the *navigation lanes of the Allies. The structure was damaged lightly, as was the nearby U-boat bunker that was still under construction. Many bombs missed their targets, costing several civilians their lives.

On 28 March 1944, two days after the heavy bombardment, the Dutch Minister of Education, Art and Science in London, G. Bolkestein (1871-1956),[107] broadcast to the Dutch people on Radio Oranje: 'History cannot be written on the basis of official decisions and documents alone. If our descendants are to understand fully what we as a nation have had to endure and overcome during these years, then what we really need are ordinary documents—a diary, letters from a worker in Germany, a collection of sermons given by a parson or priest. Not until we succeed in bringing together vast quantities of this simple, everyday material will the picture of our struggle for freedom be painted in its full depth and glory.'[108] Because of this speech, Anne decided to publish her diary as a novel after the war. Anne thought *The Secret Annexe* was an intriguing title—one that made her think of a detective novel. 'Of course, they all made a rush at my diary immediately,'[109] which sounds rather bitter in light of the knowledge we have today.

On 21-22 September 1944, the German militia destroyed the Amsterdam harbour systems.

Both outside and inside, noise was an issue. The canal house at 263 Prinsengracht had very thin walls. There was a very real chance that a noise by those in hiding would be heard; a cough, a sneeze, an argument. Other things could also draw the attention of outsiders, such as the supply of large quantities of food for those in hiding and the chimney smoke from burning waste. It is possible that, during break-ins, thieves, police, and passers-by saw something that raised questions in their minds. There were also regular visitors in Otto's office, including the owner of the house, business relations and the maid.

The pharmacy's workroom was in the kitchen directly below Anne's room. Maybe the high energy bill raised eyebrows at the utilities office. Maintenance people also did repair work. Stockroom assistants saw that the windows in the storage room looking out over the annex were blacked out. Sometimes there was a light in one of the bedrooms at night. All of this may have raised many questions. The attic window was not blacked out. From the Prinsengracht German officers in round-trip boats could get a good view of the canal house. The annex was also very visible to many of the surrounding houses.

Another danger was that Otto was being blackmailed by someone who threatened to betray him because Otto would not believe in conquest by the Germans. Some people who no longer encountered the Frank family at the Merwedeplein knew the location of Otto's company. For some, the reward money was cause to betray Jews.

The helpers sometimes made mistakes as well. 'Miep offered to take me along one evening to take a bath at her place, and to bring me back home the next evening. But that is much too dangerous for someone could easily see me.'[110] Miep fetched books for Frits Pfeffer that the Germans had banned.

Anne reproached those in hiding for sometimes not being able to resist the temptation to look outside. The pot was calling the kettle black. 'Yesterday evening I discovered something new: to peer through a powerful pair of field glasses into the lighted rooms of the houses at the back ... I never knew before that neighbors could be such interesting people, at any rate ours are, I found one couple having a meal, one family was in the act of taking a home movie, and the dentist over the way was just attending to an old lady, who was awfully scared.'[111] Perhaps Anne was able to see into P. Volders' and A. Businger's practice at 186 Keizersgracht.[112]

On the http://www.annefrank.org/en/Sitewide/Organisation/ website I read: 'The Anne Frank House is an independent organisation entrusted with the care of the Secret Annexe, the place where Anne Frank went into hiding during World War II and where she wrote her diary. It brings her life story to the attention of people all over the world to encourage them to reflect on the dangers of anti-Semitism, racism and discrimination and the importance of freedom, equal rights and democracy.'[113] Anne herself was not free from prejudices and was a product of her time and upbringing, which is logical given her young age.

From the affluent south, Anne and Margot bathed on Saturday afternoons in the office, and would look intently toward the Jordaan area and at the working class children they saw from their window.

'I'm sitting cosily in the main office, looking outside through a slit in the curtains ... The people in this neighbourhood don't look so very attractive now. The children especially are so dirty you wouldn't want to touch them with a barge pole, real slum kids with running noses ...'[114] Anne wrote about a former classmate from her *Joodsch Lyceum* grammar school: 'Sam Solomon is just a brat from the slums, a bit of riffraff.'[115] In 1943[116] Anne realised that many people ended up in poverty because of the injustice of others.

Anne sought distractions to escape boredom. From the office window she looked at everything that she thought was interesting: cars, boats, cyclists and even the rain—things that she had to miss in the annex. Anne heard the trams. In addition to lines 13 and 17, the Blue Tram ran along the Prinsengracht to Haarlem and Zandvoort. Anne could hear children calling and would look at the houseboat on the other side. 'There is a houseboat immediately opposite, where a bargeman lives with his family. He has a small yapping dog. We only know the little dog by his bark and his tail, which we can see when he runs round the deck.'[117] Today there is a houseboat in the water there as well, across from 263 Prinsengracht. Anne heard a 'bell' that played songs sung by the NSB, such as 'Upright in Body, Upright in Soul!'[118]

There was always hope for liberation. For the Frank family and many others, help came too late. The people in hiding were betrayed and, on Friday morning, 4 August 1944, they were picked up by an arresting team of the *Sicherheitsdienst* (SD, Security Service) under the command of the Austrian Karl Silberbauer (1911-1971), assisted by the Dutch Jew-hunters[119] Gezinus Gringhuis (1895-1975), Willem Grootenhorst (1889-1973) and Maarten Kuiper (1898-1948). Maarten Kuiper was a former police agent and famous for his cruelty. He was executed on 30 August 1948. Silberbauer, along with many other Nazis who had the deaths of many Jews on their conscience, worked for the West German intelligence after the war; they were often the Nazis of higher rank—those who pulled the strings in the background and ultimately got off scot-free.

The director of the Anne Frank centre in Berlin (press release 11 April 2011) thinks it is scandalous that, after all these years, there are still war tyrants walking around free. He wants the Silberbauer file to be made public. 'It is outrageous and a disgrace to our country that the man who had arrested Anne Frank and her family then later worked for the BND,' stated Thomas Heppener, Director of the Anne Frank Centre in Berlin.

'I find it very unfortunate that the BND has been actively engaged with the investigation of its own history only since 2010 and has thus covered the perpetrators of the Nazi period for a long time. I hope that the important reappraisal of the perpetrator biographies in future will not be dependent on individual efforts only, such as Peter-Ferdinand Koch's current one. Rather, I appeal to the BND and its committee of historians to promote the realisation with even greater vehemence and in particular to publish the Silberbauer file,' Heppener stated.[120]

The raiders that arrested Anne only took costly things, such as jewellery, and were not interested in *The Diaries*. Whether consciously or in panic, Anne did not take her writing with her. Miep and Bep[121] saved *The Diaries* for the future generations. During the raid, Margot's diary was probably lost. Did Miep know that Margot kept a diary as well?

Initially, it seemed as if the people in hiding were simply going to allow the raid to occur. When they began hiding, safety rules had been established; however, during the more than two years of hiding, there were no escape practices, nor was an escape route mapped out for in case they should be discovered. Those in hiding had no weapons, although Jan Gies was active in the resistance. Nor did those in hiding have a reserved alternative secret address.

The Frank family stayed in the Secret Annex the entire time and did not alternate between various hiding places, nor was there any effort made to acquire false identities. During the raid by the SD, no one attempted to distract them so the others could escape. With ropes and ladders, those in hiding could possibly have descended to the gardens. In addition, they also did not attempt to climb over the roof or escape through a window. If they had barricaded the bookcase from the inside, they could have bought themselves some time.

Importantly, the Frank family chose to stay together all the time and did not want to risk one of them getting shot during a raid.[122] In practice, during *razzias*, no escape was possible for those in hiding: the streets would be closed off.[123]

After their arrest, the eight people in hiding, along with their two helpers, Johannes and Victor, were forced to get into a *Grüne Polizei* (Green Police) vehicle. Jan and a brother of Johannes watched helplessly when the special squad car turned around on the Leliegracht.

In terms of figures, 8,500 of the 25,000 Jews in hiding fell into German hands. To date, it still is not known who betrayed the Frank family. In 2003, there was a report by the Dutch Institute for War Documentation on this issue, with no conclusive evidence available.[124]

The research gets hung-up because, after the war, incompetent investigation was performed by police and the administration of justice, permanently erasing many traces from the past—and not all sources are public. Each new hypothesis of betrayal[125] stirs dust and lacks conclusive proof. The movies and plays centred on the betrayal of Anne, including ominous soundtracks, promise an exciting evening, but ultimately fail to provide clarity on the issue.

It is striking that Miep, Jan, and Bep were not thoroughly interrogated by the Gestapo since they had helped Jews and possessed sensitive information, such as the food suppliers for the people in hiding. It is possible Silberbauer spared them partly because he, like Miep, was born in Austria and was impressed by the fact that Otto had served in the German army. Johannes was released from the Amersfoort Camp because he became seriously ill; he returned to 263 Prinsengracht. Victor escaped during a 'death march' from Wageningen to Germany in December 1944.

The Diaries end on 1 August 1944, and from that date on there are no more entries by Anne and no other good clues as to what happened.

On 4 August 1944, the ten prisoners arrived by lorry at the Gestapo Headquarters (99 Euterpestraat, now: Gerrit van der Veen Comprehensive School, 99 Gerrit van der Veenstraat).[126] Here, they were locked up in a room together with other arrestees who sat on low benches waiting for interrogation. After their interrogation, the Frank family was returned to the prison in the cellar where they stayed for two days. Miep tried in vain to buy the freedom of those captured at the Gestapo Headquarters.

Walking between the high terraces and trees in the Gerrit van der Veenstraat, I felt closed in. A statue next to the main entrance of the former Gestapo Headquarters looked at me pensively.

The building, with its high towers on the left near the jutting entrance, was opened in 1929 as a girls' secondary school, and was designed by architect Nicholas Lansdorp Jr. (1885-1968).[127] The building resembles Swedish brick architecture, and the wings have hipped roofs with a large overhang. In 1930, ten terracotta statues of rowers and clowns on gymnastic apparatuses by Hildo were placed along the side wall bordering the school yard on Anthonie van Dijckstraat. By the front wall, there is a rower above an arch. The ground plan is T-shaped.

The red-brick building had high bell-towers. During the war, the SS flag was flown in the courtyard. The cellar complex where Anne was imprisoned is now a place to park bicycles.

On Sunday 26 November 1944, the Allies bombed various locations in the Netherlands. The RAF hit the Gestapo Headquarters at 99 Euterpestraat (now: Scholengemeenschap Gerrit van der Veen, 99 Gerrit van der Veenstraat), the annex on 1 Adama van Scheltemaplein where the *Judenreferat* (IV B4) and the *Zentralstelle für jüdische Auswanderung* (now: St Ignatius Gymnasium) were located, and thirty houses. According to Karel N.L. Grazell, who saw the English aeorplanes flying over, bombs fell on Michel Angelostraat,[128] approximately 700 metres from the Gestapo Headquarters. There were 69 deaths, amongst which were four members of the SD.[129]

The Gestapo Headquarters were then moved to the hotel Apollofirst on the Apollolaan. After the war, in 1945, the

Euterpestraat was renamed after the resistance fighter Gerrit Jan van der Veen.

Department IV B4 of the *Reichssicherheitshauptambt* (Reich Security Main Office) in Berlin was the motor of the Jewish destruction. The Gestapo Headquarters were heavily damaged during the bombardment on 26 November 1944, but the annex was completely destroyed, which in 1945 was clearly visible from the Apollolaan.[130]

The Memorial to the Deported Jews in Amsterdam consists of 65 concrete tiles in a long line in the sidewalk of the Adama van Scheltemaplein. On the tile are the reactions of random Amsterdammers to the text that was placed before them by the designers of the monument.[131]

On 6 August 1944, a truck transported the Frank family from the Gestapo Headquarters to the Huis van Bewaring I (House of Detention I, Weteringschans, 14 Kleine-Gartmanplantsoen, now: Max Euweplein). The prison, where they stayed two nights, was a sombre building with two wings on a filthy canal.

Many places of entertainment are located along the Max Euweplein, including the Holland Casino. A memorial (a blue surface with glass tears), designed by Bernard Heesen (born 1958), recalls the people who were prisoners there, including Gerrit and John Post (1906-1944), both of whom were executed by the Germans. The artwork is in a passageway surrounded by some remnants of the original walls of the former prison.

Johannes 'Jo' Kleiman and Victor Kugler were brought to the Huis van Bewaring II (House of Detention II) at 6 Havenstraat and, on 7 September [1944], a good month later, were transferred to the Huis van Bewaring I. Anne was already in the Westerbork Camp at this time.

History professor Jan Romein—who lived on Daniël Willinkplein (now: 21a Victorieplein) near Anne—wrote a compelling review of Anne's diary in *Het Parool* entitled, 'A Child's Voice' on 3 April 1946: 'If all the signs do not deceive me, this girl would have become a talented writer if she had remained alive. Having arrived here at the age of four from Germany, she was able within ten years to write enviably pure and simple Dutch and showed an insight into the failings of human nature—her own not excepted—so infallible that it would have astonished one in an adult, let alone in a child.' His article stimulated interest in Anne.

After the war, Miep handed *The Diaries* over to Otto, who was very surprised at the deep thoughts of his youngest daughter. In 1947, the first edition of *Het Achterhuis* (The Secret Annex) was printed with a run of 1,500 books. At Otto's request, certain passages in which Anne writes about her sexuality were omitted. Anne's comments about her mother were also suppressed.

In his agenda, Otto noted on the day of publication: 'Book'. Later, he said about that moment, 'If she had been here, Anne would have been so proud.' Otto knew how to sell the book, and gave copies to friends and family, the Dutch Prime Minister, the Royal family, and Anne and Margot's friends.[132] The Dutch media paid no attention to the movies released at the end of the 1940s in Poland, the USA and Germany that exposed the horrors of the Holocaust, nor was there any interest in the Jewish homes that were demolished.

Het Achterhuis was translated from Dutch and was published in 1950 in both Germany and France. In 1952, *The Diaries* appeared in the United States with a foreword by Eleanor Roosevelt (1884-1962), who called it 'one of the wisest and most moving commentaries on war and its impact on human beings that I have ever read'. The book was translated into more than 60 languages.

Otto retired from business in 1953 and sold the house at 263 Prinsengracht to NV Berghaus, who wanted to pull down the building to build new houses. This led to much outrage, and the Dutch embassy in Washington received many messages from Americans who wanted the Dutch government to protect Anne's hiding place.[133] However, despite the The Hague Convention for the Protection of Cultural Property, which was to provide protection to monuments, the Dutch government showed little interest in the preservation of the building.

The public indignation with regard to the plan by the new owner to destroy the hiding place was so great that the owner donated the building to the Anne Frank Stichting, established in 1947, which sought to preserve 263 Prinsengracht, including the Secret Annex, for future generations. After a fundraiser by the Amsterdam mayor Gijs van Hall (1904-1977), it was possible for the Stichting to buy the neighbouring properties at 265-275 Prinsengracht and 16-20 Westermarkt. The Stichting had the properties at numbers 263 and 265 restored. The Anne Frank Museum was housed at number 263, whilst at 265 an international youth centre was built, which was something desired by Otto.

NV Berghaus was less accommodating with the adjacent properties, which led to the levelling of the properties at numbers 267, 269, 271, 273 and 275 on the Prinsengracht in 1959 in order to make room for a large student block that was built in 1962, impairing the historic presence of the Prinsengracht around the Secret Annex.[134] Anne's authentic living conditions were also affected. A drawing from 1901 shows that hostel *De Leeuw van Waterloo* was located at 275 Prinsengracht.[135]

A drawing from 1939 shows splendid buildings along the canal at 18-20 Westermarkt[136]; this cultural heritage is also gone forever.

In 1960, the Secret Annex opened its door, and the hiding place of Anne gradually developed into a place of pilgrimage. In the main building, the original walls were removed to create more exhibition space, which, in terms of the preservation of the material heritage of Anne, was not to be recommended.

The Anne Frank Stichting made every effort to save the chestnut tree, which had become a symbol of freedom. The student housing made way for a new wing of the museum. When the student housing was demolished, the side walls of 263 and 265 Prinsengracht became visible and the structure of the standard buildings along the canals—comprising a main building and an annex separated by a courtyard—was clearly visible. The 150-year-old chestnut tree in the garden could be seen from the street.

The architecture of the new wing did not really fit in with that of the Secret Annex. After moving the museum facilities to the new wing, the front section of the house at 263 Prinsengracht was restored to the state it was in in 1940. Many original materials, such as clinkers, wired glass, and wallpaper, had been lost. Queen Beatrix opened the 'restored' Anne Frank House on 28 September 1999. The number of visitors per year has reached the magical number of one million.

Some of the original furniture still stands in Otto's private office, such as the safe, the chest, his desk, and the filing cabinet. The radio in the private office looks old; however, it is not the original radio that the Frank family used during their period of hiding.

The stairs from the hall to the bookcase room have been made accessible and shut off at the ceiling with a glass floor panel; this was the opening that the people in hiding went through after they were betrayed. The bookcase does not contain the original documents; unfortunately, Anne's house also attracts thieves, souvenir hunters and sticky fingers.

I suspect that Anne's room does not have the original restored pictures but clever imitations that include irregularities.

Provisions have been made in order to meet the fire safety requirements for a building that has so many visitors each year: a fire-resistant plate has been inserted inside the doors, and the inner walls of the house are made of modern fire-resistant materials.

The attic of the Secret Annex is not open to the public: the stairs that lead to the attic would give way under the weight of all the visitors. With a mirror people can catch a glimpse of the attic. I felt honoured to be allowed entry to take pictures of the attic. Only rarely does one get permission to visit the attic. An old spring bed, perhaps from Peter's room, is located there. The attic contains a number of old tins, including UNOX cans of pea soup with bacon and sausage.

Otto's private office is also not usually open to the public.

During the war, many of the original old things had been stolen. Anne wrote about a beautiful clock that hung in the front office: 'The thief was also planning to steal the big electric clock; he had cleared the mantelpiece in the main office for that purpose, but he must have been disturbed.'[137] Johannes had, at one time, been a representative of the Pieter Pauwe factory.

The office of the Anne Frank Stichting is located at 10 Westermarkt. On the wall there is a plaque that reminds one of World War II: 'This building was Theo and Nel Storck's garage and house. They hid weapons, sheltered people in hiding, and fixed bicycles for countless numbers of resistance fighters. The illegal newspapers *Trouw* and *De Waarheid* were also distributed from here.' The plaque also reminds me that, whilst in hiding, Anne was in the area of a hotbed of traitors, Nazis, soldiers, and resistance fighters.

Two statues have been erected in Amsterdam in memory of Anne. Since 1977, there has been a bronze statue of Anne on the square in front of the house of the caretaker of the Westerkerk, designed by Mari Andriessen (1897-1979). Just like with the second statue of Anne at the Merwedeplein, this did not occur without strife. The socialist daily paper *Het Vrije Volk* (The Free People) protested because supposedly there were communists in the initiative committee, and the *Nieuw Israëlietisch Weekblad* (New Israelite Weekly) was afraid that this statue would make Anne a symbol for all of the Dutch Jewry.[138]

Close to the statue of Anne at the Westermarkt on the side of the Keizersgracht is a gay monument that was unveiled in 1987. The monument was designed by Karin Daan (born 1944)[139], consisting of a large triangle divided into three pink granite triangles. During World War II, homosexuals were made to wear a pink triangle in concentration camps. One of the triangles lies against the quay of the Keizersgracht whilst part of it hangs above the water. Daan placed the third triangle amongst the bricks of the street, with one of its tips pointing in the direction of the Anne Frank House. This brick contains a line of poetry: '*Naar vriendschap zulk een mateloos verlangen* (Such an endless desire for friendship)' from the poem '*Aan eenen jongen visscher*' (To a Young Fisherman) by the Dutch author Jacob Israël de Haan (1881-1924). Anne does not explicitly express her feelings about homosexuality in her works: she does, however, explore her sexual feelings and, in *The Diaries*, she writes on 6 January 1944, 'I go into ecstasies every time I see the naked figure of a woman ...'[140] Two months later, Anne writes: 'At the beginning of the New Year ... I discovered my longing, not for a girl friend, but for a boy friend ...'[141]

The Anne Frank tree—saved from a housing improvement scheme in 1993—was doomed. In 2007, the 170-year-old horse chestnut tree became world news when the owner acquired a permit to cut the sick tree down. As a precaution, the Anne Frank Stichting had already gathered chestnuts before it was cut down. In 2008, Jos Wiersema—editor of http://www.geheugenvanplanzuid.nl (memory of the Amsterdam South district)—was given a chestnut from the Anne Frank tree by Tjerk van der Veen—initiator of www.anne-in-de-buurt.nl (Anne and her neighbourhood, Dutch only).[142] In 2009, 150 offspring from the tree were donated to the *Amsterdamse Bos* (Amsterdam Forest).

The Stichting Support Anne Frank Tree tried everything it could to keep the tree alive for future generations and in memory of Anne; the judge decided that the tree was not allowed to be cut down. The newspaper *De Telegraaf* reported that the construction that supported the tree would be able to withstand wind-force 12.[143] Nevertheless, a strong wind on 24 August 2010 destroyed the monumental tree. The tree did not fall on the Secret Annex and there were no victims. The Stichting Support Anne Frank Tree claims the construction of the support was not sound.[144]

Since then, many Anne Frank Schools across Europe have a tree, as well as other organisations and locations worldwide. Elsewhere in the world, monuments recall the chestnut tree: for example, in 2011, there was one unveiled in Jerusalem—an area of rusted steel with a solid wall topped by a 'stylised chestnut tree'.[145] It is beyond the scope of this book to deal extensively with all of the monuments that have been erected in memory of Anne.

On 28 April 2010, the Anne Frank Stichting celebrated the 50th anniversary of the Anne Frank House in the presence of Her Majesty the Queen. The presentation of *Het Achterhuis Online* (The Secret Annex Online) took place in the Westerkerk. *Het Achterhuis Online*[146] allows people not able to visit the Anne Frank House to take a digital journey though the rooms of the Secret Annex.

It is because of active conservation work that the remaining authentic traces of the people hiding in the Secret Annex will be preserved for posterity. Because Otto wanted to preserve the feeling of the abandoned hiding place, the rooms are not furnished. To get an impression of the hiding place and the main building, Otto had a replica made. Due to a misunderstanding, however, the furniture was constructed on a smaller scale than the rooms so that the rooms seem larger than they actually are. I noticed that the model gave a few foreign visitors an insufficient basis for being able to find their way in the former hiding place.

After my visit to the Secret Annex, I took pictures of the hiding address from the other side of the Prinsengracht. I then took a tour through the Westerkerk and, going up the steep stairs, I reached the top from where I had a breath-taking view. From the Westerkerk I saw the Prinsengracht and the long row of visitors for the Secret Annex. The new wing and the Secret Annex are clearly visible from the Westerkerk. The small attic window from which Anne could see the Westerkerk can also be seen from the Westerkerk.

I have my suspicions that, during the war, the Germans observed the area from the Westerkerk.

The last few years, the Anne Frank House has had more than one millions visitors each year.[147]

I walked back to the Amsterdam Central station on 9 Stationsplein and took the train home.

[1] *The Diaries*, 8 July 1942. So the Franks did not receive Margot's call-up on 8 July 1942, as Hans Ulrich states (*Wie was Anne Frank? Haar leven, het Achterhuis en haar dood* (Laren, 2010), p. 56. English edition: *Who was Anne Frank? Her life, the Secret Annex and her death. A short biography for young and old.* (Verbum, 2010)).

[2] *The Diaries*, 8 July 1942. 'During the early stages of the war [10 May 1940] we, particularly the children, were not yet aware of the camps and the abuse' (translation of a Dutch email from Francien Bachra, 8 January 2010).

[3] Manfred Bierganz and Annelie Kreutz, *Juden in Aachen* [Jews in Aachen] (Aachen, 1988), p. 85 (German only).

[4] Hans Ulrich incorrectly assumes that Anne only learned of the hiding plans on 8 July 1942. (*Wie was Anne Frank? Haar leven, het Achterhuis en haar dood* (Laren, 2010), p. 56.).

[5] A decree issued on 21 May 1942 ordered all Jews to hand in their cash, stocks and other possessions in excess of 250 guilders at the Lippmann, Rosenthal & Co bank.

[6] *The Diaries*, 5 July 1942.

[7] There were several hiding places in the Rivierenbuurt area, but these were too small to house a complete family
http://www.geheugenvanplanzuid.nl/tijdtijn/schuilplaats.htm (Dutch only).

[8] Hanneli Goslar told me that if Margot would have heeded the summons, she would have been deported to the Mauthausen concentration camp and the Frank's would have been notified of her death six weeks later (telephone interview, 6 January 2011).

[9] *The Diaries*, 8 July 1942.

[10] Bob Polak mentions there were three people (*Naar buiten, lucht en lachen! Een literaire wandeling door het Amsterdam van Anne Frank* [Outside: fresh air and laughter! A literary walk through Anne Frank's Amsterdam] (Amsterdam, 2006), p. 95).

[11] *The Diaries*, 8 July 1942.

[12] *The Diaries*, 8 July 1942.

[13] *The Diaries*, 8 July 1942.

[14] *The Diaries*, 9 July 1942.

[15] http://www.portretschap.nl/jet-schepp.

[16] http://www.geheugenvanplanzuid.nl/tijdtijn/bommen.htm.

[17] http://www.tijm.nl/rubriek2a/holocaust/eindrapport_project_woii.htm (Dutch only).

[18] http://vorige.nrc.nl/100jaar_voorpaginas/article1642496.ece.

[19] *The Diaries*, 10 July 1942.

[20] *The Diaries*, 11 July 1942.

[21] The *Noord-Hollands Archief* at 40 Jansstraat in Haarlem (http://www.noord-hollandsarchief.nl/engels/71/) managed the C. Keg Firm's archives. These have not been inventoried, nor was I able to obtain permission to access these archives.

[22] http://www.winkelstories.com/.

[23] *The Diaries*, 9 July 1942.

[24] *The Diaries*, 9 July 1942.

[25] *The Diaries*, 9 July 1942.
[26] *The Diaries*, 9 July 1942.
[27] *The Diaries*, 9 July 1942.
[28] *The Diaries*, 9 July 1942.
[29] *The Diaries*, 9 July 1942.
[30] *The Diaries*, 21 August 1942.
[31] *The Diaries*, 9 July 1942.
[32] *The Diaries*, 28 October 1942.
[33] *The Diaries*, 9 July 1942.
[34] *The Diaries*, 9 July 1942.
[35] Anne Frank, *Verhaaltjes, en gebeurtenissen uit het Achterhuis* (Amsterdam, 2005), pp. 85-88. English edition: *Tales from the Secret Annex. Including her Unfinished Novel Cady's Live* (Halban Publishers, 2010)
[36] http://www.annefrank.org/en/Anne-Frank/The-Nazis-occupy-the-Netherlands/Preparations-for-a-hiding-place/.
[37] http://www.destadgeschonden.nl/?page_id=64 (Dutch only).
[38] *The Diaries*, 11 July 1942.
[39] *The Diaries*, 15 October 1942.
[40] http://www.geheugenvanplanzuid.nl/tijdtijn/razzia's.htm.
[41] http://www.geheugenvanplanzuid.nl/tijdtijn/razzia's.htm.
[42] The Dutch term used here is 'kopgeld'; on the back flap of Ad van Liempt's book (*Nederlandse premiejagers op zoek naar joden* [Dutch Premium Hunters Looking for Jews] (Amsterdam, 2009)), it says that the Germans deployed the premium weapon in 1943 because the deportation of the Jews had stagnated. According to Anne Frank's words, reward money was already being paid towards the end of 1942.
[43] *The Diaries*, 19 November 1942.
[44] *The Diaries*, 17 April 1944.
[45] *The Diaries*, 25 May 1944.
[46] Bep Voskuijl was born on 5 July 1919 and on 4 August 1944 was 25 years old, and not 23 years old as Carol Ann Lee claims (*Pluk rozen op aarde en vergeet mij niet. Anne Frank 1929-1945*, p. 9. English editon: *Roses from the Earth: The Biography of Anne Frank* (Penguin Books, 2000).
[47] *The Diaries*, 26 July 1943.
[48] Max C. van der Glas, email dated 23 December 2010.
[49] *The Diaries*, 14 August 1942.
[50] http://www.annefrank.org/en/Museum/Exhibitions/Margot-Frank-items/Interview-Jetteke-Frijda/.
[51] *The Diaries*, 14 August 1942.
[52] *The Diaries*, 22 August 1942.
[53] *The Diaries*, 21 September 1942.
[54] http://www.trouw.nl/tr/nl/4324/nieuws/archief/article/detail/1708863/2005/10/27/Het-andere-huis-van-Anne-Frank-is-hersteld.dhtml.
[55] *The Diaries*, 29 October 1942.
[56] *De Amsterdamse Gids* [The Amsterdam Guide] (Amsterdam, 1930).
[57] *The Diaries*, 15 June 1943.

[58] *The Diaries*, 29 October 1943.
[59] *The Diaries*, 15 June 1942.
[60] *The Diaries*, 23 July 1943.
[61] Anne Frank, *Verhaaltjes, en gebeurtenissen uit het Achterhuis* (Amsterdam, 2005), p. 97.
[62] *The Diaries*, 23 February 1944.
[63] *The Diaries*, 23 February 1944.
[64] *The Diaries*, 9 August 1943.
[65] *The Diaries*, 16 September 1943.
[66] *The Diaries*, 7 May 1944.
[67] Carol Ann Lee sees no connection between this incident and a letter from Anne. Carol Ann Lee, *Anne Frank. Het leven van een jong meisje* [The Life of a Young Girl. The Definitive Biography.] (Amsterdam, 2009), p. 209.
[68] Dienke Hondius, *Absent. Herinneringen aan het Joods Lyceum Amsterdam 1941-1943* [Absent. Memories of the Jewish Lyceum in Amsterdam.] (Amsterdam, 2001) p. 220 (Dutch only).
[69] http://www.dbnl.org/tekst/_han001200301_01/_han001200301_01_0006.php, Dutch only (Ton Broos, 'De boekenplank van Anne Frank,' *Colloquium Neerlandicum* 15 (2003), does not mention that Anne also read writings that were censored by the Germans.)
[70] Francesca Hart and Marinus Schroevers, *Cinema en theater: Een fascinerende selectie uit de jaargangen 1921-1944.* [Cinema & Theatre. A Fascinating Selection from the 1921-1944 Issues] (Laren, 1975), p. 49.
[71] Francesca Hart and Marinus Schroevers, *Cinema en theater: Een fascinerende selectie uit de jaargangen 1921-1944* (Laren, 1975), p. 71 (Dutch only).
[72] http://www.kb.nl/galerie/tijdschriften/295.html.
[73] Francesca Hart and Marinus Schroevers, *Cinema en theater: Een fascinerende selectie uit de jaargangen 1921-1944* (Laren, 1975), p. 137 (Dutch only).
[74] Francesca Hart and Marinus Schroevers, *Cinema & Theater. Een fascinerende selectie uit de jaargangen 1921-1944* (Laren, 1975) (Dutch only).
75 Also called Leni Riesenstahl. In *Cinema en theater: Een fascinerende selectie uit de jaargangen 1921-1944* (Laren, 1975), p. 39 (Dutch only).
[76] Anne Frank, *Verhaaltjes, en gebeurtenissen uit het Achterhuis* (Amsterdam, 2005) pp. 71-76.
[77] *The Diaries*, 21 September 1942.
[78] *The Diaries*, 14 February 1944.
[79] *The Diaries*, 18 April 1944.
[80] *The Diaries*, 28 January 1944.
[81] *Amstelodamum* (Amsterdam, 1942).
[82] *Amstelodamum* (Amsterdam, 1943).
[83] *The Diaries*, 10 August 1943.
[84] *The Diaries*, 15 June 1942.
[85] *The Diaries*, 21 September 1942.
[86] http://www.joodsmonument.nl/person/498607?lang=en.
[87] *The Diaries*, 27 February 1943.

[88] *The Diaries*, 19 November 1942.
[89] David Barnouw, *Anne Frank voor beginners en gevorderden* (Den Haag, 1998), p. 88.
[90] Many of the Jews captured lived on Prinsengracht. See also: http://www.joodsmonument.nl/search?q_mm=prinsengracht.
[91] *The Diaries*, 28 January 1944.
[92] *The Diaries*, 28 January 1944.
[93] *The Diaries*, 3 October 1942.
[94] *The Diaries*, 6 October 1942.
[95] *The Diaries*, 9 October 1942.
[96] *The Diaries*, 3 February 1944.
[97] *The Diaries*, 27 April 1943.
[98] http://www.gerritvdveen.nl/OnzeSchool/Paginas/Verzetsheld.aspx.
[99] *The Diaries*, 18 May 1943.
[100] *The Diaries*, 19 July 1943.
[101] *The Diaries*, 26 July 1943.
[102] *The Diaries*, 26 July 1943.
[103] *The Diaries*, 23 March 1944.
[104] http://www.emielros.nl/bommenwerper/index.en.html.
[105] *The Diaries*, 23 March 1944.
[106] *The Diaries*, 29 March 1944.
[107] Frits Bolkenstein's grandfather (born in 1933).
[108] *De Dagboeken van Anne Frank*. Rijksinstituut voor Oorlogsdocumentatie (Amsterdam, 2001), p. 69.
[109] *The Diaries*, 29 March 1944.
[110] *The Diaries*, 10 October 1942.
[111] *The Diaries*, 28 November 1942.
[112] www.kranten.kb.nl.
[113] http://www.annefrank.org/en/Sitewide/Organisation/.
[114] *The Diaries*, 12 December 1942.
[115] *The Diaries*, 16 June 1942.
[116] Anne Frank, *Verhaaltjes, en gebeurtenissen uit het Achterhuis* (Amsterdam, 2005), pp. 98-99.
[117] *The Diaries*, 12 December 1942.
[118] *The Diaries*, 28 February 1944.
[119] During World War II the hunting down and arresting of Jews in hiding in the Netherlands was an important part of the work of the Dutch police. Many detectives did this work with great conviction and complete commitment. Ad van Liempt and Jan Kompagnie, *Jodenjacht*[Hunting for Jews] (Amsterdam, 2011).
[120] http://www.annefrank.de/fileadmin/user_upload/downloads/presse/PM_Stellungnahme_des_Anne_Frank_Zentrums_zum_Fall_Karl_Josef_Silberbauer_110411.pdf.
[121] The literature (such as: Hans Ulrich, *Wie was Anne Frank? Haar leven, het Achterhuis en haar dood* (Laren, 2010), p. 15) often forgets that Bep Voskuijl also helped rescue *The Diaries*.

[122] Philosopher and writer Bruno Bettelheim (1903-1990) was surprised that the Frank family had not made an escape plan.
[123] Max C. van der Glas, email dated 22 October 2010.
[124] David Barnouw and Gerrold van der Stroom. *Wie verraadde Anne Frank?* (Amsterdam, 2003). English edition: *Who Betrayed Anne Frank?* (Netherlands Institute for War Documentation, 2003).
[125] 'I believe the theory of the betrayal that Carol Ann Lee researched: Ahler [Tonny Ahlers (1917-2000)] and his friends' (Buddy Elias, email 30 December 2010).
[126] According to Max C. van der Glas (email 22 October 2010), the Frank family very likely was never at the Gestapo Headquarters but was put on the transport to the Westerbork Camp directly after their arrest.
[127] http://zoeken.nai.nl/CIS/persoon/3214.
[128] http://www.geheugenvanplanzuid.nl/tijdtijn/bommen.htm.
[129] http://www.verzetsmuseum.org/tweede-wereldoorlog/nl/achtergrond/achtergrond,amsterdam/bezet_en_bevrijd.
[130] Amsterdam City Archives Image Bank. Image no: HOFM0100223000001.
[131] http://adopteereenmonument.nl/oorlogsmonumenten/zoeken/monument-detail/_rp_main_elementId/1_472156.
[132] http://www.annefrank.org/timeline#!/en/Subsites/Timeline/Postwar-period-1945--present-day/The-diary-is-published/.
[133] *De Telegraaf* national newspaper, 5 October 2008.
[134] http://grachtenboek.hetgrachtenhuis.nl/zoeken.php?search=1&straat=prinsengracht&searchtype=1&eerste=161.
[135] Amsterdam City Archives Image Bank. Image no: 010097004269 (German only).
[136] Amsterdam City Archives Image Bank. Image no.: 010097001842 (German only).
[137] *The Diaries*, 1 March 1944.
[138] At the Janskerkhof in Utrecht there is a statue of Anne (http://www.4en5mei.nl/oorlogsmonumenten/zoeken/monument-detail/_rp_main_elementId/1_10680). (Getty Images confuses the statue of Anne in Utrecht with the statue of Anne in Amsterdam at the Westermarkt.) (http://www.gettyimages.nl/detail/3420898/Hulton-Archive, Dutch only).
[139] http://www.karindaan.nl/projecten/homomonument/.
[140] *The Diaries*, 6 January 1944.
[141] *The Diaries*, 7 March 1944.
[142] http://www.geheugenvanplanzuid.nl/tijdtijn/anneindebuurt.htm#kastanje.
[143] De Telegraaf, 9 April 2008.
[144] http://www.support-annefranktree.nl/node/206.
[145] http://www.support-annefranktree.nl/node/206.
[146] http://www.annefrank.org/en/Subsites/Home/.
[147] 261, 263 and 265 Prinsengracht are listed on the Dutch national heritage list (http://monumentenregister.cultureelerfgoed.nl/php/main.php, Dutch only).

CAMP WESTERBORK

Anne must have enjoyed the fresh air and freedom of movement after years of hiding, but her fears about the future would most likely have overshadowed all else. Whilst staying in the Secret Annex, Anne already knew about the Jews being gassed in camps. 'Our many Jewish friends are being taken away by the dozen. These people are treated by the Gestapo without a shred of decency; being loaded into cattle trucks and sent to Westerbork, the big Jewish camp in Drenthe. Westerbork sounds terrible; only one washing cubicle for a hundred people and not nearly enough lavatories. (....) It is impossible to escape; most of the people in the camp are branded as inmates by their shaven heads and many also by their Jewish appearance.

If it is as bad as this in Holland whatever will it be like in the distant and barbarous regions they are sent to? We assume that most of them are murdered. The English radio speaks of their being gassed. Perhaps that is the quickest way to die.'[1]

Her former classmate Nanette Konig, who would meet Anne later in Bergen-Belsen, was apparently not aware of the German death factories as a child. 'Were you [Nanette] actually aware of the existence of the concentration and death camps?' 'No, as children we didn't know anything about them.'[2]

Anne stayed in House of Detention I for a few days. In the courtyard, Anne may have met acquaintances who would have tried to cheer her up. There are no sources for this. The tram rails were extended into the courtyard so that no one on the street could see how the prisoners were treated when they had to disembark.[3] In the courtyard, the people who had been hiding boarded tram 16 that brought them to the Amsterdam Central Station on 8 August 1944.

It was very busy at the Amsterdam Central Station. Immediately after disembarking, the prisoners were sent to a particular side of the platform that had been closed off for this purpose. It was impossible to escape: there were armed guards everywhere.

Resistance fighter Janny Brilleslijper (1916-2003, hereafter referred to as Janny) had been arrested and was at the station that morning as well, where she saw the Frank family. 'The girls looked remarkably sporty, wearing tracksuits and carrying backpacks as if they were going on winter holiday. The atmosphere was a bit surreal—the silent morning, and all these people being put into the train. The trains had compartments with closing doors on two sides; you embarked and there you were. I observed these girls attentively. We did not speak during the journey.'[4] Janny Brilleslijper and her sister Lientje saw Anne and Margot again in the Westerbork Camp and in Bergen-Belsen, and survived the war.

The Frank family had to enter a passenger train of which a number of cars were reserved for Jews who were to go to the Westerbork Camp. The train ran a regular service to Assen and Groningen, and travelled at a normal speed. The prisoners were allowed to talk amongst themselves; the Germans did not want to arouse any suspicion. Anne looked through the window at the landscape. Mown fields of grain and trees flew by. It is possible that Anne could tell from the position of the sun that they were travelling north.

The Westerbork Camp (*Polizeiliches Durchgangslager Westerbork*) had been a reception camp for Jewish refugees (*Centrale Vluchtelingenkamp Westerbork*) before the German invasion. Queen Wilhelmina encouraged the establishment of the refugee camp in the north-western part of Drente, which was very isolated at that time, as she did not want to have a refugee camp 12 kilometres from her summer residence Paleis Het Loo in Apeldoorn.

The Germans adapted the camp to function as transit quarters in the way to the camps in the east. Dutch contractors profited from the German construction contracts and used the camp prisoners as cheap labour. In order to humiliate the Jews and break down their solidarity, the Jews were required to guard their own community. 'Divide and Conquer' was the motto of the camp leadership. The site covered approximately 100 hectares and, being surrounded by swamp and moorland, was difficult to reach. With the least bit of rain, the sandy roads turned to mud. The wind whipped up the sand and grime of the moors, and there were insects everywhere.

Camp leadership attempted to camouflage the role of the Westerbork Camp as a transit camp to death by setting it up as a town with stores and such; macabre, cynical, cruel and disrespectful. There was no synagogue.

Although the Westerbork Camp did not house only Jews, it is known to many as the Jewish City of 100,000 prisoners. The prisoners were a mixed group comprising parents, children, babies, women, girls, orphans, sick people, the blind, invalids, lunatics, pregnant women, the dying, the feeble-minded, Protestants, Christians, gypsies, political prisoners, homosexuals and Jews. The Nazis treated them all like dirt.

The train ride from Amsterdam to the Westerbork Camp took a number of hours. The train arrived in Hooghalen, a little south of Assen. There the train had to be shunted into a siding because, to get into the Westerbork Camp, the train had to take a turn and a part of the train had to be uncoupled. This completely new shunting yard had been constructed especially for the transports from all of the Netherlands to Westerbork.

Because of the shunting, the train rode slowly and directly into the Westerbork Camp and to the centrally placed platform (*Rampe*) right next to the main road. A field of yellow lupine lay in the centre of the camp. The main road, which ran from west to east, was dubbed 'Boulevard des Misères'. When the train arrived, every Westerbork 'inhabitant' would look to see if there were acquaintances amongst the prisoners. Anne was most likely also curious as to whether she knew anyone from Amsterdam. The prisoners had to get off and wait to see what happened next. There was likely much shouting on the part of the camp leadership, accompanied by the barking of their dogs.

Dutch agents subsequently handed over the Franks to the *Ordedienst* (OD, militia), who brought the prisoners to the quarantine barracks close to the platform.

After 'disinfection', the prisoners went to the parade grounds (the central square) where the Jewish camp staff—the so-called Flying Column—recorded their details and confiscated their ration books.

In the quarantine barracks, the robbing bankers' team of the German bank Lippmann, Rosenthal & Co. stripped the prisoners of their valuables. The male prisoners were shaved bald and the women's hair was cut short. The 'disinfection' was of little use since the prisoners had no soap and the camp was full of lice.

After going through the quarantine barracks, the Franks ended up in penal barracks number 67. Barracks number 66 was for 'convicts' as well. These barracks housed not only people who had been hiding but also resistance fighters and those who had tried to flee; they wore blue overalls with a red patch on the shoulder. Their shoes were confiscated and replaced with clogs.[5]

These convicts had to work harder than the other prisoners, both inside and outside of the camp, and they were not allowed to go beyond the barbed-wire fence of the penal barracks. They would walk under guard to their workplace at the east side of the camp. At the rear of the penal barracks was a ditch with guards.

The convicts were given less to eat than the others, and often were made to endure punishment drills and other forms of sadism. In the summer, plagues of mosquitoes and eye infections were common. The commander of the Westerbork Camp, Albert Konrad Gemmeker (1907-1982), lived in a luxurious villa.

The villa stood in sharp contrast to the barracks. In the Westerbork Camp, surrounded by electrified barbed-wire fencing and watch towers, there were 107 barracks in total with bunk beds, three rows above each other. Altogether, 300 people 'lived' in each barracks. The light was usually broken, it was drafty, and most of the windows were broken as well. Despite the wind that blew through the barracks, it was oppressive inside and stank. Here and there, suitcases lay under the beds. The furniture consisted of rough wooden tables and narrow wooden benches. The prisoners shuffled along the narrow paths between the numbered wooden beds.

Because of the rain, mosses grew on the barracks. Relations were strained amongst the massed people who lived in uncertainty about their future and were often sick and exhausted, which led to much yelling, coughing and arguing in the barracks.

There was a fixed schedule in the Westerbork Camp; first role call and then off to work at 5 a.m. The hours spent on the parade grounds, as well as the torment at the hands of the guards, contrast sharply with my own relaxed stroll through the nature surrounding the Westerbork Camp with its moors, little pools of water, and forest.

The children, including Anne, worked in the battery demolition line where they sat at long shored-up tables, breaking open the batteries of shot-down planes with a hammer and chisel. The black tar-like substance was scooped out of the batteries by hand and gathered in a basket. The bar of carbon was collected in a basket next to it. Finally, the metal caps had to be removed with a screwdriver; they were put in a third basket.

Hitting one's own fingers was not uncommon, and at times breathing was difficult because of the poisonous vapours. Refusal to work, however, would result in deportation. The battery yard was in the eastern section of the camp behind the parade grounds.[6]

Anne and Margot received help from acquaintances they met in the Westerbork Camp. Bloeme Emden (born in 1926) knew Anne and Margot from the Joods Lyceum grammar school and higher professional education in Amsterdam, and in the battery yard they exchanged stories about their experiences during hiding. In the camp, Anne and Margot had contact with resistance fighters Janny and Lientje Brilleslijper (1912-1988, hereafter referred to as Lientje), Rachel Frankfoorder (born in 1914, hereafter referred to as Rachel) and Rose de Liema. Rachel would meet Anne later in Bergen-Belsen. The 88-year-old Rose was present at the exhibition on Anne Frank in the former Westerbork Camp on 12 June 2009.

In the camp, Anne maintained contact with her parents and the Van Pels family, with whom she had been in hiding.

Working in the battery yard did not guarantee that one would not be deported. In the penal barracks on 2 September 1944, the Jewish

OD and a German official read out the names of those who were to go on the next transport: Hermann, Auguste and Peter, Fritz, Otto, Edith, Margot and Anne. For those who thought that liberation was in sight, this was a catastrophe.

At sunrise, the 'Boulevard des Misères' was blocked off and guards sent the prisoners to the platform. Some of them had trouble getting in the train because it was so much higher than the platform. The Flying Column used brute force to get everyone on as quickly as possible. The OD chalked the number of prisoners on the outside of each carriage, which left on Sunday, 3 September 1944. It was the 93rd and also the last transport from the Westerbork Camp to Auschwitz. That same day, the allies freed Brussels; the next day, Antwerp was freed.

At Hooghalen, the train was shunted to a different track and travelled in the direction of Hoogeveen. The *Nederlandse Spoorwegen* (Dutch Railway) provided transport up to Nieuweschans. From there, the *Deutsche Reichsbahn Gesellschaft* (German National Railroad Alliance) took over the transportation to Auschwitz. Of the 1,019 Jews transported in the cattle-trucks, 127 survived the war.

The Westerbork Camp was liberated on 12 April 1945. The day before the liberation, the commander abandoned ship. By that time, Anne had already died in Bergen-Belsen. The allies did not burn the camp. In contrast to, for example, Bergen-Belsen, there were no bodies here, and there was no great danger of a contagion.

Up until 1948, the Westerbork Camp served as an internment camp for members of the *Nationaalsocialistische Beweging* (Dutch National Socialist Movement), collaborators and Germans, and from 1949 on it was a refuge for Dutch nationals who fled the former Dutch East Indies following its independence. In 1951, the Westerbork Camp was a shelter for demobilized *Koninklijk Nederlandsch-Indisch Leger* (Royal Dutch East-Indian Army) soldiers from the Maluku Islands; the camp was renamed Schattenberg. The Dutch authorities did not like to be reminded of the assistance they had given the Germans, and immediately following the war many Dutch people did not feel the need to be reminded of it either. No one made any effort to preserve penal barracks 67.[7]

Now a self-appointed protector of heritage goods, the government at that time did not exert itself to preserve the original traces of war.

In 1951, the Westerbork Camp crematorium was lost as a living memory for future generations, despite the desire of the '1940-1945 Foundation'[8] to preserve the building as '(...) a symbol of the tyranny of National Socialism and the suffering and death of Israelites and members of the resistance. The Crematorium is a historical monument and an authentic piece of war documentation.'[9]

Plans to keep the site of the former camp intact as a memorial of the past war never got off the ground. It was less scary to glance into space than face one's own past. In 1967, the Provincial Executive of Drenthe approved placing satellite dishes on the site.

The need for commemoration gradually arose amongst the (grand)children of the camp survivors and the younger generation. On 4 May 1970, approximately a year before the last South Moluccans left Schattenberg, the National Westerbork Monument was unveiled by Queen Juliana in the presence of several dignitaries and the press. In September of 1970, a number of camp survivors were present at the unveiling of the National Westerbork Monument, organised by *Het Nederlands Auschwitz Comité* (The Dutch Auschwitz Committee). A memorial service is held on 4 May each year at the National Westerbork Monument.

I took the A28 in the direction of Assen and reached Hooghalen by exit 31, direction Westerbork. The site of the former concentration camp is relatively accessible in the early morning, which allowed me the opportunity to take some photographs. Not many people were there; only a few enthusiasts playing a traditional Dutch outdoor bowling game along the educational route. Is this an outing or am I working?

I walked along the educational route to the Westerbork observatory situated on the former camp site—observing the stars while the pain of the past has not yet been properly dealt with. My walk in this quiet misty environment is quite a contrast to the suffering that took place here and the shouts of the guards. The prisoners had very different things on their mind than the beauty of nature, the way the light falls, composition and contrast management.

Camp survivor Ralph Prins (born 1926) designed the National Westerbork Monument representing the thirty-nine trains that left the transit camp to go to the extermination camps in the east. The monument consists of a forty-metre-long train line, 93 railway sleepers, and rails that end rising toward the skies. Four railway sleepers left loose symbolise the four transports that left from somewhere else to go to Eastern Europe. From a distance, the wall of local boulders seems to be a pile of skulls: this wall prevents the monument from being seen, as it were. In front of it is the buffer stop, close to where the track from Hooghalen to the camp ended during the war as well. Ralph Prins purposely did not use the original buffer stop that still stands behind the wall. The same is true for all the materials of the monument; nothing is originally from the camp itself—not even the rails. Inscribed on two marble slabs is the Biblical text of Lamentations 4:18[10]: 'They hunt our steps, that we cannot go in our streets; our end is near, our days are fulfilled; for our end is come.'

In 1971, the last South Moluccans families left and all the barracks were demolished, including the penal barracks of the Frank family. Right under the nose of the National Westerbork Monument, so to speak, the original traces of war were demolished. I find this action difficult to reconcile with preserving our cultural heritage, providing space for mourning, and facing up to history.

Now there is only a scale model of the barracks. Commerce was fixated on Anne's Diaries and the Secret Annex, and saving the other buildings that were reminders of Anne just was not important. In 1983, the Westerbork Camp Memorial Centre was opened by the then Queen Beatrix. A private initiative began the Memorial Centre, but, since the opening, the national government has viewed it as a national institution. The National Westerbork Monument is the property of the province Drenthe, and the management and maintenance of the monument, the camp site and the Memorial Centre are subsidised.

In the Memorial Centre, a barracks, including its interior, has been reconstructed. The barracks looks quite comfortable as I walk around in the heated Memorial Centre. In reality, Anne's barracks was filthy and overcrowded. I sincerely hope that Anne's penal barracks will be reconstructed on the former camp site. Now there are only a few concrete wall panels (not the original ones) to serve as a reminder of that barracks. The concrete construction has windows without glass, and there are many cracks; it does not require much imagination to picture how draughty the original barracks would have been. Next to the location of the former penal barracks, part of the private house (lavatory) has been reconstructed in order to demonstrate the lack of privacy.

In the Memorial Centre, the story of the inhabitants of the Westerbork Camp is illustrated through photographs, objects, personal stories, drawings, letters and diaries.

At the entrance, I come across a photograph of Anne. 'A suitcase full of hope' tells the story of the Jewish refugees from Germany. I do not know if Anne wrote letters in the Westerbork Camp. In any case, they were not saved: my inquiries at the Anne Frank Stichting and the Westerbork Camp proved fruitless.

According to Hanneli Goslar, the prisoners in the Westerbork Camp were allowed to write a postcard once a week.[11] Buddy Elias states that Jews in concentration camps were not allowed to write letters,[12] nor were any letters or cards from Anne that she might have written in Auschwitz-Birkenau or Bergen-Belsen saved. When striving to garner insight into her experiences in the Secret Annex, we rely on, for the most part, Anne's diaries; for the seven-month period she spent in camp we mainly rely on eyewitness reports.

Despite the severe censoring of letters, prisoners sometimes succeeded (through smuggling) in writing letters to their friends or family outside of the camp. Marianne (Marleen) Helena Godschalk (1927-1943) wrote to Ilse Jacobsen about her memories of her school, the Joods Lyceum.

Marianne lived at Millestraat 40 II in Amsterdam and perished in Sobibor. Esther (Etty) Hillesum (1914-1943)—a good fifteen years older than Anne—had studied law and worked for the Jewish Council. At first, in connection with her work, she was permitted simply to walk in and out of the Westerbork Camp; however, in July 1943, she lost this special privilege. On 7 September 1943, Etty Hillesum, together with her parents and her brother Mischa, was deported by the Nazis to the Auschwitz concentration camp where she died on 30 November 1943 at the age of 29. In 1981, 38 years after her death, her diary was published and translated into many languages. The diary is a very personal document that reveals the madness of the Holocaust.

In cooperation with the KNBLO Wandelsportorganisatie Nederland (Netherlands Hiking Organisation), the Memorial Centre organises an annual Westerbork Camp Walking Tour. The purpose of the walk is to draw attention to the history of the camp through sports. 'At this historical place, the lives of more than a hundred thousand Jewish Dutch people are commemorated,' the Westerbork Camp Memorial Centre website states.[13] Unfortunately, however, the former camp site contains few tangible memories of World War II. Incidentally, Anne was not actually Dutch but a German refugee.

Another reference to the history of the camp is the Westerbork Trail. The Westerbork Trail follows a path of about 336 kilometres from the Hollandsche Schouwburg—a depot for Jews in Amsterdam during the war—to the Westerbork Camp.

Eyewitness accounts are biased at times, and often are dated years after the liberation of the Westerbork Camp. Moreover, the fact that much of the original layout has disappeared makes it even more difficult to reconstruct Anne's life. This is a missed opportunity, especially since it was not necessary to burn down the camp immediately after its liberation.

During Anne's time, the Westerbork Camp was filled with barracks, ranging from an orphanage to a German Security Service bunker,[14] and unpaved roads. Now the Westerbork Camp is paved, neatly divided into perfectly manicured lawns, an abundance of symbols and an ever-present silence. 'I no longer recognise it as Camp Westerbork,' Nanette Konig states.[15]

Silent Witnesses could make a significant contribution to Anne's memory and that of the other prisoners—most certainly once the last people who have known Anne will have passed away. Then there will be only 'indirect' materials, such as photographs, drawings and archive items.

With the exception of the commander's villa, there are only a few remainders of the original platform that remind one of the raw reality. The tree along the main road, with Anne's barracks in the background, dates from after the war. The watchtower, with its barbed-wire fence, was reconstructed following the war. The barbed wire is a clear sign that the Westerbork Camp was a place where people were locked up.

The Resistance Monument in the south-western section reminds us of the ten resistance fighters executed by a firing squad of the German occupying forces on 20 September 1943 at Witterveld near Assen. The monument consists of a large cross and is inscribed with the names of the resistance fighters. The crematorium, which was demolished, is not on the *Explanation of the Numbers on the Map of the Westerbork Camp* dated June 1944.

The original buildings, such as the kitchen and workshops, have been demolished and are marked by means of low grassy mounds, stones and signs. The slopes give an idea as to the original location and size of the buildings. The structure of the old (originally unpaved) plan of pathways has been restored. Information plates indicate the function of the barracks at that time.

I find it bitter that the former wooden villa of the camp commander has remained standing, whereas a fire in Veendam in 2009 destroyed the barracks in which Anne dismantled batteries. 'It is a cruel twist of history that the residence of the camp commander still stands,' the website of the Westerbork Camp states. It is, however, not history but human actions and failures that are responsible for this.

In 2012, archaeologists excavated the former camp site in preparation for the renovation of the residence of the camp commander. Perhaps the excavations of the garbage site will reveal former prisoners' belongings.[16]

Close to the entrance of the camp and the residence of the former camp commander stand the Markers of Westerbork,[17] designed by Victor Levie (born 1955) and brought into being on the initiative of Jules Schelvis (born 1921),[18] survivor of Sobibor. For every destination camp of the deportations—Sobibor, Mauthausen, Bergen-Belsen, Auschwitz-Birkenau and Theresienstadt—a marker has been erected in memory of those deported and the victims. Almost 107,000 Jews in total were deported from the Westerbork Camp to the concentration and extermination camps. In Bergen-Belsen, more than 1,700 Jews (from the Netherlands) were killed, including Anne. Most of the Jews were murdered in Auschwitz-Birkenau; more than 56,500 Jews, and more than 200 Sinti and Roma people from the Netherlands.

The Westerbork Portraits exhibition in the Memorial Centre gives a face to the victims; however, there is no portrait of Anne.

A central information point in the middle of the site provides some background information as to the history of the camp, and a scale model provides a good overview of the layout of the Westerbork Camp. Right next to it is the Jerusalem Stone, an Israeli Holocaust monument. This stone, hewn from the hills of Jerusalem, is a gift from the State of Israel. The memorial stone was unveiled on 3 March 1993 by the Israeli president at that time, Chaim Herzog, in the presence of the then Queen Beatrix and many other interested parties. A similar stone can also be found in Auschwitz and in Bergen-Belsen. The Jerusalem Stone commemorates the victims of Nazi terror and the Westerbork Camp. The stone has a Bible quotation inscribed:

'… their image shall be forever before my eyes' (Psalm 38:18).

On the original parade grounds of the Westerbork Camp, 102,000 stones were placed at the initiative of former camp prisoners: 102,000 times a mother, a father, a grandfather, a sister, a friend, a classmate, a … were killed in the extermination camps. The monument was erected with the support of Dutch municipalities. The stones were placed at various heights; the persecution of the Jews entails the story of one person—but then told 102,000 times over. The red stones have a silver Star of David on the top.

Moreover, 200 stones have a flame on the top, symbolising the Sinti and Roma people imprisoned in the Westerbork Camp and murdered. Importantly, 100 stones have no symbol, representing the resistance fighters who were held captive in the Westerbork Camp and deported. The stones are positioned within the outlines of a map of the Netherlands.

Over time, the names of the victims of the Holocaust were collected. In the Memorial Centre, these names, along with the dates and places of birth and places and dates of death (read: murder), are continuously projected onto a special Name Wall.

Of note is the fact that 5,000 of the 107,000 Jews (from the Westerbork Camp) returned to the Netherlands. As stated earlier, of the 140,000 Jews, 102,000 did not survive the war. In comparison to other countries, a relatively large number of Jews from the Netherlands were murdered, which is due to various factors including the many officials cooperating with the Germans, the high concentration of Jews in Amsterdam, the cooperation of the Jewish Council, and the fact that the resistance, which has done much good, started relatively late in the Netherlands.

[1] *The Diaries*, 9 October 1942.
[2] Theo Coster, *Klasgenoten van Anne Frank* (Amsterdam, 2009), pp. 145-146 English edition: *We All Wore Stars. Memories of Anne Frank from Her Classmates* (Macmillan, 2011).
[3] Leny Boeken-Velleman, *Breekbaar, maar niet gebroken* [Fragile, but not Broken] (Laren, 2008), p. 60.
[4] Willy Lindwer, *De laatste zeven maanden van Anne Frank. Het ongeschreven laatste hoofdstuk van het Dagboek* (Hilversum, 2008), p. 75. English edition: *The last Seven Months of Anne Frank. The stories of six women who knew Anne Frank.* (MacMillan, 2004).
[5] Carol Ann Lee, *Anne Frank. Het leven van een jong meisje* [The Life of a Youngj girl. The Definitive Biography] (Amsterdam, 2009), p. 222.
[6] Explanation of the numbers on the map of the Westerbork Camp, June 1944.
[7] I follow the order of numbers of the objects on 'Explanation of the numbers on the map of the Westerbork Camp' dated June 1944.
[8] http://www.st4045.nl/ (Dutch only).
[9] http://www.kampwesterbork.nl/en/museum/camp-grounds/resistance-memorial/index.html#/index
[10] http://www.kampwesterbork.nl/en/museum/camp-grounds/the-national-westerbork-memorial/index.html#/index
[11] Hannah Goslar (telephone interview 6 January 2011).
[12] Buddy Elias, email dated 30 December 2010.
[13] http://historiek.net/wandeltochten-bij-kamp-westerbork/12572/
[14] Map of the Westerbork Camp situation in June 1944.
[15] Theo Coster, *Klasgenoten van Anne Frank* (Amsterdam, 2009), p. 140.
[16] www.volkskrant.nl 6 December 2011.
[17] http://www.4en5mei.nl/oorlogsmonumenten/zoeken/monument-detail/_rp_main_elementId/1_6768 (Dutch only),
[18] http://www.sobiborinterviews.nl/index.php?option=com_content&view=article&id=14.

AUSCHWITZ-BIRKENAU

'No one is spared—old people, children, babies, expectant mothers, the sick—each and all join in the march of death. (...) And all because they are Jews!'[1]

Hours went by after the departure from the Westerbork Camp. On its way, the packed train stood still for hours in Germany when an air raid by the Allies was anticipated. It was summer, the sun was hot and everyone was terribly thirsty. The prisoners relieved themselves in a bucket and people collapsed from exhaustion.

The train made a sharp turn in the direction of a long, low building with a gabled roof, and arrived at the Auschwitz-Birkenau platform (hereafter referred to as Auschwitz II) in the village of Brezinka during the night of 5-6 September 1944, after a horrible three-day trip.

The sight of the crematory chimney spewing fire, the stink, the barking of dogs, the searchlights and shouting Germans must have been very frightening for Anne.

Auschwitz II covered a good 2 square kilometres. East of Auschwitz II was Auschwitz I and the Buna Werken IG Farbenindustrie (Auschwitz III). Together, Auschwitz I, II and III covered sixty square kilometres.[2] Auschwitz II was a death factory where Jews were treated not as people but as a means of production.

The camp doctor Josef Mengele (1911-1979, hereafter referred to as Mengele), who was nicknamed the Angel of Death, decided on life or death. Upon arrival at the platform, the first selection was made: those who were sent to the left went directly to the gas chambers; this would often be children under fifteen and older adults. Hermann van Pels, aged 46 at the time, was gassed directly upon arrival. Otto was 55 when he arrived in Auschwitz, Anne was 15. Mengele assessed the prisoners on the basis of looks: apparently, he thought Otto could contribute to productivity.

The Frank family probably looked relatively healthy because they came from the relatively 'comfortable' Westerbork Camp. The Frank family was separated on the platform of Auschwitz II. Otto would never see his daughters and wife again.

Subsequently, the prisoners who survived the first selection walked from the platform to the *Zentralsauna* (Central Sauna) in the western part of Auschwitz II. Prisoners who volunteered to use the truck to get to the *Zentralsauna* ended up in the gas chambers after all, which were situated close to the *Zentralsauna*.

The warehouses with the prisoners' belongings—the so-called 'Canada barracks'—were also in the western part of the camp.

In the *Zentralsauna*, the prisoners were robbed of the rest of their personal property, gold teeth included, and a number was tattooed on their lower arm. The guards forced the women to undress and made them stand under a freezing cold or boiling hot stream of water. In the 'beauty parlour', underarm and pubic hair was removed, and the head was shaved bald with dull scissors. Prisoners were handled roughly so that many of them were injured or suffered hypothermia.

The stuffing of the German soldiers' sleeping bags at the war front consisted of prisoners' hair. Good clothing from the prisoners was washed in a disinfectant and given to German families.

I was deeply impressed by my visit to the *Zentralsauna*. The building, the floor and the halls were still the original ones. I could feel the despair of the prisoners, including Anne, who also had to undergo the humiliating walk through the *Zentralsauna*.

After the *Zentralsauna*, Anne, Margot and Edith ended up in one of the quarantine barracks (BIIa) on the east side of Auschwitz II. Following the quarantine, Anne was in one of the 27 barracks in the women's camp (BIb) located in the south-western part of the camp. The tracks led from BIIa to BIb.[3] The platform was somewhat north-east of the women's camp.[4]

A barracks measured approximately 44 x 8 metres, and was built on marshy grounds without a foundation, causing much rain to stream into the building. The latrine was a row of holes. There was no privacy at all. Rows of three wooden beds above each other left little room to sit up straight. Each bed usually accommodated two prisoners. The beds were built of unprocessed wood with a straw mattress or just some loose straw, and two blankets per bed. The blankets and straw mattresses were filthy from bleeding and festering sores. Moreover, faeces and urine from prisoners suffering from diarrhoea and polyuria (increased urine discharge) often dripped down from the bed above.

Whoever could not get a place on a bed had to lie on the mucky ground. The prisoners' thin clothing—the so-called zebra clothes—did not protect the prisoners from the draught. It was already chilly in September, especially at night, whereas during the summer it was hot and stuffy, and mosquito plagues were prevalent. The mosquitoes came from the surrounding moist swamps.

The prisoners washed themselves with the filthy water in the huts located on the south side of the camp. They were undernourished and weak and thus vulnerable to many diseases. The damaged skin of the prisoners could not tolerate sunlight. Diseases were also spread by the filthy water and the rats. Many prisoners suffered from malaria, typhoid fever, paratyphoid fever and scabies.

Despite the fact that the prisoners often had become very weak, they were exposed to a severe regime by the sadistic camp leadership. At 03:30 a.m., the shrill whistles sounded, upon which the prisoners were driven outside by the camp guards. After a meagre breakfast the camp prisoners were forced to do heavy labour. No machines were used for work in the camp. Many prisoners died during the hard labour, which included pulling heavy cement rollers. Anne, Margot and Edith cut sod and lugged heavy stones.[5] Another torment was having to stand still for prolonged periods on the parade grounds at random times.

The German company IG Farben, which made Zyklon B in Frankfurt am Main, used labourers from Auschwitz and had a factory (the *Bunawerke*, Auschwitz III) in Monowitz, close to Oświęcim, where synthetic rubber and petrol were manufactured. Many ancillary camps of Auschwitz were in Silesia, near furnaces, mines and factories, where prisoners were doing the heavy work in coal mines, arms factories and chemical manufacturing plants. Prisoners were not allowed to take breaks: instead, they received whiplashes and beatings. The fast pace, the heavy work, little food, thirst, diseases, the beatings and other degrading conditions caused many prisoners to die prematurely from exhaustion and disease. Dead prisoners or those abused with shovels or sticks were dragged away on wheelbarrows. Prisoners who could no longer work were sent to the infirmary or the gas chambers.

The evening meal was also meagre. Anne fairly doled out the food to the prisoners so that there were no arguments. Many other prisoners stole, beat and cheated their fellow prisoners in order to stay alive. Anne and Margot received much support from friends they knew from the Westerbork Camp. Anne, Margot and their mother helped one another in the struggle to survive, and the arguments in the Secret Annex had probably been forgiven and forgotten.

Anne was most likely a witness to many terrors in the camp, such as the regular executions and hangings of prisoners. Terrible things also happened behind closed doors. Mengele carried out felonious medical experiments on twins. Adult prisoners were forced to sit in ice baths for the purpose of army experiments. Essentially, there was no human dimension at all. Anne cried when she saw Hungarian gypsy girls standing in the streaming rain outside of the gas chambers.[6]

The camp leadership in Auschwitz felt the Russians breathing down its neck and were preparing to evacuate the camps in the east.

On 7 October 1944, the young and strong women from Anne's block number 29 were selected to work in a munitions factory in Czechoslovakia. Anne, Margot and Edith remained in Auschwitz II. Edith became more and more ill.

Anne had scabies and was sent to the *Krätzeblock*—the scabies barracks. Scabies was caused by mites that would burrow into the skin, resulting in very painful sores. Margot volunteered to go with Anne and got scabies as well. Anne and Margot were selected to go to Bergen-Belsen on 30 October 1944. Rootje de Winter witnessed: Anne and Margot step forward: 'Then it was both girls' turn… And there they stood for a moment, naked and bald. Anne looked straight at us with her innocent eyes, and then they were gone. We weren't able to see what happened to them next. We heard Mrs Frank cry out: "The children! O God."[7] Anne and Margot were separated from their mother for good. Auschwitz was not the last judgment for Anne, but it proved to be death's gate.

Edith remained in Auschwitz where she died on 6 January 1945—three weeks before its liberation. Notably, 6 January 1945 was also the day of the last execution in Auschwitz: 70 Polish people and four Jewish women were sentenced to death because of their (alleged) contribution to an uprising in Auschwitz (II). They were hanged on the scaffold.

Auschwitz was liberated by the Soviet army on 27 January 1945.

The Allies, who had taken aerial photographs of Auschwitz in May and August 1944 and had bombarded the IG Farben factory, made no attempt to destroy the railway lines that led to the extermination camp, even though the Americans and the British were well aware of the mass murder of Jews. More than one and a half million Jews died in Auschwitz.

In 1986, the *Nederlands Auschwitz Comité* (Dutch Auschwitz Committee) began organising trips to the various concentration and extermination camps in Poland centred on commemoration and keeping the memory alive. Prior to my own trip, I became acquainted with the other participants and the contents of the programme during a visit to Amsterdam.

During this trip in 2008, I met employees of the Anne Frank Stichting, the *Nederlands Instituut voor Oorlogsdocumentatie* (NIOD Institute for War, Holocaust and Genocide Studies), the *Joods Maatschappelijk Werk* (JMW, Jewish Social Work) and the *Nationaal Comité 4 en 5 mei* (National Committee for 4 and 5 May).

For the relatives of the Holocaust victims, this trip was a difficult and very emotional event. During our stay, camp survivors and resistance fighters related their experiences. My attention was specifically directed towards Anne. Everyone could share their experiences with the others. The trip was purposely organised in November so that we could experience the Polish cold.

During the trip to Poland I visited various concentration camps, a number of Polish cities, and Jewish monuments and synagogues. Cracow, situated on the Vistula River, is the largest city in Poland after Warsaw, and was the capital of Poland until 1609. At present, Cracow is recognised as one of the most important cultural cities in Europe and is referred to as the 'Florence of the North'. Poland and its inhabitants and soldiers suffered greatly during the war, but Cracow was one of the few cities in Poland that remained intact throughout World War II.

I also visited the Jewish cemetery in Warsaw. One of my travelling companions pointed out that I had to cover my head. It did not have to be a *yarmulka* (skull cap). I put on my woollen hat. It was cold and dusky. Another traveller directed my attention to a portrait of Anne at the children's monument where I saw pictures of other children as well. I did not know these children, but their lives undoubtedly ended tragically as well. There were candles burning; children were being commemorated by their family and friends.

The cemetery seemed dismal to me. Autumn leaves lay on the ground. There were many tombstones, some of which were damaged, had fallen over, or were grown over by bushes. The cemetery looks out on a concrete block of flats.

World War II brought tragedy to the Polish capital Warsaw; the Jewish ghetto in the city was destroyed by the Germans. In the post-war period, the old centre was rebuilt in the old style, and the city, like Cracow, is now included on the UNESCO World Heritage List.

Poland has been harassed by various powers—not only by Germany but also by Russia. Moreover, other population groups besides the Germans persecuted the Jews in Eastern Europe. The Jewish Cemetery, the Nożyk synagogue in Warsaw and the Jewish quarter *Kazimierz* in Cracow are reminders of the rich Jewish life of yesteryear, now gone forever.

The Jews in Poland (and elsewhere) were driven from their houses and eventually ended up in Auschwitz. Whilst the former Westerbork and Bergen-Belsen concentration camps are currently dominated by symbols, Auschwitz is marked by the grey (black) reality that is to be seen in the ruins of the gas chambers and crematories.

I could walk freely through the gates that led to one of the former crematories. There were tourists walking around in tracksuits. During the war, however, those entering the gates to the gas chambers were doomed.

There was a beautiful tree dressed in autumn colours next to an old water reservoir. People were milling around the former main entrance to Auschwitz II. I saw a group of young people from Israel holding in their hands white flags with the image of the Star of David and two blue stripes. They placed wreaths with a blue and a white horizontal stripe and carnations at the end of the platform on the buffer stop and between the rails to commemorate their people.

From 1943, prisoners were transported directly into Auschwitz II by train. Contrary to the claims of some, Anne therefore did not pass through the famous gate of Auschwitz I with its text *Arbeit macht frei*.[8] It is not only the remains of the five former gas chambers and crematories that remind us of the madness of the past: details such as the hatch in a gas chambers' ceiling through which the Germans threw Zyklon B are also well preserved.

Even beyond the museum boundaries, there are visible traces in the urban landscape of Oświęcim, indicating the destruction of the Jews supported by industrial resources, such as the railway line that runs right through the houses' backyards.

Luckily, attention is being directed to the preservation of the original camp site and authentic reminders so that there will not be countless models of concentration camps reconstructed throughout the world outside of the context. However, the Auschwitz-Birkenau Foundation needs more money for a long-lasting restoration of the former extermination camp.

The Dutch Pavilion pays special attention to the fate of the Dutch Jews during World War II. Attention is also paid to Anne's history, and quotations from Anne's diary are displayed. There are photographs of her time at the Merwedeplein in Amsterdam.

I remained somewhat aloof from the memorial service of the *Nederlands Auschwitz Comité*. Preferring to walk alone for a while, I headed in the direction of the main office of the camp commander. On both sides of the long paths there are ruins of barracks, crematories and gas chambers. The desolate surroundings were more compelling without the distraction of visitors. The sun was already sinking in the late afternoon sky as a red glow swept over the barbed wire.

[1] *The Diaries,* 19 November 1942.
[2] The photograph of two tourists in tracksuits on page 15 (Erik Borgman and Liesbeth Hoeven, *Sporen van afwezigheid. Gedenken in stemmen, stenen en stilte* [Traces of Absence: Commemorating in Voices, Stones and Silence] (Zoetermeer, 2011)) was not taken in Auschwitz-Birkenau (Auschwitz II), but in Auschwitz I. The Auschwitz complex consisted of three parts: Auschwitz I, the concentration camp famous for the gruesome text hanging above the entrance 'ARBEIT MACHT FREI' [WORK MAKES ONE FREE]; the second part, Auschwitz II (Birkenau), the extermination camp; and the third part (Monowitz), the work camp with its subcamps. Only the concentration camp and the extermination camp (Auschwitz I and II) were open to visitors.
[3] Map of the former concentration camp Auschwitz II-Birkenau (Brezinka).
[4] My gratitude goes out to Mrs Wojciech Plosa (Head of Archive Państwowe Muzeum Auschwitz-Birkenau), who drew the position of the women's camp (BIb), the platform, the quarantine barracks (BIIa), the *Zentralsauna* and the main entrance of Auschwitz-Birkenau for me on a 1943 map (letter, 5 January 2009). No maps of Auschwitz-Birkenau dating from 1944 have been preserved.
[5] http://www.annefrank.org/en/Anne-Frank/Discovery-and-arrest/The-destiny-of-the-people-in-hiding/The-fate-of-the-women-from-the-Secret-Annex/.
[6] Carol Ann Lee, *Anne Frank. Het leven van een jong meisje* [The life of a young Girl. The Definitive Biography] (Amsterdam, 2009), p. 237.
[7] http://www.annefrank.org/en/Anne-Frank/Discovery-and-arrest/The-destiny-of-the-people-in-hiding/The-fate-of-the-women-from-the-Secret-Annex/.
[8] According to Max C. van der Glas (email 22 December 2010), Anne was never in Auschwitz I. According to Carol Ann Lee (*Pluk rozen op aarde en vergeet mij niet. Anne Frank 1929-1945,* p. 198), the women, including Anne, walked through the arched gateway with the text *Arbeit macht frei* and this was the entrance gate to Birkenau. That had to have been in Auschwitz I. Buddy Elias (email 30 December 2010) also believes that Anne walked through the gate with the famous inscription. The train that Anne was on, however, rode straight through the gate of the main entrance of Auschwitz-Birkenau to the platform. The claim by Hans Ulricht (*Wie was Anne Frank? Haar leven, het Achterhuis en haar dood* (Verbum, 2010, p. 88) English edition: *Who was Anne Frank? Her life, the Secret Annex and her death. A short biography for young and old* (Verbum, 2010)) that Anne and the other prisoners were made to walk to the extermination camp Auschwitz-Birkenau is also incorrect.

BERGEN-BELSEN

'I simply can't build up my hopes on a foundation consisting of confusion, misery and death. I see the world gradually being turned into a wilderness, I hear the ever approaching thunder, which will destroy us too, I can feel the suffering of millions (...).'[1]

Like the Westerbork Camp, Bergen-Belsen has a history that precedes its being arranged as a concentration camp by the Nazis. The former concentration camp lies 23 kilometres north of Celle and 6 kilometres west of Bergen on the Luneburg Heath. In 1936, it was a drill ground for the German army and trains with army materials arrived at the platform between Bergen and Belsen.

Following the German invasion in Belgium and France in June of 1940, the Germans used it to house prisoners of war.

After Germany invaded Russia on 22 June 1941, over 21,000 Russians soldiers were held in the camp—known as *Stalag* at the time—under abominable circumstances: out in the open, surrounded by barbed-wire and lacking in sanitary provisions. In early 1942, 13,500 Russians died of hardship, dysentery and typhoid fever. In April 1943 the SS turned Bergen-Belsen into a concentration camp. Like the Westerbork Camp, Bergen-Belsen lay isolated on the heath. The camp covered about 30 square kilometres.

Already before Anne arrived here it was chaos, as attested to by Renate Laqueur (1919-2011), who arrived in Bergen-Belsen on 15 March 1944 and described its horrors in a diary. Unlike Anne, she lived to experience the liberation of the camp. It is possible they met in Bergen-Belsen. Notably, Bergen-Belsen was not a extermination camp; there was a crematory but no gas chamber. Nonetheless, many people died in Bergen-Belsen of disease and undernourishment.[2]

On 1 November 1944, Anne travelled on one of the last transports from Auschwitz to Bergen-Belsen. It was bitterly cold. On 3 November 1944, the train stopped between Bergen and Belsen.[3] The exhausted women were forced to leave the cattle-cars and walk the last six kilometres to the concentration camp in the pouring rain, under the sharp eye of the guards—shaven bald, covered in blankets and terribly thin. The prisoners passed through the barrier of the main entrance in the north-eastern section that was surrounded by barbed-wire.

If Anne had not been betrayed and had remained hidden in the Secret Annex, she would have had to suffer during the Dutch famine.[4] After an urgent appeal by Radio Orange, the employees of the Dutch Railway ceased their work. In retaliation, the German invaders blocked all food transport to the Netherlands for weeks, causing an extensive famine in the west of the Netherlands.

Feeling the Russians breathing down their necks, the Germans were busy evacuating camps in the east and bringing prisoners to camps in the west. When the prisoners arrived in Bergen-Belsen, they were very weak because of the hardships in the east. Overpopulation and the lack of any medical provisions in Bergen-Belsen furthered the spread of disease. Even simple complaints refused to heal. The camp was 'guided' by the sadistic commander Josef Kramer (1906-1945).

The commander's villa and the residences of the SS were situated close to the main entrance. The officers had a sauna and a swimming pool. Also at the entrance of the camp were the administration, an office and other buildings, including an area for *Entlausung* (delousing). The prisoners were deloused by walking through a hall with hot steam that poured out of openings in the floor. Clothing of the prisoners, as far as present, was gathered in a wagon and disinfected. A strange arrangement: due to the lack of hygienic circumstances, the camp itself was a paradise for lice. Many prisoners contracted pneumonia because they had to wait naked and wet in the cold for their prison garments. Following delousing, the prisoners walked along the camp street to the other side of the camp where the women's camp and the crematory were situated.

After their personal data had been noted down, the new batch of prisoners had to bivouac in overcrowded military tents. Anne's tent was in a part of the concentration camp where the *Haus der Stille* (House of Silence) and the Jewish monument now stand. In the improvised tents the prisoners lay on a layer of dirty straw. The winter cold penetrated the weak bodies from below as they lay on the ground. Nights were pitch-black. There were no sanitary provisions, with only open pits that served as latrines. There was much screaming and panic.

An autumn storm destroyed the tent camp, and Anne and Margot ended up in a wooden barracks in the women's camp, in approximately the same location as where the tents had stood. The women's camp bordered the *Sternlager* (Star Camp), which housed 4,000 Jews to be traded for cash or German prisoners of war. On the north-western side, the women's camp bordered the labour barracks, where Anne was forced to work. The women's camp held many prisoners who were seriously weakened or dying, and who often did not have the strength to drag themselves to the latrines. The bed linen on the wooden beds was often filthy because of diarrhoea. The hygienic circumstances reached a gruesome low when the bodies of thousands of victims were left unburied at the site.

According to the *Stiftung niedersaechsische Gedenkstaetten Welfenallee* (Lower Saxony Memorials Foundation on Welfenallee), the shoe barracks[5] were only operational until August 1944,[6] yet eyewitnesses claim that Anne worked here in a shoe barracks. In Bergen-Belsen Anne met acquaintances. Rachel and Rosa de Liema knew Anne from the Westerbork Camp and the Brilleslijper sisters knew her from Auschwitz II and the Westerbork Camp. The Frank sisters and the Brilleslijper sisters sometimes spoke with one another during the heavy work in the shoe barracks, where the prisoners had to separate and collect the useful parts of the soldiers' boots covered in blood and mud. Lientje and Anne's hands bled and had blisters because of the dirty work; many people died of blood poisoning.

In Bergen-Belsen in November 1944, Anne met Nanette, who had been a prisoner in the Westerbork Camp and with whom Anne had gone to the Joods Lyceum grammar school. A fellow prisoner told Nanette that Edith was still alive; she communicated this to Anne.[7]

Anne and Margot would never see their parents again and in Bergen-Belsen they depended on each other a lot. The Frank sisters and the Brilleslijper sisters kept up their courage by singing Jewish songs[8] and exchanging thoughts as to what they would do after the war. Anne told them that they would all go to a banquet in one of the most expensive restaurants in Amsterdam. Just as in the Secret Annex, it was mainly the hope of liberation that sustained them.

The people who had hidden for so long were no longer afraid of being betrayed, and yet each day held the threat of the gas chambers.

At home, Anne had always dressed neatly and had had beautiful black hair. In the Secret Annex, Anne dreamed of a career as a film star. Nanette and Rachel were shocked at Anne's appearance in Bergen-Belsen: she was bald, had sunken cheeks, and was nothing but skin and bones.

Auguste van Pels, with whom Anne had often had arguments in the Secret Annex, made sure that Anne got into contact with her friend Hanneli, who had been deported from the Westerbork Camp to Bergen-Belsen on 15 February 1943 and who was in the *Sternlager* as an exchange Jew.[9] The prisoners in the *Sternlager* had certain privileges: some possessions, more food, no prison garments, and parents and children were not separated from each other.

The women's camp in which Anne sat was separated from the *Sternlager* by a barbed-wire fence with watchtowers. From the *Sternlager*, the prisoners sometimes threw food packages over the fence for the prisoners in the women's camp. Anne met Hanneli at night by the fence, where both had to take care not to stand in the light of the searchlights or most likely they would have been shot by a guard.

Anne and Hanneli's meeting at the fence in Bergen-Belsen probably occurred at the end of 1944 or beginning of 1945. Perhaps they had seen each other earlier at the parade grounds. Hanneli could not see Anne very well from the *Sternlager* because there was straw between the fence: 'She [Anne] started crying immediately, and told me: "I have no parents anymore." I remember that for sure,' Hanneli says.[10] Hanneli cried as well. They had last spoken over two years ago.

Anne told Hanneli that she had hidden in the Secret Annex, had been betrayed and deported to the Westerbork Camp, and then sent to

Auschwitz. Anne was not well. It was winter, but Anne had thrown away her lice-ridden clothes. When Hanneli threw a bundle over the fence with a woollen sweater and food for Anne, Hanneli heard a cry of despair from Anne; another woman had grabbed the bundle and would not give it back. The bundle that Hanneli threw over the fence a couple of days later Anne did manage to grab. Anne shared the contents with Margot.

Anne apparently did not speak to Hanneli in Bergen-Belsen about the passage in her diary where she had written: 'Dear Kitty, yesterday before I fell asleep, who should suddenly appear before my eyes but Hanneli! 'I saw her in front of me, clothes in rags, her face thin and worn. Her eyes were very big and she looked so sadly and reproachfully at me that I could read in her eyes: Oh, Anne, why have you deserted me? Help, oh, help me, rescue me from this Hell!'[11] It was not Anne, however, but Hanneli who would survive the war. This diary fragment made a deep impression on Hanneli after the war. According to Nanette, who met Anne in Bergen-Belsen, Anne spoke of wanting to publish her diary in an adapted form.[12] Apparently, the idea that her diary had been saved after the betrayal in the Secret Annex and would survive the war sustained Anne. Anne most likely did not keep a diary in Bergen-Belsen.

At the end of 1944, a typhoid epidemic[13] hit the overcrowded camp killing tens of thousands of victims, including Anne and Margot. Hanny Lévy-Hass (born in 1913) survived Bergen-Belsen and, in her diary, describes her struggle to survive and the miseries in the camp in March and April 1945, when the food supply was delayed and the prisoners cooked grass to stay alive with most likely some cannibalism amongst the prisoners.

Soon after Hanneli's father died in Bergen-Belsen on 23 February 1945,[14] the contact between Hanneli and Anne ceased. Maybe the contact stopped because the Russian camp was dismantled to make way for the large women's camp.[15] The smaller women's camp in the south-western part where Anne was originally held was shut down completely in April 1945.

From April 1945 latest[16], the women's camp no longer bordered the *Sternlager*. The shortest distance between the large women's camp and the *Sternlager* was 100 metres at the time. The camps were separated by some barracks and the main street (*Lagerstrasse*). Perhaps the contact between Anne and Hanneli stopped because Anne was sick and staying in one of the barracks of the (small) women's camp or maybe in one of the sick barracks in Bergen-Belsen, close to the small men's camp.[17]

In addition to typhoid fever, Margot also had dysentery and could no longer stand. The Brilleslijper sisters stole aspirin tablets from the SS chemists for the Frank sisters. Terminally ill, Anne and Margot suffered because of the cold and the draught in the barracks. The Allies had already flown over the site with aeroplanes, but help was not forthcoming.

Margot was very weak and did not survive a fall from her bed. After the war, a number of prisoners, all women, stated that Margot died before Anne. Three days before her death, Anne suffered from intens and terrifying hallucinations as a result of her illness.[18]

Anne died in Janny Brilleslijper's arms.[19] The Brilleslijper sisters laid the bodies of the Frank sisters on a blanket and buried them in one of the mass graves the prisoners had dug. In this sad way ended the lives of the 15-year-old Anne and the 18- or 19-year-old Margot. Two young, promising lives were taken before they could blossom; murdered simply because they were Jews. Their mother died a lonely death in Auschwitz without knowing the fate of her children and husband. Anne did not know that her father was still alive.

Despite the destruction of the camp archives by the SS just before its liberation, 50,000 names of the roughly 120,000 prisoners in Bergen-Belsen have already been retrieved. Of many, the exact date of their death is not known. Many others are known to have died during the last few days before the liberation. Most of the dead lie in mass graves. Symbolic gravestones are inscribed with dates of death. Shortly before the British liberated Bergen-Belsen on 15 April 1945, about 35,000 more prisoners died in this camp. The Red Cross estimates Anne's date of death to be 31 March 1945. It is possible, however, that Anne died in February.

The British found stacks of bodies that had not yet been buried. The shocking images of the emaciated (yet living) bodies went around the world after the liberation, whereas the Allies had taken photographs of the camp already in mid-1944 without taking any action.

The Allies burned the Bergen-Belsen camp shortly after the liberation because of the very high risk of being infected with typhus and lice. The last barracks were burned on 24 May 1945 in the presence of the former prisoners, who partook in a small ceremony.

After a three-and-a-half-hour ride, I arrived at the Anne Frank Memorial Square in Bergen-Belsen. The spacious square holds a documentation centre, where the history of the prison and concentration camp and its victims is revealed. Here, video interviews about Anne can be viewed. At the entrance of the documentation centre there is also a book store.

The train platform south of Bergen is still used by the German and English army and no entry is permitted.[20] Visitors can take a pathway outside of the fence to view a wagon on a section of old track.

On dead tracks: a rusty plaque reminds one of the *Rampe* (ramp), where the march began for the exhausted people, Anne included, who died in Bergen-Belsen. Part of the platform—the oldest track dates to 1936—is being cared for as national heritage. The *Arbeitsgemeinschaft* (AG, Cooperation) of Bergen-Belsen holds an annual ceremony at the platform to commemorate the dead.

Upon entering the former camp site, I was reminded by a sign to behave respectfully: 'To all visitors of the memorial site. Respect the dignity of this site and preserve the peace of the deceased.' (translated from the German). I perceived a stone with the inscription: 'Bergen-Belsen 1940-1945'. On a plateau there were two replicas: one of the former concentration camp (1943 situation) and one of the current memorial (after renovation). A stone-paved road ran along the former parade grounds of the camp.

I walked along the hardened pathways and saw the vast heath, bushes and sandy paths. The site within has been landscaped with slopes (mass graves) and symbolic graves. It was beautiful weather. The sun was shining; blue sky with white clouds.

An oppressive silence ruled. Everything looked so 'neat' in contrast to the mess that would have prevailed in the camp.

On 15 April 1946, the *Belsener Jüdische Komitee* (Belsen Jewish Committee) unveiled a memorial stone with Hebrew and English inscriptions: a large square stone with Jewish symbols on a triangular pedestal.

At the initiative of the British military administration, a central monument was erected in 1947—a 24-metre-high obelisk with a 50-metre-long wall upon which there are inscriptions from countries that lost citizens in Bergen-Belsen. The Dutch text reads: 'The heaviest artillery and the finest gun can give an advantage on the battlefield; here, no force of arms could help any more. No battle, just a people suffering for life.'[21] At the location of the obelisk, a memorial service is held each year on the anniversary of the liberation, organised by the AG Bergen-Belsen in cooperation with young people who participate in international work camps and with survivors of the Bergen-Belsen concentration camp.[22]

There are birch trees in the woods. A wooden cross reminds us of the cross that the Bergen-Belsen survivors made of birch wood in memory of the camp's deceased.

On a plaque by the wooden cross I read: 'On this spot, survivors of the Bergen-Belsen concentration camp erected a simple cross made of birch wood a day after their release on 16 April 1945. In an ecumenical service they remembered the children, women and men murdered in the concentration camp.'

With the passage of time, the remains of the barracks, old foundations and latrines have been excavated and are now overgrown with plants, and there are many fragments of old buildings and walls. Behind the former women's camp in the woods, the remains of the latrines can be seen: holes covered by a plank. The steps to the water reservoir are still partially preserved and between the seams of the steps grow daisies; nature has covered the horrors of the war.

At the former entrance of the camp, closed off with a red-white gate, a canvas tent protects the old foundations of the so-called decontamination room. Spread throughout the former concentration camp site and concentrated in the area of the obelisk are fourteen mass graves in the form of burial mounds. A memorial stone indicates how many people are buried here. This number is missing for a couple of the mass graves. Spread throughout the site there are a number of anonymous graves. On one of those graves is written *Ein Unbekannter Toter* (an unknown dead). Here and there, as reminders of someone, are crosses with the text 'In remembrance'.

The location of the mass grave where Anne and Margot are buried is not known. A symbolic gravestone, displaying a Star of David, close to the obelisk and the Jewish memorial, which can almost be considered a warning sign, reminds one of Anne and Margot. The students of the Anne-Frank-Schule (Amtland 28, Bergen)[23] were present at the unveiling of Anne and Margot's gravestone in Bergen-Belsen on 15 June 1999, as was Buddy Elias and representatives of the Anne Frank Fonds and the Anne Frank Stichting.

At Anne and Margot's grave there are letters, flowers, jewellery and stones that have been placed in their memory by students from all corners of the earth.

The stones often have the Star of David, a message or a flower painted on them. I am glad that I am not alone in remembering Anne Frank.

Little stones lie on Anne and Margot's grave—an old Jewish custom: it is said that whoever places a stone at someone's grave takes the deceased with them in their heart. In ancient times, Jews buried their dead in the desert. Because there are no flowers in the desert, they would place stones on the grave. Silent witnesses remind us of the Nazi's victims. Let us keep these memories alive.

[1] *The Diaries*, 15 July 1944.
[2] http://Bergen-Belsen.stiftung-ng.de/de/geschichte.html
[3] Anne arrived at the platform just south of Bergen [between Bergen and Belsen] (Silvia Rathman, email 27 January 2011). Thus, Anne did not arrive in Celle [via the *Reichsbahn*] as Carol Ann Lee maintains (*Het leven van een jong meisje* (Amsterdam, 2009), p. 20, p. 206).
[4] Inhabitants of the Rivierenbuurt recount stories about the 1944 Dutch famine (http://www.zuidelijkewandelweg.nl/tijdtijn/hongerwinter.htm).
[5] Barracks number 42 is on the map that sketches the situation at the beginning of April 1945 (Die Topografie des Lagers Bergen-Belsen Sechs Karten).
[6] Karin Theilen, email 9 October 2008.
[7] Theo Coster, *Klasgenoten van Anne Frank* (Amsterdam, 2009), p. 86. English edition: *We All Wore Stars. Memories of Anne Frank from her Classmates* (Macmillan, 2011).
[8] Lee, Carol Ann. *Anne Frank. Het leven van een jong meisje* [The life of a young girl. The Definitive Biography] (Amsterdam, 2009), p. 26.
[9] Exchange Jews were, for the Nazis, Jews that could be exchanged for German prisoners of war or cash. On the basis of this 'horse trading', several hundred Jews obtained an exit visa to Palestine.
[10] Willy Lindwer, *De laatste zeven maanden van Anne Frank. Het ongeschreven laatste hoofdstuk van het Dagboek* (Hilversum, 2008), p. 49. English edition: *The Last Seven Months of Anne Frank. The Stories of Six Women who Knew Anne Frank* (Macmillan, 2004).
[11] *The Diaries*, 27 November 1943.
[12] Theo Coster, *Klasgenoten van Anne Frank* (Amsterdam, 2009), p. 85.
[13] Symptoms of paratyphoid fever were: skin rash, fever, headache, joint pain, kidney problems, blood vessel stoppages and an impaired immune system.
[14] http://www.communityjoodsmonument.nl/person/215693/nl
[15] According to *Stiftung niedersaechsische Gedenkstaetten Welfenallee* the small women's camp where Anne was held already existed in November 1944 (email 9 October 2008).
[16] *Die Topografie des Lagers Bergen-Belsen* (The Topography of the Bergen-Belsen Concentration Camp) by the *Stiftung niedersächsische Gedenkstätten* in Bergen-Belsen has, among other things, a map that shows the situation in September 1944 and again in early April 1945.
[17] *Die Topografie des Lagers Bergen-Belsen*, Stiftung niedersächsische Gedenkstätten Bergen-Belsen.
[18] Willy Lindwer, *De laatste zeven maanden van Anne Frank. Het ongeschreven laatste hoofdstuk van het Dagboek* (Hilversum, 2008), p. 100
[19] Willy Lindwer, *De laatste zeven maanden van Anne Frank. Het ongeschreven laatste hoofdstuk van het Dagboek* (Hilversum, 2008), p. 13.
[20] Silvia Rathmann, email 27 January 2011.
[21] http://bergen-belsen.stiftung-ng.de/de/geschichte.html.
[22] http://www.ag-bergen-belsen.de/rondleiding.html.
[23] http://anne-frank-schule-bergen.de/index.php.

EPILOGUE

Before WWII, private parties were already interested in preserving monumental sites. The Athens Charter (1931) was the first initiative in which a number of principles were laid down, serving as a guideline for the protection and restoration of monuments worldwide. The Protection of Monuments and the Landscape Act dating from 7 August 1931, formally established that important monuments and landscapes be protected by the government. This often turned out to be lip service only. Prinsengracht, for instance, was not on the Amsterdam heritage list in 1935. Private parties could not prevent the houses on 219-231 Prinsengracht from being demolished in 1938.[1]

Many monuments and houses were destroyed during the war. During the Dutch famine of 1944/1945, Amsterdammers would remove the wood from the houses of Jewish people who had been arrested and deported—not to harm the Jews in any way, but simply to survive the bitter cold of winter. They used the wood to burn in their stoves and for other purposes.[2] By order of the occupiers, the moving company Puls emptied the secret Annex after the betrayal.

Some held the Jews responsible for the hardships of war. In 1944, even before the Dutch famine broke out, Anne mentions the rise of anti-Semitism. 'To our great horror and regret we hear that the attitude of a great many people towards us Jews has changed.'[3]

When the war had just broken out, some would still support the Jews: 'The people of Amsterdam prefer their own city to all others (…) But perhaps this love is greater and more deeply rooted in the Jews of Amsterdam than in anyone else.'[4]

Many Jewish residences were emptied by the occupying forces during the war and the Frank family's possessions have also disappeared.

Allied bombings caused great damage in Germany. The Aachen and Frankfurt am Main city centres were destroyed by heavy Allied bombings in 1944.

Nor did the residence on 4 Mertonstrasse in Frankfurt, where Anne and her family had lived in 1933, survive the war.

When it became clear that Germany would lose the war, the Germans started successfully erasing any traces of their crimes in the concentration and extermination camps. The Germans burnt the camps' records and blew up many of their crematoria and gas chambers in Auschwitz. After the liberation, the allied forces burnt down Bergen-Belsen in order to prevent the spread of contagious diseases. The barracks at the Westerbork camp initially remained intact, serving as prisons for (alleged) war criminals and NSB members.

The period immediately following the war was spent clearing up the rubble. Nobody had heard of Anne Frank yet, she was still one of the many anonymous victims. Many people had lost their family, friends and acquaintances. The people who had stayed home, who had looked on from the sidelines without being able to help, wanted to repress the emerging feeling of guilt and not be confronted with reminders of the war. Concentration camps brought back horrid memories for many people.

The Dutch government did not want to look back and focused instead on rebuilding the country. This meant demolishing the houses in the Jewish areas in Amsterdam that had been badly damaged during the war and therefore many of the Jews who had survived the war could not return to their houses.[5] The apartment of the Franks on Merwedeplein, had been let to new tenants. Only some of the canal houses that had been damaged by incendiary bombs were restored. Jewish life had (largely) disappeared.

Amsterdammers missed the liveliness of the Jewish markets and the typically Jewish sense of humour in the Jewish corner of the Sunday morning market and the market on Amstelveld. Both literally and figuratively, the Jews left behind a great void in Amsterdam.[6] Some felt (vicarious) shame with regard to the deportations of their Jewish fellow Amsterdammers: 'The city's ancient tradition of providing refuge to the oppressed was trampled down, its entire, remarkable Jewish district was depopulated, ransacked and left to fall apart.'[7]

Otto Frank dedicated himself to promoting the works of his daughter Anne. The publication of her diaries turned out to be a commercial success and following their first 1947 edition, Anne became world famous.[8] During the Cold War, however, her popularity was also misused for political purposes. In 1958, the Polish film director Joachim Hellwig (born in 1932) produced a black and white documentary on Anne Frank. Following its release, the *Staatliche Komittee für Filmwesen* remarked that Hellwig's documentary poignantly unveiled the fascist character of 'des Bonner Staates'.[9]

Because of the focus on the commercial success of the diaries and its byproducts, mainly films and theatre plays, there was very little interest in preserving the material heritage reminiscent of Anne. 'The Diary of Anne Frank',[10] a film directed by George Stevens (1904-1975), was shot in a replica of the Secret Annex in Beverly Hills. Former member of the Dutch resistance Tony van Renterghem (born in 1919) made sure clogs and tulips were not the dominant subjects on display. 'The Diary of Anne Frank' premiered in 1959 (not in its actual location). In the film, Milly Perkins walks through artificial snow down Staalstraat in Amsterdam, as Anne. The film won three Oscars.

American writer and psychologist Bruno Bettelheim (1903-1990) showed very little regard for the situation the Franks were in and accused them of having a passive attitude towards the Nazis—which is similar to what actress Shelly Winters (1920-2006) was told at the 1962 Moscow Film Festival. She attended the screening of 'The Diary of Anne Frank' and was told that the behaviour of Anne and her family was not in accordance with the Communist Party guidelines. Identifying themselves with 'unspoiled' Anne, many denied their own faults and looked for them in others instead.

With respect to the Anne hype, Mrs. L.H. Isselman-Flatow writes 'I came to The Hague after the war, following my marriage with a journalist who was born and raised there. But I wanted to spend the holidays in Amsterdam, at the Muzieklyceum that had been hired especially for survivors [2 Albert Hahnplantsoen, Amsterdam[11]]. My husband, who is not a Jew, wanted to come along. When we entered the hall, Otto Frank met us at the entrance. I (…) greeted him and introduced him to my husband. Otto was moved and said "I am so glad you survived". It was only later that I realised that Anne had been overtaken by commerce. I thought this was awful. Even though we were not exactly what you would call friends, I am and at that time already was against mythologization".[12] [13]

This fixation with the diaries, which have been listed as UNESCO world heritage since 2009, is still prevalent today. Extreme right-wing circles keep denying the holocaust despite the definitive scientific editions proving otherwise.

Fortunately, there are also those who stress that Anne is more than *The Diaries* and the Secret Annex. Since 1960, the Secret Annex has had many visitors who want to see the hiding place where Anne wrote her diaries. Finally, 40 years after the war, there has been growing interest in the Netherlands in preserving Anne's 'second' home on Merwedeplein and other locations Anne (liked to) visit.

We may thank heavens that from the 1980s onwards, there has been an increased interest in Anne as a person and a historical figure as well. Anne was not a saint, but she was a talented adolescent with a complicated character who could not fully blossom before she died a miserable death in Bergen-Belsen.

It would be disrespectful to Anne not to acknowledge this and attribute traits to her that she did not really have.

Because the diaries and their exploitation dominate interest, additional tangible traces Anne left in the current (urban) landscape have still not been sufficiently highlighted. It is very unfortunate that the Westerbork barracks in which Anne worked burnt down in 2009.

It is also evident that the material heritage evocative of Anne has been insufficiently documented and inventoried, which means that the background of some of Anne's photographs cannot always be established any longer. The traces in the sand have been washed away.

It is a pity that material traces in the cityscape reminiscent of Anne have been lost, because the homes, hiding place and concentration camps where Anne lived are living monuments that, unlike objects in a museum, are located in a fixed place and situated directly in their historical context—the context in which Anne lived her (brief) life.

Keeping alive the tangible cultural heritage reminiscent of Anne is important since it also makes us realize that many of her surroundings have been lost forever after she was snatched away and eventually murdered by the Nazis.

I sincerely hope that some of Anne's more personal belongings,[14] [15] such as her hairdressing cape and necklace, will also be displayed to the public. I am not aware of whether her ballroom dress[16] and red shoes[17] survived the war. The bickering between various parties and persons on the usage rights of various items does not help to present these pieces of cultural heritage in a manner that benefits the public.[18]

Family members, friends and museums possess personal items and letters from Anne that are not always on 'live' display.

For me, Anne came to life when I traced her footsteps and combined this experience with other sources of knowledge. In this way, Silent Witnesses such as buildings, streets and squares came to life.

Every façade harbours a story. I am glad that more attention is being invested lately in the tangible cultural heritage of WWII in general and that of the Jewish citizens in particular.[19] More attention is now also being paid to the other children who became or who are currently victims of the persecution of the Jews.[20] Anne was one of many thousands of Jewish children who were murdered in the camps.

I particularly felt the void Anne left behind in the landscape when I took a photograph from the same perspective as an old photo with Anne in it and when I recognized the houses and buildings on the historical image.

I am glad that some of the monuments that remind us of Anne have been preserved, mainly thanks to private efforts. The former homes of Anne in Aachen and Frankfurt am Main now house private individuals and companies.

Anne's living environment in the Aachen and Frankfurt am Main city centres was destroyed by bombs during WWII. The area around the building on 1 Pastorplatz and the Aachen and Frankfurt am Main inner cities were particularly affected and have become run down over the years.

Anne mainly lives on in Amsterdam, which is confirmed by the international standing of the Secret Annex. The building itself is a museum although much of the original interior and furniture has been lost. The Secret Annex has the distinct character of a deserted house. Otto wanted the hiding place to remain unfurnished.

Unfortunately, some of the canal houses adjacent to 263 Prinsengracht, which were part of Anne's living environment and the historical Prinsengracht ring of canals, have been demolished. In this case, short-term thinking overruled the long-term preservation of heritage for posterity.

The identity of the Frank family and the distinct thirties atmosphere can best be felt in their home on Merwedeplein. The buildings' architecture and the street layout of the Rivierenbuurt area have been well-preserved, bringing Anne's world to life.[21] In 2011, the Frank's apartment was briefly opened to the public.

Due to a conscious effort, Anne is more visible in the cityscape in the Netherlands than in Germany. There is no prominent statue of Anne in her place of birth. The current residents of 24 Ganghoferstrasse in Frankfurt am Main are open about Anne's life and death, as evidenced by a clearly visible memorial plaque.

In the Westerbork and Bergen-Belsen camps, there are hardly any tangible reminders of Anne. The bleak reality of wartime is acutely evident in the gas chamber ruins of Auschwitz-Birkenau. As mentioned earlier, the foundation in Poland unfortunately does not have the funds to properly maintain the former extermination camp, in spite of its being placed on the UNESCO world heritage list in 1979. Every stone that crumbles is lost to posterity, reducing Auschwitz to a myth without history. The popularity of the Secret Annex is partly due to the fact that Anne also wrote her diary here. Anne did not leave behind any writing from her period at the camps; one could almost forget that she had a horrific time in Auschwitz-Birkenau and Bergen-Belsen.

There are still children being dragged from their houses, children who die a miserable death because of war violence. Let us learn from Anne's story so that we may protect children from such fates.

[1] *Amstelodamum* (Amsterdam, 1938). Therefore, 219-231 Prinsengracht are not metnioned in the Museum of the Canals on http://grachtenboek.hetgrachtenhuis.nl/
[2] http://www.dedokwerker.nl/joodse_huizen.html
[3] *The Diaries*, 22 May 1944.
[4] *Amstelodamum* (Amsterdam, 1940)
[5] Many Jewish houses (in Amsterdam) were demolished in order to make way for newly built housing districts, without any research into the Jews who had lived there. Fortunately, the Jewish Historical Museum and the Foundation 4/5 May are developing initiatives that stress the importance of preserving Jewish houses (in Amsterdam). Also see http://www.communityjoodsmonument.nl/page/249245/nl
[6] *Amstelodamum* (Amsterdam, 1946).
[7] *Amstelodamum* (Amsterdam, 1944-1945).
[8] The fact that Anne's diary gained so much popularity in so little time is also due to the fact that her diaries contain relatively few horrifying details and are therefore suitable for younger readers as well.
[9] Barnouw David and Gerrold van der Stroom, *Wie verraadde Anne Frank?* (Amsterdam, 2003) p. 55. English edition: *Who Betrayed Anne Frank?* (Netherlands Institute for War Documentation, 2003).
[10] http://www.freebase.com/view/en/the_diary_of_anne_frank
[11] http://beeldbank.amsterdam.nl/beeldbank/weergave/search/layout/result/indeling/detail/start/6?q_searchfield=muzieklyceum
[12] Letter by Mrs L.II. Isselmann-Flatow dated 8 February 2011.
[13] '[Anne Frank] is currently being romanticised, mainly by young people. Or is this just me? As I mentioned earlier, I never could nor wanted to read the diary [by Anne Frank]. We have been to Auschwitz several times. There, too, commerce has increased over the past few years. I guess one cannot avoid this.' (translation of a Dutch email from Francien Bachra dated 8 January 2011).
[14] 'A few items of Anne have been saved.' Buddy Elias, email dated 30 December 2010.
[15] A couple of images of properties in some way related to the people hiding in the annex and their helpers can be found on the internet: http://www.musip.nl/brief.aspx. Some images are barely or not at all legible and some items do not have images available.
[16] *The Diaries*, 12 January 1944.
[17] *The Diaries*, 10 August 1943.
[18] In 1981, an anonymous benefactor donated a necklace that belonged to Anne to the NIOD. In 2006, the Anne Frank Fonds in Switzerland successfully claimed these artefacts after an intervention by the then minister Maria van der Hoeven (born in 1949) and the *Restitutiecommissie* (http://vorige.nrc.nl/kunst/article1753007.ece/Spullen_Anne_Frank_terug_en_weer_uitgeleend). Since January 2002, this restitution committee has been researching and assessing individual requests to return cultural items that have disappeared during WWII (http://www.restitutiecommissie.nl/)

[19] There is also an increased recent interest in the material items that are reminiscent of Jewish life in the Netherlands. 'Jewish homes' constitute a section of the Jewish Monument Community website. This site connects the people of the past to the people of today through active contributions by visitors. Zij geven een gezicht aan de namen van alle in de oorlog omgekomen Nederlandse joden (http://www.communityjoodsmonument.nl/page/249245/nl). This site lists addresses where Jews lived before they were killed and recent pictures of their façades, including the Merwedeplein apartment (http://www.communityjoodsmonument.nl/search/250221/nl?start=0). Elsewhere in the Netherlands, digital monuments have also been set up (http://www.joodsmonumentmeppel.nl/sitemap/main.html)
The leaflet *Prosecution and resistance in Amsterdam. Reminders of the Second World War. A walk from the Anne Frank House to the Resistance Museum.* (Amsterdam, 2006) by historian Ineke van Tol describes a walk from the Anne Frank House to the Resistance Museum.
The Bornmeer publishing house produced a booklet on Jewish life in the Dutch province of Friesland (*Joods leven in Friesland* (Gorredijk 2010)) containing an overview of what is currently still visible of the pratically extinct Jewish culture in Friesland, including homes, shops and streets, hospitals and Jewish cemeteries. In that same year, the Leeuwarden Historical Center (HCL) (http://www.historischcentrumleeuwarden.nl/text/nl/1097/Nieuw_in_onze_winkel) and the Leeuwarden tourist office collaboratively published a city walks booklet: *Stadswandeling Leeuwarden. Sporen van joods leven* (Leeuwarden City Walk. Traces of Jewish Life.) (Leeuwarden, 2010).
The Westerbork Remembrance Center (http://www.kampwesterbork.nl/) in collaboration with the Drents Plateau (http://www.drentsplateau.nl/) highlights the preservation of tangible traces of the war in the Drenthe province.
Together with Jewish working groups and foundations for the Jewish labour camps, the Westerbork Remembrance Center pays particular attention to visible traces in the current landscape that are reminiscent of Jewish camp life. In 1942, hundreds of Jewish men were force to leave there home and hearth in order to work in special labour camps. They were deported to over forty labour camps, mostly located in the north or the east of the Netherlands, which turned out to be the gate to deportation to Camp Westerbork or the extermination camps in the east. (http://www.joodsewerkkampen.nl/).
Moreover, excursions and tours (of varying quality) are being organized in Amsterdam and elsewhere, visiting places that are reminiscent of Anne Frank and Jewish life during the war. Hopefully, this will raise an interest in preserving the cultural and material heritage amongst the general public.

[20] Marcel Prins and Peter Henk Steenhuis, *Andere Achterhuizen. Verhalen van Joodse onderduikers* (Amsterdam, 2010). English edition: *Hidden Like Anne Frank* (Scholastic, 2014). This book contains the stories of fifteen people who, unlike Anne, did survive the war, including that of Bloeme Evers-Emden (born in 1927) who knew Anne. Esther was Max C. van der Glas' niece. She lived on 38-II Holendrechtstraat (600 metres from Merwedeplein) in Amsterdam and kept a

friendship album containing beautiful poems by friends and family. Esther was arrested on 22 February 1942 and murdered in Auschwitz on 21 September 1942. Max C. van der Glas, email dated 23 December 2010.

[21] Not everyone shares my enthusiasm: 'And the restored house? I saw a picture on the internet and thought: new is not old.' (Karel N.L. Grazell, email dated 28 December 2010).

307 Marbachweg, Frankfurt am Main, Frank family residence

1 Pastorplatz, Aachen, Stolpersteine

Amstellaan (as of 1956: Vrijheidslaan)
with the Wolkenkrabber (Skyscraper) in the background

Berlagebrug, 1932

Collection Ad Tiggeler

*Blommestein bakery,
26 Noorder Amstellaan (currently 26 Churchilllaan)*

*Classroom Anne Frank,
6ᵉ Montessorischool (Anne Frankschool), Niersstraat 41*

Blankevoort bookshop, (currently Jimmink bookshop)
62 Zuider Amstellaan, (now 62 Rooseveltlaan)

Daniël Willinkplein (currently Victorieplein), around 1935

Collection Jos Wiersema, Amsterdam Trams

*View on Amstellaan (as of 1956: Vrijheidslaan)
from the Wolkenkrabber, around 1935*

Collection Jos Wiersema, Amsterdam Trams

Lijn 8, Daniël Willinkplein (currently Victorieplein), around 1935

Collection Jos Wiersema, Amsterdam Trams

Line 8

Collection Jos Wiersema, Amsterdam Trams

Maasstraat, around 1935

Collection Ad Tiggeler

Magere Brug ['Skinny Bridge'], around 1935

Collection Ad Tiggeler

Noorder Amstellaan (currently Churchilllaan), around 1940

Collection Ad Tiggeler

*Police station, 5 Pieter Aertszstraat
(currently Public Space Services, City of Amsterdam, Zuid District,)*

Jewish Synagogue, 160 Tolstraat (currently Zuid Library – Cinetol)

*Wolkenkrabber and Daniël Willinkplein
(currently Victorieplein), around 1935*

Collection Ad Tiggeler

View from the Wolkenkrabber on Merwedeplein

Collection Ad Tiggeler

Merwedeplein, roof terrace, Frank family residence

Merwedeplein, entrance, apartment of the Franks

Amsterdam Central Station, 9 Stationsplein, around 1920

Collection Ad Tiggeler

Keizersgracht, Amsterdam.

Raadhuisstraat ['Town Hall Street'] with tram line 13 and the Westerkerk in the background

Collection Jos Wiersema, Amsterdam Trams

Restaurant D'Vijff Vlieghen, 294-302 Spuistraat

View from the Westerkerk towards De Jordaan area before WWII

Collection Ad Tiggeler

View from the Westerkerk towards De Jordaan area after WWII

Collection Ad Tiggeler

View of the Westerkerk from the attic of the Secret Annex

The chestnut tree, back garden of 188 Keizersgracht

Barbed-wire fence with the outline of Anne Frank's penal barracks in the background, Camp Westerbork

Photo of Anne Frank at the children's monument, Jewish cemetery, Warshaw, Poland

Zentralsauna, Auschwitz II

Gas chamber ruins, Auschwitz II

Remembering the deceased, Auschwitz II

Symbolic tombstone Anne en Margot Frank, Bergen-Belsen

ITINERARY

TRAVELLING SCHEDULE

23 December 2007	Camp Westerbork
17 February 2008	Amsterdam
8 May 2008	Amsterdam
18 May 2008	Amsterdam
28 May 2008	Amsterdam
28 May 2008	Zandvoort aan Zee.
22 June 2008	Bergen-Belsen
27 July 2008	Aachen
29 August 2008	Frankfurt am Main
30 August 2008	Frankfurt am Main
31 August 2008	Frankfurt am Main
4 September 2008	Amsterdam
18 September 2008	Amsterdam
3 November 2008	Poland
4 November 2008	Poland
5 November 2008	Poland
6 November 2008	Poland
7 November 2008	Poland
8 November 2008	Poland
9 November 2008	Poland
18 December 2009	Amsterdam
21 October 2010	Aachen
10 July 2011	Amsterdam
2 September 2011	Arnhem
24 September 2011	Arnhem

PHOTOGRAPHIC EQUIPMENT

I took photo's using a Canon 30D camera with matching EF-S 17-35 mm 1:4-5.6 IS USM objective. I prefer to take photographs using the existing daylight, since using a flash looks unnatural and often results in harsh lighting and shadows. Moreover, using a flash is not always permitted and may damage old documents and paintings, as well as disturb other (museum) visitors. I used a stable tripod and a cable release if there was too little light to allow me to photograph by hand without moving, which otherwise would cause a blur. I used Photoshop to adjust contrast, brightness, details, colours, horizon, frame and sharpness where necessary.

PHOTO ACCESSORIES

Batteries plus charger
Memory cards
Lens hood

MAPS

ANWB Amsterdam City Map
Falk Citymap Center of Amsterdam
Falk Citymap Classic Arnhem
Maps with marked routes printed using http://maps.google.nl/
Routes planned using http://maps.google.nl/

OVERVIEW OF MONUMENTS

Preserved monuments

Anne's home addresses

5 Liebfrauenstrasse (currently 5 Elsa-Brändström-Strasse), residence of grandmother Rosa Holländer	Aachen
1 Pastorplatz, residence of grandmother Rosa Holländer	Aachen
37-II Merwedeplein, residence of Frank family	Amsterdam-Zuid area
24 Ganghoferstrasse, residence of the Frank family.	Frankfurt am Main
307 Marbachweg, residence of the Frank family.	Frankfurt am Main

Preserved monuments Anne definitely visited

Jewish Synagogue, 160 Tolstraat
(currently Library Zuid – Cinetol)
www.joodsamsterdam.nl/gebsynagogetolstraat.htm

188 Keizersgracht back garden (during the hiding period)   Centre of Amsterdam
http://grachtenboek.hetgrachtenresidence
of.nl/objecten.php?id=1425
http://www.support-annefranktree.nl/

Cineac cinema, 31 Reguliersbreestraat   Centre of Amsterdam
http://www.architectenweb.nl/aweb/archipedia/archipedia.asp?ID=4989, http://zoeken.nai.nl/CIS/project/7490,
www.bma.amsterdam.nl/@99864/cineac/

The Secret Annex, 263 Prinsengracht (while hiding)   Centre of Amsterdam
http://www.annefrank.org/en/Subsites/Home/

Hollandsche Schouwburg, 24 Plantage Middenlaan.   Centre of Amsterdam
http://www.hollandscheschouwburg.nl/

Preserved monuments Anne definitely visited (continued)

Joodsch Lyceum, 1-2 Voormalige Stadstimmertuin (now ROC van Amsterdam, 1-2 Voormalige Stadstimmertuin) http://www.jhm.nl/cultuur-en-geschiedenis/amsterdam/joodse-hbs-en-joods-lyceum, http://www.rocva.nl/Mbo/Contact/DeScholen/Pages/Voormalige_Stadstimmertuin_1-2.aspx	Centre of Amsterdam
M. Frank & Zonen, 604 Keizersgracht (currently houses multiple businesses) http://grachtenboek.hetgrachtenresidenceof.nl/objecten.php?id=1258	Centre of Amsterdam
Opekta, 120-126 Nieuwezijds Voorburgwal (Candida building) (currently houses multiple businesses) http://grachtenboek.hetgrachtenhuis.nl/objecten.php?id=6863	Centre of Amsterdam
Opekta, 400 Singel (currently Meertens, T.I.) http://grachtenboek.hetgrachtenhuis.nl/objecten.php?id=584	Centre of Amsterdam
Restaurant D'Vijff Vlieghen, 294-302 Spuistraat http://www.vijffvlieghen.nl/	Centre of Amsterdam
Amsterdam Central Station, 9 Stationsplein http://zoeken.nai.nl/CIS/archief/83, www.nl.wikipedia.org/wiki/Station_Amsterdam_Centraal	Centre of Amsterdam
6th Montessori School 'Anne Frank', 41 Niersstraat http://www.annefrank-montessori.nl/	Amsterdam Zuid area
Amstelparkbad (currently De Mirandabad, 9 Mirandalaan) http://www.zuid.amsterdam.nl/vrije_tijd_en_sport/de_mirandabad/, http://www.mirandabad.nl	Amsterdam Zuid area
1-5 Apollohal Stadionweg (currently 4 Apollolaan) www.alphons.net/apollohal	Amsterdam Zuid area
Blommestein bakery, 26 Noorder Amstellaan (currently 26 Churchilllaan) http://www.zuidelijkewandelweg.nl/winkels/blommestein.htm	Amsterdam Zuid area
P. de Munk bakery, corner Waalstraat and Zuider Amstellaan (currently Rooseveltlaan)	Amsterdam Zuid area

Preserved monuments Anne definitely visited (continued)

Berlagebrug across the Amstel, Amstellaan (Vrijheidslaan) http://www.geheugenvanplanzuid.nl/architectuur/berlagebrug.htm	Amsterdam Zuid area
Blankevoort bookshop, 62 Zuider Amstellaan (currently Boekhandel Jimmink, 62 Rooseveltlaan) http://www.jimminkboek.nl/, http://www.zuidelijkewandelweg.nl/architectuur/boekhandelblankevoort/index.htm	Amsterdam Zuid area
Bridges Muzenplein Kinderhof http://www.kunstwacht.nl/publiek/oudzuid/kunstwerken.php?kunstID=203	Amsterdam Zuid area
Amstelrust estate, 319 Amsteldijk http://www.buitenplaatseninnederland.nl/NoordHolland_beschrijvingen/Amsterdam_Amstelrust.html, http://www.gettyimages.com/detail/3229076/Premium-Archive	Amsterdam Zuid area
Kahn family, 59-I Michelangelostraat http://www.freebase.com/view/m/0h2t9ky, http://www.freebase.com/view/en/old_phoebe_halliwell	Amsterdam Zuid area
Bike shed, 2 Deltastraat (currently FysioPlus) http://www.fysioplus.nl/	Amsterdam Zuid area
Gestapo headquarters, 99 Euterpestraat (currently Gerrit van der Veen comprehensive school, 99 Gerrit van der Veenstraat) www.zoeken.nai.nl/CIS/project/16088	Amsterdam Zuid area
Koco ice-cream parlour, 71 Rijnstraat (currently Pamba DIY launderette, 71-73 Rijnstraat) http://www.geheugenvanplanzuid.nl/tijdtijn/koco.htm http://www.pamba.nl/inbrengstations/index.html	Amsterdam Zuid area
Oase ice-cream parlour, 1 Geleenstraat (currently snack counter Oase, 1 Geleenstraat) http://www.zuidelijkewandelweg.nl/ingezonden/127.htm, http://www.kindermonument.nl/wandeling/snackbar.htm	Amsterdam Zuid area

Preserved monuments Anne definitely visited (continued)

Jewish synagogue, 63 Lekstraat (currently Arts & Antiques Group AAG, Netherlands Israelite Main Synagogue Seminary on 63 Lekstraat) http://www.jhm.nl/, http://www.architectuurgids.nl/, www.joodsamsterdam.nl/gebsynagogelekstr.htm	Amsterdam Zuid area
Lunchroom Delphi, 1 Victorieplein (currently Waarlé Graphic design) www.annefrankdiaryreference.org/places/delphi.htm	Amsterdam Zuid area
Police station (currently Public Space Services City of Amsterdam, Zuid district, 5 Pieter Aertszstraat) http://beeldbank.amsterdam.nl/beeldbank/weergave/search/layout/result/indeling/detail/start/1?q_searchfield=Pieter%20Aertszstraat%205	Amsterdam Zuid area
Vondelpark http://www.zuid.amsterdam.nl/wonen_en/natuur_en_milieu/parken_in_zuid/vondelpark	Amsterdam Zuid area
Former city hall (currently Hotel The Grand, 197 Oudezijds Voorburgwal) http://grachtenboek.hetgrachtenresidenceof.nl/objecten.php?id=6347	Amsterdam Zuid area
Wolkenkrabber (Skyskraper), Daniël Willinkplein (currently Victorieplein) www.geheugenvanplanzuid.nl/architectuur/wolkenkrabber.htm	Amsterdam Zuid area
Central-Bahnhof, Im Hauptbahnhof http://en.wikipedia.org/wiki/Frankfurt_(Main)_Hauptbahnhof	Frankfurt am Main
303 Marbachweg, residence of neighbour Gertrud Naumann (1917-2002) http://www.freebase.com/view/en/gertrud_naumann	Frankfurt am Main
Villa Larêt in the Sils Maria http://www.trouw.nl/tr/nl/5009/Archief/archief/article/detail/2700386/1999/05/01/Monument-voor-Anne-Frank-in-Zwitserland.dhtml	Switzerland

Other important preserved monuments Anne may have visited

The Dom, Münsterplatz, http://www.aachen.de/DE/kultur_freizeit/kultur/dom_rathaus/index.html	Aachen
Rathaus, Markt http://www.aachen.de/DE/kultur_freizeit/kultur/dom_rathaus/index.html	Aachen
Theatre, Theaterplatz http://www.aachen.de/DE/kultur_freizeit/kultur/theater/theater_aachen/index.html	Aachen
The post office (currently Magna Plaza, 192 Nieuwezijds Voorburgwal) http://www.magnaplaza.nl/index.php?objectID=389#	Centre of Amsterdam
Artis Zoo, 38-40 Plantage Kerklaan http://www.artis.nl/ontdek-artis/de-tuin/van-toen-tot-nu/	Centre of Amsterdam
Library, 42 Stadhouderskade (currently Rijksmuseum depot) http://www.gevelstenen.net/kerninventarisatie/plaatsenNed/Amsterdam-s4.htm	Centre of Amsterdam
Bijenkorf department store, 1 Dam Square http://nl.wikipedia.org/wiki/De_Bijenkorf_(Amsterdam)	Centre of Amsterdam
Binnengasthuis hospital, 237 Oudezijds Achterburgwal (currently University of Amsterdam) (Anne mentions the hospital in her diary on 27 May 1943 in connection with Johannes 'Johan' Hendrik Voskuijl's illness) http://stadsarchief.amsterdam.nl/onderwijs/buurt_en_stad/centrum/oudestad/binnengastresidence of/agnietenkapel/	Centre of Amsterdam
Carlton Hotel (now NH Carlton Amsterdam, 4 Vijzelstraat) http://nl.wikipedia.org/wiki/Carlton_Hotel_(Amsterdam)	Centre of Amsterdam
De Westerkerk, 28 Prinsengracht, http://www.westerkerk.nl/	Centre of Amsterdam
Hendrik van Hoeve greengrocers (currently houses private residents and furniture maker De Lely Sluys BV), 58 Leliegracht http://beeldbank.amsterdam.nl/beeldbank/weergave/search/layout/result/indeling/detail/start/6?q_searchfield=leliegracht%2058	Centre of Amsterdam

Other important preserved monuments
Anne may have visited (continued)

Royal Palace Amsterdam, Dam square (147 Nieuwezijds Voorburgwal) http://www.paleisamsterdam.nl/, http://grachtenboek.hetgrachtenhuis.nl/objecten.php?id=2384	Centre of Amsterdam
Carré theatre (currently Koninklijk Theater Carré), 115 Amstel http://www.carre.nl/nl/over-carre/carr-istorie	Centre of Amsterdam
De Centrale Markthallen (covered market), Jan van Galenstraat (currently Food Center Amsterdam) http://www.bma.amsterdam.nl/@300448/pagina/	Amsterdam West area
Library on 16b Coöperatiehof (currently ARVH Marketing & Communication) http://www.dbnl.org/tekst/sten009monu11_01/sten009monu11_01_0015.php	Amsterdam Zuid area
Rialto cinema, 338-340 Ceintuurbaan http://nl.wikipedia.org/wiki/Rialto_(filmtheater)	Amsterdam Zuid area
Como bookshop, 227 Rijnstraat (currently Evy daycare centre)	Amsterdam Zuid area
Municipal Girls' School, 62 Reijnier Vinkeleskade http://zoeken.nai.nl/CIS/project/16071	Amsterdam Zuid area
Koco ice-cream parlour, 149 Van Woustraat http://www.zuidelijkewandelweg.nl/tijdtijn/koco.htm	Amsterdam Zuid area
Jewish Invalid, 100 Nieuwe Achtergracht http://www.jhm.nl/cultuur-en-geschiedenis/amsterdam/joodse-invalide	Amsterdam Zuid area
Rosel-Wronkler-Goldschmidt (Frank family housekeeper), 59-II Michelangelostraat http://www.freebase.com/view/m/0gmm3qc, http://www.freebase.com/view/m/0gmkcm0	Amsterdam Zuid area
Theater Tuschinski cinema, 26-28 Regulierbreestraat http://www.geschiedenis24.nl/nieuws/2011/oktober/Theater-Tuschinski-in-de-jaren-30.html	Amsterdam Zuid area
Otto Frank's temporary residence, 24 Stadionkade http://www.annefrank.org/en/Anne-Frank/Emigrating-to-the-Netherlands/A-new-start/	Amsterdam Zuid area

Other important preserved monuments Anne may have visited (continued)

Vondelschool, 84 Jekerstraat (currently Robbeburg   Amsterdam Zuid area
International Playgroup) (Margot Frank's school)
http://www.communityjoodsmonument.nl/page/280560/nl

Zuiderbad, Hobbemastraat 26   Amsterdam Zuid area
http://www.zuid.amsterdam.nl/vrije_tijd_en_sport/zuiderbad,
http://nl.wikipedia.org/wiki/Zuiderbad

Zentralstelle für jüdische Auswanderung   Amsterdam Zuid area
(1 Adama van Scheltemaplein, currently a supermarket)
http://www.annefrank.org/nl/Subsites/Amsterdam/Tijdlijn/Oorl
og/1942/1942/Oproepen-voor-
tewerkstelling/#!/nl/Subsites/Amsterdam/Tijdlijn/Oorlog/1942/
1942/Oproepen-voor-tewerkstelling/

The University of Frankfurt   Frankfurt am Main
(since 1932 Goethe-Universität, on 31 Senckenberganlage)
http://www.uni-frankfurt.de/ueber/geschichte/index.html

Der Jüdische Friedhof (currently Der neue Jüdische Friedhof),   Frankfurt am Main
238 Eckenheimer Landstrasse http://www.jg-
ffm.de/index.php/juedische-friedhoefe

Grossmarkthalle, 2-6 Rückertstrasse   Frankfurt am Main
http://www.frankfurt.de/sixcms/detail.php?id=3793411&_ffmp
ar%5B_id_inhalt%5D=32561

IG Farben (Interessen Gemeinschaft Farbenindustrie   Frankfurt am Main
Aktiengesellschaft), currently
I. G. Farben-Hochhaus, 1 Grüneburgplatz http://www.fritz-
bauer-institut.de/
(not very probable Anne has been inside this building)

Ludwig Richter Schule, 10 Hinter den Ulmen   Frankfurt am Main
http://ludwigrichterschule.de/2009/

Westend Synagogue, 30 Freiherr-vom-Stein-Straße   Frankfurt am Main
http://www.frankfurt.de/sixcms/detail.php?id=3866&_ffmpar[_
id_inhalt]=32659, http://www.jg-
ffm.de/images/jgffm/startseite/100_Jahre_Westend_Synagoge_
100_ani.pdf

Other important preserved monuments Anne may have visited (continued)

Jewish cemetery Gan Hasjalom Hoofddorp
http://www.dodenakkers.nl/beroemd/algemeen/28-hollander.html

Anne's direct neighbours on Merwedeplein

31 Merwedeplein, 'Goslar-Dr. Ledermann' consultancy (for Jews) Merwedeplein
http://kranten.kb.nl/view/article/id/ddd%3A010673179%3Ampeg21%3Ap007%3Aa0032 , http://www.berlin-judentum.de/geschichte/goslar.htm

37-III Merwedeplein Merwedeplein
Marianne Veerman family
http://www.joodsmonument.nl/page/386922

37-III Merwedeplein, Rebecca Trijtel-Berlijn Merwedeplein
http://www.joodsmonument.nl/person/510593

39 Merwedeplein, parents of Tiny Burger, the bride who married dentist A.J.D. van Kalken Merwedeplein

39-1 Merwedeplein, Bernard Wolff Beffie, Joods arts Merwedeplein
http://www.joodsmonument.nl/person/305852/nl

41 Merwedeplein, Leonhard Alexander Levy Merwedeplein
http://www.joodsmonument.nl/person/567531

41 Merwedeplein, Julius Freudenberger family Merwedeplein
http://www.joodsmonument.nl/page/386916

44-1 Merwedeplein, Erich Geiringer family Merwedeplein
http://www.joodsmonument.nl/page/386909

44-II Merwedeplein Merwedeplein
Rudolf Jacob family
http://www.joodsmonument.nl/page/386903

Anne's direct neighbours on Merwedeplein (continued)

49 Merwedeplein Samuel Rosenthal family http://www.joodsmonument.nl/page/386897	Merwedeplein
49 Merwedeplein, Ludwig Schoenthal family http://www.joodsmonument.nl/page/386898	Merwedeplein
49 Merwedeplein, Asser de Boers family http://www.joodsmonument.nl/page/386896	Merwedeplein
57-I Merwedeplein, Louis Asscher family http://www.joodsmonument.nl/page/386886	Merwedeplein
59 Merwedeplein Prof. Ben-Ali-Libi, magician http://kranten.kb.nl/view/article/id/ddd%3A010318321%3Amp eg21%3Ap007%3Aa0041	Merwedeplein

Memorials to Anne

Monheimsallee, square memorial plaque highlighting Anne's home address www.wgdv.de/wege/monheimsallee.htm	Aachen
1 Pastorplatz, Stolpersteine, small brass memorial plates in the pavement commemorating the (deportation of) the Frank family http://www.stolpersteine.com/	Aachen
Anne Frank statue, Westermarkt http://www.annefrankguide.net/nl-nl/bronnenbank.asp?oid=2702	Centre of Amsterdam
Memorial plaque in the hall of the 6th Montessori School 'Anne Frank', 41 Niersstraat) http://www.annefrank-montessori.nl/	Amsterdam Zuid area
Anne Frank statue, Merwedeplein www.portretschap.nl/jet-schepp, http://www.geheugenvanplanzuid.nl/tijdtijn/monument.htm	Amsterdam Zuid area

Memorials to Anne (continued)

Symbolic tombstone Anne and Margot Frank	Bergen-Belsen
24 Ganghoferstrasse, Frank family residence, memorial plaque	Frankfurt am Main
Photo of Anne at the children's monument, Jewish cemetery, Warshaw	Warshaw, Poland

Lost monuments where Anne stayed

Residence of grandmother Rosalie Stern, 42-44 Monheimsallee http://www.aachen.de/de/kultur_freizeit/pdf_kultur_freizeit/gedenktafeln.pdf	Aachen
Huis van Bewaring I (Weteringschans) (prison), 14 Kleine-Gartmanplantsoen (currently Max Euweplein) Part of the original building has been preserved and this part contains a memorial (a blue area with tears of glass)	Centre of Amsterdam
Hotel Groot Warnsborn (277 Bakenbergseweg, Arnhem) www.grootwarnsborn.nl	Arnhem
Op den Driest (5 Koningsweg, Beekbergen) (near Apeldoorn)	Beekbergen
Der Klinik des Vaterländischen Frauenvereins in der Eschenheimer Anlage, (where Anne was born on 12 June 1929)	Frankfurt am Main
Residence of Otto Frank's parents, 4 Jordanstrasse (currently 4 Dantestrasse)	Frankfurt am Main
Anne Frank's penal barracks, Camp Westerbork	Hooghalen, Drenthe
Anne Frank's labour barracks, Camp Westerbork	Hooghalen, Drenthe

Lost monuments where Anne may have stayed

Synagogue (Promenadenstraße, currently 23 Synagogenplatz) (This is where Otto and Edith married) http://www.aachen.de/DE/stadt_buerger/gesellschaft_soziales/integration/dialog_der_religionen/judentum/juedische_gemeinde/index.html/	Aachen

OVERVIEW OF PEOPLE

Frank family members

Annelies Marie 'Anne' Frank

http://anne-frank.startpagina.nl/
http://teacher.scholastic.com/frank/index.htm
http://www.annefrank.ch/
http://www.annefrank.com/
http://www.annefrank.de/
http://www.annefrank.org.uk/
http://www.annefrank.org/
http://www.annefrankdiaryreference.org/
http://www.annefrankguide.net/
http://www.anne-in-de-buurt.nl/
http://www.biografischportaal.nl/persoon/05308737
http://www.jbs-anne-frank.de/
http://www.joodsmonument.nl/person/510596/nl
http://www.kb.nl/dossiers/annefrank/annefrank.html
http://www.uen.org/annefrank/

Frank Family

http://www.joodsmonument.nl/page/305996/nl?lang=en

Alice Betty Stern

http://www.freebase.com/view/en/alice_betty_stern

Bernard 'Buddy' Elias

http://www.freebase.com/view/en/buddy_elias
http://www.pr.com/article/1099

Edith Frank

http://www.annefrank.org/nl/anne-franks-historie/personen-overzicht/edith-frank/
http://www.joodsmonument.nl/person/510598?lang=en

Margot Betti Frank

http://www.annefrank.org/nl/anne-franks-historie/personen-overzicht/margot-frank/
http://www.joodsmonument.nl/person/510597?lang=en

Frank family members (continued)

Otto Heinrich Frank

http://www.annefrank.org/nl/anne-franks-historie/personen-overzicht/otto-frank/

Rosalie 'Rosa' Holländer-Stern

http://www.joodsmonument.nl/person/551099

Stephan Elias

http://www.freebase.com/view/m/073k2tt

Other people in the Secret Annex

Auguste van Pels

http://www.annefrank.org/nl/anne-franks-historie/personen-overzicht/auguste-van-pels/
http://www.joodsmonument.nl/person/476862?lang=en

Friedrich 'Fritz' Pfeffer

http://www.annefrank.org/nl/anne-franks-historie/personen-overzicht/fritz-pfeffer/
http://www.joodsmonument.nl/person/540498/nl

Hermann van Pels

http://www.annefrank.org/nl/anne-franks-historie/personen-overzicht/hermann-van-pels/
http://www.joodsmonument.nl/person/476863?lang=en

Peter van Pels

http://www.annefrank.org/nl/anne-franks-historie/personen-overzicht/peter-van-pels1/
http://www.joodsmonument.nl/person/371708/en

Helpers

General

http://www.annefrank.org/nl/Zoek/Zoek-overzicht/?query=helpers
http://www.auschwitz.nl/paviljoen/onderduiken/onderduiken/lichtbak-1

Bep (Elisabeth) 'Elli' Voskuijl

http://www.annefrank.org/nl/Anne-Franks-historie/Personen-overzicht/Bep-Voskuijl/
http://www.freebase.com/view/en/bep_voskuijl

Jan Gies

http://www.annefrank.org/nl/Anne-Franks-historie/Personen-overzicht/Jan-Gies/
http://www.freebase.com/view/en/jan_gies

Johannes 'Jo' Kleiman

http://www.annefrank.org/nl/Anne-Franks-historie/Personen-overzicht/Jo-Kleiman/
http://www.freebase.com/view/en/johannes_kleiman

Johannes 'Johan' Hendrik Voskuijl

http://www.annefrank.org/nl/anne-franks-historie/personen-overzicht/johannes-voskuijl/
http://www.freebase.com/view/m/0cw_06q

Hermine 'Miep' Santruschitz

http://www.geheugenvanplanzuid.nl/tijdtijn/miepgies/miepgies.htm
http://www.miepgies.nl/
http://www.freebase.com/search?limit=30&start=0&query=miep+gies

Victor Kugler

http://www.annefrank.org/nl/Anne-Franks-historie/Personen-overzicht/Victor-Kugler/
http://www.freebase.com/view/en/victor_kugler

Friends

Merwedeplein.

Bertha 'Betty' Louise Bloemendal

http://www.joodsmonument.nl/person/498607

Eva Goldberg

http://www.freebase.com/view/m/0h25k4m

Gertrud Naumann

http://www.freebase.com/view/en/gertrud_naumann

Hannah 'Hanneli' Elisabeth Goslar

http://www.annefrank.org/nl/Wereldwijd/Educatie/Basisschool/Vriendinnen/Intro1/Hanneli/
http://www.freebase.com/view/en/hanneli_goslar

Hannelore 'Hansi' Klein (Laureen Nussbaum)

http://www.freebase.com/view/en/hannelore_klein

Helmuth 'Hello' Silberberg

http://www.annefrank.org/nl/Wereldwijd/Educatie/Basisschool/Verliefd/
http://www.freebase.com/view/en/matthew_j_perry

Ilse Wagner

http://www.freebase.com/view/en/ilse_wagner
http://www.joodsmonument.nl/person/522477/en

Jacqueline van Maarsen

http://www.freebase.com/view/en/jacqueline_van_maarsen

Juliette 'Juultje' Nanny Ketellapper

http://www.annefrank.org/nl/Wereldwijd/Educatie/Basisschool/Poeziealbum/
http://www.freebase.com/view/en/david_olsen

Merwedeplein (continued)

Käthe 'Kitty' Egyedie

http://www.annefrank.org/nl/Wereldwijd/Educatie/Basisschool/Vriendinnen/
http://www.freebase.com/search?limit=30&start=0&query=Egyedie

Lucia 'Lucie' van Dijk

http://www.annefrank.org/nl/Wereldwijd/Educatie/Basisschool/Vriendinnen/
http://www.freebase.com/view/en/lucia_van_dijk

Lutz Peter Schiff

http://www.annefrank.org/nl/Wereldwijd/Educatie/Basisschool/Verliefd/
http://www.freebase.com/view/m/05y6ppz
http://www.joodsmonument.nl/person/533337/nl

Martha van den Berg

http://www.annefrank.org/nl/Wereldwijd/Educatie/Basisschool/Vriendinnen/

Mary Bos

http://www.annefrank.org/nl/Wereldwijd/Educatie/Basisschool/Poeziealbum/
http://www.freebase.com/view/en/mary_bos

Nanette 'Nanny' Konig

http://www.annefrankdiaryreference.org/livingclassmates/Nanette_Blitz.htm
http://www.freebase.com/view/en/nanette_blitz

Rie 'Ietje' Swillens

http://www.annefrank.org/nl/Wereldwijd/Educatie/Basisschool/Vriendinnen/

Sol 'Sally' Kim(m)el

http://www.freebase.com/view/m/0cxr2n6

Susanna 'Sanne' Ledermann

http://www.joodsmonument.nl/person/504629/en

Wilma de Jonge

http://www.freebase.com/view/en/eefje_de_jong

People Anne met in the concentration camps

Bloeme Emden

http://www.freebase.com/view/m/0gh76zm

Frieda Brommet

http://www.kampwesterbork.nl/jodenvervolging/onderduik/ervaringen/

Janny Brilleslijper

http://www.freebase.com/view/m/075v25w

Judith de Winter

http://ckean.wordpress.com/2007/09/22/crushed-flowers-how-the-nazis-murdered-edith-margot-and-anne-frank/

Lenie van Naarden

http://www.freebase.com/view/m/0dwtqg4

Lientje Brilleslijper

http://www.freebase.com/view/en/lientje_brilslijper

Rachel Frankfoorder

http://www.freebase.com/view/m/0dm58yp

Ronnie van Cleef

http://www.auschwitz.nl/paviljoen/nederlanders-in-auschwitz/overlevenden/ronnie-goldstein

Rootje de Winter

http://www.freebase.com/view/m/0gvpgy6

Rose de Liema

Ruth Wiener

http://www.weinsteinmortuary.com/obit.cfm?step=2&id=2059

Other contacts

Barbara Ledermann

http://www.freebase.com/view/en/barbara_ledermann

Charlotta Kaletta

http://www.freebase.com/view/en/charlotta_kaletta

Elfriede Geiringer

http://www.freebase.com/view/en/elfriede_geiringer

Eline van Maarsen

http://www.freebase.com/view/en/eline_van_maarsen

Eva Geiringer

http://www.freebase.com/view/en/eva_geiringer

Gabi Goslar

http://www.freebase.com/view/en/gabi_goslar

Jetteke Frijda

http://www.freebase.com/view/en/jetteke_frijda

Juanita Wagner

http://www.freebase.com/view/en/natalia_felicia_anastasia_romanov

Paul Wronker

http://www.joodsmonument.nl/person/529156/nl

Other contacts (continued)

Rosel Wronker-Goldschmidt

http://www.joodsmonument.nl/person/510358/nl

Ruth Judith Klee

http://www.freebase.com/view/en/ruth_klee

Ursula 'Ursul' 'Ulla' Emelia Gallasch

http://www.freebase.com/view/m/0h1q4h1

BIBLIOGRAPHY

Translator's note: Works that have been translated from or into English are listed in bold with reference to their English-language publisher and year of publication. For works that are not available in English, a translation of the Dutch/German title is given in square brackets for reference.

Books	**ISBN**
Gies, Miep, *Herinneringen aan Anne Frank. Het verhaal van Miep Gies, de steun en toeverlaat van de familie Frank in het Achterhuis* (Amsterdam, 1987) **Anne Frank Remembered: The Story of the Woman Who Helped to Hide the Frank Family (Simon and Schuster, 2011)**	9035104897
Pol, Ruud, van der and Rian Voorhoeven, *Anne Frank* (Amsterdam, 1992)	9038403291
6^e Montessorischool Anne Frank. 75 Jaar en springlevend! **[6th Montessori School 'Anne Frank', 75 Years and Alive!]** (Amsterdam, 2008)	9789090225142
Anne Frank Stichting, *Anne Frank in the World. De wereld van Anne Frank 1929-1945* (Amsterdam, 1985) **The World of Anne Frank (Macmillan, 2003)**	9035109139
Anne Frank Stichting, *Anne Frank. Haar leven in brieven* **[Her Life in Letters]** (Amsterdam, 2006)	9086670016

Books (continued)

	ISBN
Anne Frank Stichting, *Vijftig vragen over antisemitisme* (Amsterdam, 2005) **Fifty Questions on Antisemitisme (Anne Frank House, 2005)**	9085060958
Anne Frank Stichting, *Anne Frank Huis. Een museum met een verhaal* (Amsterdam, 1999) **Anne Frank House. A Museum with a Story (Anne Frank House, 1999)**	9072972619
Arnoldussen, Paul and Alice van Diepen, *Bibliotheek van Amsterdamse herinneringen 02: Nieuw-Zuid* **[Library of Amsterdam Memories 02: The New 'Zuid' District]** (Amsterdam, 2003)	9789059370258
Barnouw, David and Gerrold van der Stroom, *Wie verraadde Anne Frank?* (Amsterdam, 2003) **Who Betrayed Anne Frank? (Netherlands Institute for War Documentation, 2003)**	9789053529324
Bekker M.M. and F.M. van de Poll, *Architectuur en stedenbouw in Amsterdam* **[Architecture and Urban Development in Amsterdam]** (1992)	9789066303089
Bierganz, Manfred and Annelie Kreutz, *Juden in Aachen* **[Jews in Aachen]** (Aachen, 1988)	3924007756
Blumenthal Lazan, Marion, *Vier gelijke stenen. Op de vlucht voor de Holocaust* (Laren, 2006) **Four Perfect Pebbles. A Holocaust Story (HarperCollins Publishers, 1999)**	9074274021

Books (continued) ISBN

Boeken-Velleman, Leny, *Breekbaar,* 9789074274227
maar niet gebroken [Fragile, but not broken]
(Laren, 2008)

Borgman, Erik and Liesbeth Hoeven, *Sporen* 9789086870844
van afwezigheid. Gedenken in stemmen, stenen
en stilte [Traces of Absence: Commemorating
in Voices, Stones and Silence] (Zoetermeer,
2011)

Bregstein, Philo. *Herinnering aan joods* 9789023415565
Amsterdam (Amsterdam, 1999)
Remembering Jewish Amsterdam
(Holmes & Meier Pub 2004)

Citroen D. and R. Mendel, *Eén verhaal uit* 9789085066422
duizenden. Kleinkinderen over de erfenis van
de Shoah [One telling story out of thousands.
Grandchildren on inheriting the Shoah]
(Amsterdam, 2009)

Coster, Theo, *Klasgenoten van Anne Frank* 9789048803217
(Amsterdam, 2009)
We All Wore Stars: Memories of Anne Frank
from Her Classmates (Macmillan, 2011)

De Dagboeken van Anne Frank. 903510921X/
Rijksinstituut voor oorlogsdocumentatie 9789035121997
(Amsterdam, 1990/2001)
The Diary of Anne Frank. The Revised
Critical Edition (The Netherlands Institute
for War Documentation, Doubleday 2003)

Lachendro, Jacek (ed.), *Duitse* 9788374191074
vernietigingskampen in Polen (2008)
German Places of Extermination in Poland
(Parma Press, 2010)

Books (continued)	**ISBN**
Frank, Anne, *Het Achterhuis. Dagboekbrieven 14 juni 1942 – 1 augustus 1944* (Amsterdam, 1996) **Anne Frank. The diary of a young girl (Doubleday & Valentine Mitchell, 1952)**	9035109996
Frank, Anne, *Mooie-zinnenboek* **[The Book of Beautiful Sentences]** (Amsterdam, 2004)	9035126475
Frank, Anne, *Verhaaltjes, en gebeurtenissen uit het Achterhuis. Met de roman in wording Cady's leven* (Amsterdam, 2005) **Tales from the Secret Annex. Including her Unfinished Novel Cady's Live (Halban Publishers, 2010***)*	9035128044
Gold, Alison Leslie, *Anne Frank. Mijn beste vriendin. Het verhaal van Hannah Goslar* (Alkmaar, 1997) **Hannah Goslar and Alison Gold, *Memories of Anne Frank: Reflections of a Childhood Friend* (Scholastic Paperbacks, 1999)**	9020620991
Hart, Francesca and Marinus Schroevers, *Cinema & Theater. Een fascinerende selectie uit de jaargangen 1921-1944* **[Cinema & Theatre. A Fascinating Selection from the 1921-1944 Issues]** (Laren, 1975)	9060711602
Acherchour, E.M., *Het andere huis van Anne Frank. Geschiedenis en toekomst van een schrijvershuis* **[Anne Frank's Other Home. Past and Future of a Writer's Refuge]** (Bussum, 2006)	9068684280

Books (continued)	ISBN
Heuberger, Rachel and Helgo Krohn, *Hinaus aus dem ghetto...Juden in Frankfurt am Main 1800-1950* **[Out of the Ghetto: Jews in Frankfurt am Main 1800-1950]** (Frankfurt am Main, 1988)	3100314077
Hillesum E. Etty, *De nagelaten geschriften van Etty Hillesum 1941-1943* **[Etty Hillesum's Written Legacy 1941-1943]** (Amsterdam, 2008)	9789050188128
Hondius, Dienke, *Absent. Herinneringen aan het Joods Lyceum Amsterdam 1941-1943* **[Absent: Memories of the Jewish Lyceum in Amsterdam]** (Amsterdam, 2001)	9050003222
Jacobsen S. and E. Colón, *Het leven van Anne Frank. De grafische biografie geautoriseerd door het Anne Frank Huis* (Amsterdam, 2010) **Anne Frank: The Anne Frank House Authorized Graphic Biography (Anne Frank House, 2010)**	9789024532438
Jansen, Ronald Wilfred, *Anne Frank* (Hoogeveen, 2011)	9789491080432
Jansen, Ronald Wilfred, *In de voetsporen van Anne Frank* (Hoogeveen, 2011) **Following the Footsteps of Anne Frank (RWJ-Publishing, 2011)**	9789081423847
Jansen, Ronald Wilfred. *Anne Frank* (Hoogeveen, 2011)	9781463714345
Jansen, Ronald Wilfred. *Anne Frank* (Hoogeveen, 2011)	9781466281936

Books (continued)	ISBN
Jansen, Ronald Wilfred. Stille Getuigen. Sporen van Anne Frank in het (stedelijke) landschap **[Silent Witnesses. Reminders of Anne in the (Urban) Landscape]**, in: *Monumenten. Hèt tijdschrift voor cultureel erfgoed* **[*Monuments.* The *Cultural Heritage Magazine]* (Issue 32, no. 5, May 2011)	
Van der Woude, Siem (ed.), *Joods leven in Friesland* **[*Jewish Life in Friesland]*** (Leeuwarden, 2010)	9789056152390
Lans, Jos van der and Herman Vuijsje, *Het Anne Frank Huis. Een biografie* (Amsterdam, 2010) **The Anne Frank House. A Biography (Anne Frank House, 2010)**	9789085069393
Lee, Carol Ann, *Anne Frank. Het leven van een jong meisje* (Amsterdam, 2009) **The Life of a Young Girl. The Definitive Biography**	9789460030123
Lee, Carol Ann, *Het verborgen leven van Otto Frank. De biografie* (Amsterdam, 2002) **The Hidden Life of Otto Frank (Goodreads, 2003)**	9789050185554
Lee, Carol Ann, *Pluk rozen op aarde en vergeet mij niet. Anne Frank 1929-1945* (Amsterdam, 1998) **Roses from the Earth: The Biography of Anne Frank (Penguin Books, 2000)**	9050185320

Books (continued)	ISBN
Liempt, Ad van, *Nederlandse premiejagers op zoek naar joden* **[Dutch Premium Hunters Looking for Jews]** (Amsterdam, 2009)	9789041707758
Liempt, Ad van, and Jan Kompagnie, *Jodenjacht* **[Hunting for Jews]** (Amsterdam, 2011)	9789760033681
Lindwer, Willy, *De laatste zeven maanden van Anne Frank. Het ongeschreven laatste hoofdstuk van het Dagboek* (Hilversum, 2008) **The Last Seven Months of Anne Frank. The stories of six women who knew Anne Frank (Macmillan, 2004)**	9789077895726
Maarsen, Jacqueline Jopie van, *Anne en Jopie. Leven met Anne Frank* **[Anne and Jopie. Living with Anne Frank]** (Amsterdam, 1990)	9050181104
Maarsen, Jacqueline van, *De erflaters. Herinneringen van de jeugdvriendin van Anne Frank* (Amsterdam, 2004) **Inheriting Anne Frank (Arcadia Books, 2010)**	9059360575
Maarsen, Jacqueline van, *Ik heet Anne, zei ze, Anne Frank. Herinneringen van Jacqueline van Maarsen* (Amsterdam, 2003) **My Name Is Anne, She Said, Anne Frank, The Memoirs of Anne Frank's Best Friend (Arcadia Books 2007)**	9789041705242
Mali, Anco, *Margot Frank en de anderen* **[Margot Frank and the others]** (Soesterberg, 2005)	9059111923

Books (continued)	ISBN

Müller, Melissa. *Anne Frank. De biografie* (Amsterdam, 1998)
Original German title: *Das Mädchen Anne Frank. Die Biographie.*
English edition: **Anne Frank: The Biography (Macmillan 2013)** — 9035119908

Polak, Bob, *Naar buiten, lucht en lachen! Een literaire wandeling door het Amsterdam van Anne Frank **[Outside: fresh air and laughter! A literary walk through Anne Frank's Amsterdam]*** (Amsterdam, 2006) — 9059371240

Presser, J. *Ondergang. De vervolging en verdelging van het Nederlandse Jodendom 1940-1945 I & II **[Destruction. The Persecution and Extermination of Dutch Judaism I & II]*** (The Hague, 1965)

Prins, Marcel and Peter Henk Steenhuis, *Andere Achterhuizen. Verhalen van Joodse onderduikers* (Amsterdam, 2010)
Hidden Like Anne Frank (Scholastic, 2014) — 9789025367398

Prose, Francine, *Anne Frank. Leven en werk van een schrijfster* (Amsterdam, 2009)
Anne Frank: The Book, The Life, The Afterlife (Harper Collins Books, 2009) — 9789045010946

Schloss, Eva, *Herinneringen van een joods meisje **[Memories of a Jewish Girl]*** (Breda, 2005) — 9789062221844

Schuter, Jane, *Bezoek aan het verleden. Auschwitz **[Visiting the Past: Auschwitz]*** (Harmelen, 1999) — 9054954019

Books (continued)

ISBN

Smith, Lyn, *Vergeten stemmen van de Holocaust* **[Forgotten Voices of the Holocaust]** (Amsterdam, 2005)

9789022544174

Ulrich, Hans, *Wie was Anne Frank ? Haar leven, het Achterhuis en haar dood* (Laren, 2010)
Who was Anne Frank ? Her life, the Secret Annex and her death. A short biography for young and old (Verbum, 2010)

9789074274524

Vermeer Gerrit, Ben Rebel and Vladimir Stissi, *D'Ailly's Historische gids van Amsterdam. De stadsuitbreidingen 1860-1935* **[D'Ailly's Historical Guide to Amsterdam: City Extensions 1860-1935]** (Amsterdam, 2010)

9789059372290

Werkman, G, *Amsterdam. Stad te water* **[Amsterdam. City on Water]** (Bussum, 1943)

Zee, Manda van der, *De kamergenoot van Anne Frank* (Soesterberg, 2001)
The Roommate of Anne Frank (Aspekt, 2003)

9059110250

Resources from archives

Jewish Historical Museum Archives, (Various) Labels with Antisemitic texts from the Kölner Hof Hotel, Frankfurt a.m., dated around 1900, Inventory number 00004698

German National Archives (Bundesarchiv). *Das Gedenkbuch des Bundesarchivs für die Opfer der nationalsozialistischen Judenverfolgung in Deutschland (1933-1945)*

[The National Archives Memorial Book to the Victims of National-Socialist Persecution of the Jews in Germany (1933-1945)]

Het Joodsch Weekblad **[The Jewish Weekly]** (22 August 1941) National Library of the Netherlands, Inventory number 9158 A6

Het Joodsch Weekblad **[The Jewish Weekly]** (23 July 1943) National Library of the Netherlands, Inventory number 9158 A7

Het Joodsch Weekblad **[The Jewish Weekly]** (27 February 1942) National Library of the Netherlands, Inventory number 9158A7

Periodicals, newspapers and brochures

AG Bergen Belsen e.V. Führung. Gedenkstätte Bergen-Belsen mit Erklärungen **[Bergen-Belsen Memorial Site with Explanations]** (Lohheide)

AG Bergen Belsen e.V. *Informatie over de geschiedenis. Krijgsgevangenenkamp. Concentratiekamp. Gedenkplaats Bergen-Belsen met uitgebreide plattegrond* **[Information about the history. Prisoner of war camp. Concentration camp. Bergen-Belsen Memorial Site containing a detailed map]** (Lohheide)

Algemeen Handelsblad (Amsterdam-based semi-national newspaper) 15 July 1939

Algemeen Handelsblad (Amsterdam-based semi-national newspaper) 26 February 1932

Periodicals, newspapers and brochures (continued)

Amstelodamum (Amsterdam, 1933)
Amsterdam City Archives
Inventory number 15030: 15841

Amstelodamum (Amsterdam, 1935)
Amsterdam City Archives
Inventory number 15030: 15843

Amstelodamum (Amsterdam, 1936)
Amsterdam City Archives
Inventory number 15030: 15844

Amstelodamum (Amsterdam, 1939)
Amsterdam City Archives
Inventory number 15030: 15847

Amstelodamum (Amsterdam, 1940)
Amsterdam City Archives
Inventory number 15030: 15848

Amstelodamum (Amsterdam, 1941)
Amsterdam City Archives
Inventory number 15030: 15849

Amstelodamum (Amsterdam, 1942)
Amsterdam City Archives
Inventory number 15030: 15850

Amstelodamum (Amsterdam, 1946)
Amsterdam City Archives
Inventory number 15030: 15854

CVJM. Oldauer Hefte No. 2.
Anne Frank in Bergen-Belsen

Periodicals, newspapers and brochures (continued)

Dagblad van het Noorden (Regional Newspaper) 4 May 1936

De Amsterdamse Gids **[The Amsterdam Guide]** (Amsterdam, 1930)

De Telegraaf (National Newspaper) 5 October 2008

De Telegraaf (National Newspaper) 9 April 2008

De Telegraaf (National Newspaper) 26 February 2008

Het Parool (National Newspaper) 3 April 1946

Het Parool (National Newspaper) 16 June 2004

Het Vaderland (National Newspaper) 25 May 1939

Jewish Historical Museum. *Jodenvervolging in Amsterdam 1940-45* **[Persecution of Jews in Amsterdam 1940-45]** (Zwolle, 1993)

Nieuwsbrief Dachau **[Dachau Newsletter]** (Stichting Vriendenkring van Oud-Dachauers [Foundation of supporters of former Dachau prisoners], No. 9 – December 1994), pp. 8-9

NRC (National Newspaper) 10 November 2008

Periodicals, newspapers and brochures (continued)

NRC (National Newspaper)
13 March 2001

Sonderzüge in den Tod. Die Deportationen mit der Deutschen Reichsbahn **[Special Express to Death. Deportation on the German National Railway]** (Exhibition at the Central-Bahnhof, 2008)

State Museum in Oświęcim. 8388526588
Auschwitz-Birkenau (Oświęcim, 2006)

Stiftung niedersächsische Gedenkstätten 9783981161755
Gedenkstätte Bergen-Belsen. Die Topografie des Lagers Bergen-Belsen **[Bergen-Belsen Memorial Site. Bergen-Belsen Site Topography]** (2008)

Süddeutsche Zeitung (German National Newspaper), 10 August 1994

Velden, Jolly van der, *Edith Frank-Holländer, de moeder van Anne* **[Edith Frank-Holländer, Anne's mother]** in: Nederlands Auschwitz Comité. Auschwitz Bulletin (Issue 55, no. 4, December 2011) pp. 18-19

Verenigingsblad Waffel **[Waffel Society Magazine]** (June 2010, no. 44)

Vervolging en verzet in Amsterdam. Herinneringen aan de Tweede Wereldoorlog. Een wandeling van het Anne Frank Huis naar het Verzetsmuseum **[Persecution and Resistance in Amsterdam. Reminders of the Second World War. A walk from the Anne**

Frank House to the Resistance Museum]
(Amsterdam, 2006)

Videos

Anne Frank Remembered Video version of the film (UK, 1995)

Anne Frank. De laatste zeven maanden van Anne Frank. Het ongeschreven laatste hoofdstuk van het Dagboek **[The Last Seven Months of Anne Frank. The stories of six women who knew Anne Frank]** (Just Publishers)   9789077895726

WEBSITES

Home addresses, hiding place and concentration camps

1. Frankfurt am Main

http://www.frankfurt1933-1945.de

2. Aachen

http://www.aachen.de/DE/kultur_freizeit/kultur/index.html

3. Merwedeplein.

http://www.geheugenvanplanzuid.nl/tijdtijn/restauratiemerwedeplein37.htm

4. Rivierenbuurt and Amsterdam Zuid areas

http://www.geheugenvanplanzuid.nl/
http://www.zuidelijkewandelweg.nl/

5. Centre of Amsterdam

http://www.onsamsterdam.nl/
http://www.annefrank.org/Amsterdam

6. The Secret Annex

http://www.annefrank.org/en/Subsites/Home/
http://www.bouwbrowser.nl/leveranciers/110/461/cor%20bouwstra.pdf

7. Camp Westerbork

http://www.kampwesterbork.nl
http://www.westerbork.nl/

8. Auschwitz-Birkenau

http://www.auschwitz.nl/
www.auschwitz.pl

9. Bergen-Belsen

http://bergen-belsen.stiftung-ng.de/
http://www.ag-bergen-belsen.de/

Anne's living environment

http://buurtwinkels.amsterdammuseum.nl/search?q_mm=prinsengracht
http://joodsactueel.be/2011/01/03/in-de-voetsporen-van-anne-frank-1929-1945
http://members.casema.nl/a.tiggeler/
http://members.chello.nl/wiers/amsterdam/stadsgezichten.htm
http://www.amsterdamsetrams.nl/
http://www.edenamsterdamamericanhotel.com/nl/restaurant.aspx
http://www.februaristaking.nl/
http://www.geheugenvanplanzuid.nl/
http://www.geheugenvanplanzuid.nl/tijdtijn/pontje.htm
http://www.kindermonument.nl/wandeling/
http://www.spoorzoekenderivierenbuurt.nl/
http://www.zuid.amsterdam.nl/wonen_en/natuur_en_milieu/parken_in_zuid/vondelpark/
http://www.zuidelijkewandelweg.nl/

Resources from archives

http://d-nb.info/998592757
http://hetverhalenarchief.nl/
http://kranten.kb.nl
http://stadsarchief.amsterdam.nl/archieven/index.nl.html
http://www.4en5mei.nl/oorlogsmonumenten
http://www.aachen.de/DE/stadt_buerger/bildung/oeffentliche_bibliothek/index.html
http://www.aachen.de/DE/wirtschaft_technologie/archiv/index.html
http://www.archieven.nl/nl/
http://www.archievenwo2.nl/
http://www.beeldbank.amsterdam.nl/
http://www.beeldbankwo2.nl/index.jsp
http://www.bundesarchiv.de/gedenkbuch/
http://www.centrumjudaicum.de/de/archiv
http://www.d-nb.de/
http://www.dodenakkers.nl/
http://www.freebase.com/
http://www.gettyimages.nl/
http://www.historici.nl/
http://www.jhm.nl/collectie/zoeken
http://www.joodsmonument.nl/
http://www.kamparchieven.nl/
http://www.kb.nl/dossiers/annefrank/annefrank.html
http://www.musip.nl/
http://www.nai.nl/
http://www.nationaalarchief.nl/
http://www.oorlogsgetroffenen.nl/
http://www.stadtgeschichte-ffm.de/

Cultural heritage

http://grachtenboek.hetgrachtenhuis.nl/
http://monumentenregister.cultureelerfgoed.nl/
http://ver-bouwkunst.nl/over
http://www.amsterdam.nl/kunst-cultuur-sport/
http://www.andereachterhuizen.nl/#/kaart
http://www.bewoondbewaard.nl/
http://www.bma.amsterdam.nl/
http://www.bouwhistorie.nl/
http://www.communityjoodsmonument.nl/page/249245/nl
http://www.cultureelerfgoed.nl/
http://www.drentsplateau.nl/
http://www.erfgoednederland.nl/
http://www.icn.nl/
http://www.jewisheritage.org/jh/index.php
http://www.joodsamsterdam.nl/
http://www.joodsewerkkampen.nl/
http://www.knob.nl/
http://www.monumentenwacht.nl/
http://www.monumentenwachtnoordholland.nl/index.html
http://www.nirov.nl/
http://www.nvmz.nl/
http://www.openmonumentendag.nl/
http://www.raap.nl/
http://www.restauratiecentrum.nl/
http://www.restauratiefonds.nl/Paginas/default.aspx
http://www.restitutiecommissie.nl/
http://www.shni.nl/
http://www.sporenvandeoorlog.nl/
http://www.torenuurwerk.nl/
http://www.unesco.nl/
http://www.vakgroeprestauratie.nl/
http://www.westerborkpad.nl/

Judaism

http://dornsife.usc.edu/vhi/
http://joodsactueel.be/
http://nihs.nl/
http://www.bethshalom.nl/bsnieuw/
http://www.bnaibrith-amsterdam.org/
http://www.bundjuedischersoldaten-online.com/39994.html
http://www.c-hef.org/index2.htm
http://www.cjo.nl/
http://www.holocaust-memorial-day.nl/
http://www.jg-ffm.de/
http://www.jhm.nl/cultuur-en-geschiedenis/amsterdam
http://www.jhm.nl/cultuur-en-geschiedenis/gebouwen
http://www.j-o-k.nl/
http://www.jonag.nl/
http://www.jonet.nl/
http://www.joodseomroep.nl/
http://www.joodswelzijn.nl/
http://www.joodszorgcircuit.nl/
http://juedischesmuseum.de/startseite.html?&L=1
http://www.lechaimtolife.nl/page/stichting-l-chaim-to-life
http://www.ljgamsterdam.nl/
http://www.museumoftolerance.com/
http://www.nik.nl/
http://www.niw.nl/
http://www.urban.ne.jp/home/hecjpn/indexENGLISH.html
http://www.ushmm.org/
http://www.verbond.eu/
http://www.wiesenthal.com/
http://www.yadvashem.org/
http://www.yivo.org/
http://www.zentralratdjuden.de/

War

http://deoorlog.nps.nl/
http://www.20eeuwennederland.nl/periodes/Tweede%20Wereldoorlog
http://www.innl.nl/
http://www.stiwot.nl/
http://www.verzetsmuseum.org/

Additional resources

http://www.nlpvf.nl/
http://www.ymere.nl/ymere/home.asp
http://www.cidi.nl/
http://www.cogis.nl/Index.aspx
http://www.cvjm.de/
http://www.osce.org/
http://haeuser.cvjm-lvh.de/anne-frank-haus--oldau
http://www.letterenfonds.nl/
http://www.abc.nl/
http://www.eurohistour.com/
http://www.dachau.nl/en_verder/ouddachauers/content.html#vriendenkring
http://www.stiftung-bg.de/gums/en/index.htm
http://www.bijbelaantekeningen.nl/
http://www.dichtbij.nl/amsterdam-zuid/home/amsterdam-zuid.aspx
http://www.dichtbij.nl/amsterdam-centrum/home/amsterdam-centrum.aspx?pr=1&cid=1649
http://rivierenbuurt.weblog.nl/
http://www.seniorennet.nl/
http://www.deweekkrant.nl/pages.php?page=1528934
http://www.jbs-anne-frank.de/
http://www.architectenweb.nl/aweb/archipedia/archipedia.asp?ID=829
http://www.hildokrop.nl/
http://www.oranjehotel.org/
http://www.dodenakkers.nl/oorlog/algemeen/23-waalsdorpervlakte.html
http://www.antiken-kabinett.de/
http://www.willylindwer.com/
http://www.herdenking.nl/
http://www.portretschap.nl/jet-schepp
http://www.karindaan.nl/projecten/homomonument/

SPECIAL THANKS TO...

Moll B.	6th Montessori School 'Anne Frank', Amsterdam
Ruijtenburg C.	6th Montessori School 'Anne Frank', Amsterdam
Grazell Karel N.L.	Amsterdam Municipal Poet from the Zuid area
Eldridge, B.	Anne Frank Fonds, Basel
Elias B.	Anne Frank Fonds, Basel
Nykl D.	Anne Frank expert, the Netherlands
Morine S.	Anne Frank expert, USA
Bekker A.	Anne Frank Stichting
Broek G.	Anne Frank Stichting
Prins E.	Anne Frank Stichting
Veen T. van der	Anne-in-de-buurt.nl
Tiggeler A.	Postcards and photos of Amsterdam
Arends J.	Resident, Rivierenbuurt area
Bachra F.	Resident, Rivierenbuurt area
Geiringer E.	Resident, Rivierenbuurt area
Hendriks J.	Resident, Rivierenbuurt area
Holten A.	Resident, Rivierenbuurt area
Isselmann L.H.	Resident, Rivierenbuurt area
Liefboer L.	Resident, Rivierenbuurt area
Tuijl L. van	Resident, Rivierenbuurt area
Wijk E. van	Resident, Rivierenbuurt area
Giessen J.P. van de	Bijbelaantekeningen.nl
Sar M. van der	The Netherlands Central Jewish Consulting Body, Amsterdam
Dannel H.	Centrum Judaicum, Berlijn
Volkers L.	Dé Weekkrant Amsterdam (weekly), Amsterdam
Heimer I.	German National Library, Leipzig
Lindwer W.	Documentary maker
Ooijen W. van	P. de Munk bakery, Amsterdam
Michels C.	Frankfurter Rundschau
Becker K.	Resident, 24 Ganghoferstrasse, Frankfurt am Main
Gackstätter B.	Resident, 24 Ganghoferstrasse, Frankfurt am Main

SPECIAL THANKS TO...
(CONTINUED)

Hummel J.	Bergen-Belsen Memorial Site
Rathmann S.	Bergen-Belsen Memorial Site
Hartwig G.	Bergen-Belsen Memorial Site
Rahe T.	Bergen-Belsen Memorial Site
Theilen K.	Bergen-Belsen Memorial Site
Nolte A.	Goethe-Institut, Amsterdam
Doorten W.	Camp Westerbork Memorial Centre
Meijering W.	Camp Westerbork Memorial Centre
Kras J.	Jewish Historical Museum, Amsterdam
Zwiers A.	Jewish Historical Museum, Amsterdam
Boer J. de	Jewish Social Work
Schepp J.	Artist, Amsterdam
Demnig G.	Artist, Duitsland
Vries L.J. de	Hotel Groot Warnsborn Estate, Arnhem
Marcus A.	Liberal Jewish Congregation, Amsterdam
Claudy E.	Ludwig Richter School, Frankfurt am Main
Dolly en Nolly	Massage Practice
Korzeniowska M.	Auschwitz Memorial and Museum
Lech J.	Auschwitz Memorial and Museum
Plosa W.	Auschwitz Memorial and Museum
Urbaniak M.	Auschwitz Memorial and Museum
Henzen T.	Meppeler Courant Newspaper
Glas, van der M.C.	Holocaust survivor and writer
Todorovic G.	Editor at the Echo weekly, Amsterdam
Graaf B. de	Restaurant d'Vijff Vlieghen, Amsterdam
Wijgergangs H.	Rijksbureau voor Kunsthistorische Documentatie [Netherlands Institute for Art History]
Bijlsma H.	Regional Education Centre (ROC), Amsterdam
Broefkhoff W.J.M.	Regional Education Centre (ROC), Amsterdam
Hal M. van	Regional Education Centre (ROC), Amsterdam
Pravilović G.	Amsterdam City Archives
Staal C.	Amsterdam City Archives

SPECIAL THANKS TO...
(CONTINUED)

Lambrechtsen E.	Stadsarchief, Amsterdam
Bister F.	Aachen City Archives
Wyborny I.	Aachen Municipal Library
Perez T.	Amsterdam City of Refugees Association
Lassche L.	L'Chaim Foundation, Meppel
Roxlau T.A.	United States Holocaust Memorial Museum
Heuberger R.	University Library Frankfurt
Jansen W.	Father, Hoogeveen
Bonn R.	Waffel Society Magazine
Rubbens A.	Resistance Museum, Amsterdam
Rij S. van	Former official at the city of Amsterdam
Suijk C.	Former Director Anne Frank Stichting
Streef W.	Friend
Goslar H.	Friend of Anne Frank
Maarsen J. van	Friend of Anne Frank
Mali A.	Friend of Margot Frank
Wageningen E. van	WinkelStories.nl
Mulder H.	Ymere Group Services (housing corporation), Amsterdam
Wiersema J.	zuidelijkewandelweg.nl, Amsterdam

COLOPHON

Text: Ronald Wilfred Jansen
Translation: Dutch Direct Translation Services

Photos:

Collection Ad Tiggeler
Collection Jos Wiersema, Amsterdam Trams
Collection Ronald Wilfred Jansen

Print:

RWJ-Publishing has requested proprietors of images, in as far as they were known, for permission for publication. Whomever claims to have title to any of the images in this book is requested to contact RWJ-Publishing.

© 2014, RWJ-Publishing.

All rights reserved. No part of this publication may be reproduced, stored in a database or retrieval system, or published, in any form or or by any means, electronically mechanically, by print, photoprint, recording or otherwise without prior written permission from RWJ-Publishing.

ISBN: 9789490482084

NUR code: 508.